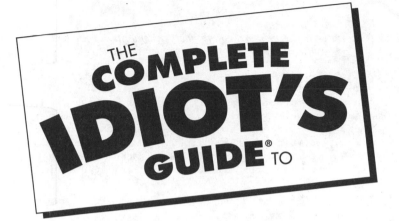

THE **COMPLETE IDIOT'S GUIDE®** TO

American Cooking

by Ronnie Fein

ALPHA

A Pearson Education Company

This book is dedicated to the memories of my mother, who taught me how to cook,
and my father, who taught me how to eat.

Copyright © 2003 by Ronnie Fein

International Standard Book Number: 0-02-864391-7
Library of Congress Catalog Card Number: 2002111659

04 03 02   8 7 6 5 4 3 2 1

Interpretation of the printing code: The rightmost number of the first series of numbers is the year of the book's printing; the rightmost number of the second series of numbers is the number of the book's printing. For example, a printing code of 02-1 shows that the first printing occurred in 2002.

Printed in the United States of America

For marketing and publicity, please call: 317-581-3722

The publisher offers discounts on this book when ordered in quantity for bulk purchases and special sales.

For sales within the United States, please contact: Corporate and Government Sales, 1-800-382-3419 or corpsales@pearsontechgroup.com

Outside the United States, please contact: International Sales, 317-581-3793 or international@pearsontechgroup.com

Publisher: *Marie Butler-Knight*
Product Manager: *Phil Kitchel*
Managing Editor: *Jennifer Chisholm*
Senior Acquisitions Editor: *Renee Wilmeth*
Development Editor: *Lynn Northrup*
Production Editor: *Katherin Bidwell*
Copy Editor: *Jan Zunkel*
Illustrator: *Chris Eliopoulos*
Cover/Book Designer: *Trina Wurst*
Indexer: *Angie Bess*
Layout/Proofreading: *Angela Calvert, John Etchison*

Contents at a Glance

Contents

10   Invention, Innovation, and Culture   249

Foreword

This is a book whose time has come! There are lots of books on American food, but Ronnie Fein has gone beyond the recipe to give us a delicious history of America through our culinary heritage and traditions.

Many of us who write seriously about food feel strongly that the communal breaking of bread is indeed the fabric by which history is written and cultures develop. It's likely that when the cave dwellers discovered fire and its use for cooking, the nuclear family took hold as a group whose survival depended on sharing the meal with each other. In the Bible, it was Eve's passion for apples that changed the course of the world, and the biblical history of the Jews is detailed and reconstructed every single year in the Passover Seder. Christianity has its roots in the same Seder feast, and this breaking of the bread has been re-created millions of times since. Indeed, all major religions intertwine rituals and tradition through the preparation and serving of food.

Every country in the world "writes" its history through its recipes, and this history is documented in the family meal. I tell my grandchildren about my great-grandma, whose pies were legendary, and how she passed down the gene for making good pastry to me and on to them. They will never meet great-grandma, but they know her through her apple pie. I also tell them about their other great-grandma, who brought the family's recipes tucked into her bodice over on the boat from Sicily. They will never know this courageous woman, but they will know how to make her braciole. Family reunions are not about games, they are about the food. And when Aunt Eloise died, it was most poignant as her bowl of potato salad went unprepared the first year, but cousin Patty took over next year saying always that it was Aunt Eloise's recipe, not hers. The grandchildren will know Aunt Eloise through her potato salad, and so will their children.

Ronnie Fein, a talented cook, is also a strong believer in the importance of the family table. She has passed her cultural traditions to her two grown daughters, who are now adapting them with contemporary ingredients to times in which they live and cook. Ronnie is also a gifted teacher with an extraordinary sense of detail and the patience to pass on her knowledge with clarity and style.

True to her reputation, Ronnie has thoroughly researched every detail and fully tested every recipe in this book. But even more, she brings alive the stories and the history of American food, both in the text and in the recipes.

The Complete Idiot's Guide to American Cooking can teach you to cook, and it will teach you about America. A melting pot of cuisines and cultures, America is really about each and every family who sits down to supper. In giving us American recipes to enjoy together and American history to learn together, Ronnie has made an important contribution to the future of our families and our valued culture.

—Melanie Barnard

Melanie Barnard is author or co-author of 13 cookbooks, including the James Beard award-winning *The American Medical Association Family Cookbook*, and her most recently published work, *Short & Sweet*. Her newest book, with Brooke Dojny, is *A Flash in the Pan*, to be published in early 2003. She is also co-author of "Every-Night Cooking," the monthly column in *Bon Appétit*. Melanie hosted a weekly food segment on WCBS-TV in New York for more than two years, and appears often on local and national television. She has for 20 years been the restaurant critic for the *Stamford Advocate* and *Greenwich Time* daily newspapers. Melanie lives in Connecticut with her husband, and does much of her writing in between ambulance calls while working as a volunteer Emergency Medical Technician.

Introduction

American food, once the Rodney Dangerfield of cuisines, finally gets respect. Our country's innovative chefs are world renowned, and our palates are sophisticated. American recipes integrate flavors from places as diverse as the Asia, the Mediterranean, and the West Indies. We are willing to taste whatever new foods come along.

Still, when July 4th rolls around, do we want a smart Oven-Roasted Salmon with Horseradish Crust? On Thanksgiving, do we forego Roasted Turkey for Lime-Marinated Turkey Cutlets with Fruit Salsa? Would John Wayne have swapped his spurs and chaps for Goat Cheese and Walnut Salad with Balsamic Vinaigrette?

Not likely. Yet, these dishes are as American as fried chicken and hot dogs. Or maybe I should say, these are among the newer additions to the American treasure house of recipes. American food has a wide reach.

Fast food and recipes based on canned, packaged, and processed items are also part of our cooking heritage. These are the foods that helped home cooks get out of the kitchen quickly. American food is hamburgers and fries. It's also Tuna Casserole, Jell-O Molds, and Lipton's Onion Soup Dip.

Consider our country's indigenous products. Corn, squash, peppers, beans, avocados, tomatoes, maple syrup, wild mushrooms, and salmon, among others, were staples used by Native Americans and by the first settlers. Regional recipes developed as people took advantage of the produce and wildlife that flourished locally. American food is New England Clam Chowder, Pecan Pie, Cherry Cobbler, Baked Potatoes, and Chili Con Carne.

Our country has always been a land of immigrants. From the beginning, our foods reflected the nations of our ancestors, our religious beliefs, and our cultural values. American food is Dutch Doughnuts, German Potato Salad, Italian Pizza, Jewish Stuffed Cabbage, Swedish Meatballs, and Irish Oat Scones.

We have gone through boom times and bad times in America. When life has been flush, we have eaten like royalty. During troubled times, we budgeted together, stretched meat to make it into more, and made do with less. We ate dishes that nourished us emotionally. American food is Meatloaf, Mashed Potatoes, Chocolate Pudding, Macaroni and Cheese, and Chocolate Chip Cookies.

Restaurants have been influential in defining American cuisine, too. In days gone by, the influential chefs were at such well-known establishments as Delmonico's, Antoine's, and the Waldorf; today's star chefs may be in charge of several restaurants at one time. We see them on TV; we buy their cookbooks. Americans have always been eager to cook the dishes invented by professionals. American food is Waldorf

Salad, Vichyssoise, Pasta Primavera, Chicken à la King, Blackened Redfish, Caesar Salad, and Baked Alaska.

We are lucky to live in a country so abundant in resources, so generous with its liberties, so accepting of variety. It has given us confidence and enabled us to develop as individuals and as a nation. It has nurtured our appetites and encouraged the vastness, the bounty, and the diversity of American food. I hope you enjoy this journey through the cuisines of America. Good luck and bon appétit!

How This Book Is Organized

This book was designed to give you a notion of how our vast, bountiful, and diverse American cuisine developed. **Part 1, "The Regional Cuisines of America,"** is divided into eight chapters, each of which deals with a specific region of the country. **Part 2, "An Emerging National Cuisine,"** explains the factors that helped define a national American cuisine. It covers such topics as immigration, innovation, and technological advances.

At the end of each chapter I've included pertinent recipes. Some recipes are well-loved classics: Angel Food Cake, Coleslaw, White Bread, and Potato Salad. Some are regional favorites: Maine Lobster Pie, Country Captain, and Manhattan Clam Chowder. There are recipes inspired by restaurants: Caesar Salad, Boston Cream Pie, and Pasta Primavera; and recipes out of the immigrant melting pot: Chicken Cacciatore, Borscht, and Cuban Black Beans and Rice. I've included a few contemporary American dishes, and I've adapted and updated some recipes for the modern table.

A few of the recipes take some time, but most can be prepared in half an hour or less. And while some of the recipes can be challenging, most of the ones I've chosen can be prepared successfully even by inexperienced cooks.

Extras

In addition to the background information and recipes from each region, you'll find the following sidebars sprinkled throughout the text:

Hot Tip

Within the recipes, you'll find tips for making recipe preparation easier or more understandable; suggestions on how to vary a recipe; or cautions about possible dangers or pitfalls such as chopping chili peppers without protecting your skin.

What Is It?
Here you'll find definitions of cooking and ingredient terms—which are also compiled in the book's glossary.

 Mini-Recipe
Here you'll find tasty and easy-to-make recipes for some of the foods featured in the text.

 Fein on Food
Check these boxes for fascinating tidbits of history and folklore that complement the text. They aren't necessary for cooking, but they make for great dinner conversation!

 Kitchen Clue
Check these boxes for useful information about food, as well as tips for making cooking simpler, more accurate, more organized, and more understandable.

 **Did You Know ...**
In these boxes I offer suggestions for making ingredient and utensil substitutions.

Acknowledgments

I owe many thanks to Renee Wilmeth and Marie Butler-Knight, for their encouragement and enthusiasm in going forward with this book. I would also like to thank Lynn Northrup, Katherin Bidwell, and Jan Zunkel, the hard-working professionals at Pearson, for the insightful questions and comments that show their fine editorial leadership.

Special Thanks to the Technical Reviewer

The Complete Idiot's Guide to American Cooking was reviewed by an culinary expert who double-checked the accuracy of what you'll learn here, to help us ensure that this book gives you everything you need to know about America's food traditions. Many special thanks are extended to my colleague Mary Goodbody.

Mary Goodbody is a nationally known food writer and editor who has worked on more than 45 books. Her most recent credits include *Williams-Sonoma Kitchen*

Companion (Time-Life Books), *The Garden Entertaining Cookbook* (Chronicle Books), and *Back to the Table* (Hyperion). She has contributed significantly to other books, including *Prime Time*, *The Lobels' Guide to Great Grilled Meats*, *The Naked Chef*, *How to Be a Domestic Goddess*, and *Alfred Portale's Twelve Seasons Cookbook*. She is the editor of the *IACP Food Forum Quarterly*, and was the first editor-in-chief of *Cooks* magazine.

Trademarks

All terms mentioned in this book that are known to be or are suspected of being trademarks or service marks have been appropriately capitalized. Alpha Books and Pearson Education, Inc., cannot attest to the accuracy of this information. Use of a term in this book should not be regarded as affecting the validity of any trademark or service mark.

Part 1

The Regional Cuisines of America

American cuisine began in several places. The food that the first settlers and pioneers ate depended upon where they lived, the indigenous foods that were available to them, and their own particular religious and cultural backgrounds. Recipes developed on a regional basis, and a variety of cooking styles developed alongside one another.

The following chapters will familiarize you with culinary traditions in the eight regions of America: New England, the mid-Atlantic, the South, the Midwest, Louisiana, the Southwest, the great West, and the Northwest. You'll find that, while some dishes overlap from region to region, each area has its own distinctive—and delicious!—culinary characteristics.

Chapter 1

New England

In This Chapter

- Corn, beans, and pumpkins: the American lifesavers
- Cranberries, the crimson harvest
- Pies, cobblers, grunts, slumps, and pandowdies
- A sweet tooth: maple syrup and molasses
- Sea of plenty: lobsters, codfish, and clams

New England's foods are at the core of American cooking. Schoolchildren learn about the Pilgrims braving it out in the New World, adapting to the rocky soil, growing unfamiliar crops. Thanksgiving, one of our most beloved holidays, centers around a feast that began in Massachusetts a year after the colonists landed at Plymouth Rock. Many of our country's most enduring recipes go as far back as the earnest settlers who made their home in the region.

There are six states in New England, and each has its own particular specialties: Maine is famous for lobster, Massachusetts for codfish and cranberries. The Connecticut River is abundant with shad. Maple trees, with their sweet, delicate sap, flourish in the forests of Vermont. Rhode Island grows Greening apples, still the first choice for pie; and New Hampshire boasts pea soup, the food of folk who emigrated from French Canada hundreds of years ago.

Yet there is a wholeness about traditional New England cuisine, all dating back to the very first few years that Europeans made a home on its shores.

First There Were Pilgrims

The Pilgrims were the first permanent European settlers in New England. Before them, fishermen from Europe had come for short periods as far back as the sixteenth century to load up their boats with codfish. But Native Americans had lived in the area for thousands of years.

The *Mayflower* Arrives

The colonists who came on the *Mayflower* and landed at Plymouth Rock in 1620 were English who were fleeing religious persecution. They were plain people whose religious ethic was reflected in their simple cooking style. They were frugal, too. Leftovers from a New England Boiled Dinner became the next night's Red Flannel Hash; day-old cornmeal mush was fried and served with maple syrup for breakfast. The bitterly cold winters also influenced their cooking. *Chowders* and other hot, hearty foods were typical.

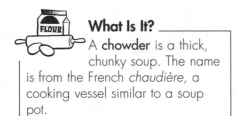

What Is It?

A **chowder** is a thick, chunky soup. The name is from the French *chaudière*, a cooking vessel similar to a soup pot.

Chowders are still popular, and if you plan to prepare them or any other kind of soup, don't worry about buying an expensive pot. On the other hand, avoid cheap, thin-gauge cookware, which warps easily and can burn the ingredients. Look for pots with an aluminum core or a thick disc at the bottom. Be sure that the handles are secured very well. Riveted handles are preferable because they offer more support.

How Corny

The Pilgrims came to Plymouth in the dead of winter. They would all have starved if they hadn't found some dried corn. But corn is native to the Americas, and the English had never seen it. It was fortunate for the Pilgrims that Squanto, a Native American neighbor, spoke English. He and other natives befriended the newcomers and showed them how to plant and to cook the grain.

Mostly Meal

The Pilgrims learned to roast fresh summer corn and use it for soups, side dishes, and relishes, but a good deal of the crop was dried and made into meal. Meal was used for flat breads called ashcakes, hoecakes, or jonnycakes.

Unlike wheat, corn has no gluten and you can't make regular breads with the dried meal. There are yellow, white, and blue cornmeals available (blue varieties are typical in recipes of America's Southwest). Cornmeal is available in several textures, but finely ground is best for cornbreads, mush, muffins, and puddings.

Yankee Ingenuity and Frugality

The Pilgrims learned quickly and adapted cornmeal to some of their familiar recipes. Pudding was always an English favorite. The cornmeal mush, or "hasty pudding," that the natives taught them how to make was transformed into several delicious dishes including Indian Pudding, which is cornmeal mush mixed with eggs, milk, molasses, and spices, and Brown Bread, a tender, grainy loaf that contains some rye and wheat flours and molasses.

 **Fein on Food**
Harvard's Hasty Pudding Club was founded in 1795 by students who hated college food—imagine that!—and wanted to make their beloved hasty puddings in their dorm fireplaces.

The First Thanksgiving

After a first hard winter, the Pilgrims who survived were so grateful that they invited their Native American friends to share in a feast. The first Thanksgiving wasn't anything like the traditional one we have today. No one recorded the actual meal, but Governor Bradford's history *Of Plimoth Plantation* mentions wild turkey. Most likely the natives and colonists also ate venison, lobster, squash, cornmeal mush, and cranberries sweetened with maple syrup. Over the years, the traditional dinner took on a more English style with stuffings for the bird and pumpkin made into pie.

In 1863, President Lincoln issued a Proclamation, setting the last Thursday in November as a national Thanksgiving Day. It was changed in 1941 to fall on the fourth Thursday in November.

All About Beans

Most beans are native to the Americas and were important to Pilgrim survival the first years. They are still one of our country's most important foods.

Going Together

In colonial days, beans and corn were grown together and eaten together, too, in Succotash, an original Native American dish still popular throughout the United States. In the summer, succotash is made with fresh vegetables, but the dish is a winter staple, too, made from dried corn and beans.

An American Classic

Baked Beans is one of our country's most cherished dishes and is the reason that Boston got the nickname Beantown. (You probably wouldn't be surprised to learn that the first successful commercial convenience food in the United States was Van Kamp's canned baked beans in 1861!) This dish was one of the first recipes the colonists learned from the Native American. The English, who had a love for all things sweet, knew the stuff would taste better with molasses, and they preferred salt pork to the bear fat the natives used. Baked beans satisfied the religious Puritans, who refrained from working on the Sabbath; the dish cooked all day Saturday and was done in time for the evening meal. Leftovers stayed warm in the hearth for the Sunday meal after church.

The recipe for baked beans traveled with the pioneers, and different versions of it emerged throughout America. Bostonians insist that theirs is the proper one and consider the addition of tomatoes or ketchup a heresy dreamed up by some misguided cook in Pennsylvania. Out West, cooks flavor the beans with chili peppers. Vermont Baked Beans are always made with maple syrup. People have strong opinions everywhere about what kind of beans to use: Most New Englanders like navy beans, except for Rhode Islanders, who prefer yellow-eyes. Midwesterners opt for kidney beans; southerners use red beans; Texans, pinto beans; and folks from Pennsylvania, lima beans. Actually, all these are delicious options. Try several variations to see which is your favorite.

Did You Know ...

Fresh lima beans are classic for succotash, although some New Englanders insist on cranberry beans. If you can't find fresh lima beans, use thawed, frozen ones. Most early settlers enriched the dish with salt pork, but modern palates may find that pancetta works even better: It's tastier and has less fat.

Kitchen Clue

Dried beans need soaking before you cook them. You can cover them with water and let them rest for about eight hours, but here's a quicker method: Place the beans in a large saucepan and cover them with water. Bring the water to boil over high heat. Lower the heat and let the beans boil gently for two minutes. Remove the pan from the heat and let the beans soak for one hour.

Baked Bean recipes usually call for salt pork, which gives the sauce a rich, luxurious flavor. But you can use a variety of substitutes, including bacon, kielbasa, a ham bone, a chunk of corned beef, cut-up hot dogs, or even smoked turkey.

Crimson Harvest

It's likely that cranberries were served at the first Thanksgiving. This bright red fruit, which grew profusely in bogs on the shores of Massachusetts, would have been ready for harvest in mid-autumn. The Pilgrims ate the berries plain or with maple syrup. It wasn't until generations later, when sugar became less expensive, that cranberry sauce became a beloved staple. Most people use cranberries for sauce or relish, but the fruit is more versatile: Use it for pies, breads, and muffins, or to accent pork or poultry. You can freeze cranberries in the plastic bag they're wrapped in. You don't have to thaw them before using in recipes unless the berries need chopping.

Pumpkins and Squashes and Pies, Oh My!

Pumpkins were as important to the Puritans as corn and beans. In fact, the colonists would have starved to death without these bright orange gourds. The settlers had never seen pumpkins, but they quickly learned how to cook them and other indigenous winter squashes. They boiled pumpkin and used it as a vegetable with dinner. They also mashed the pulp for use in biscuits.

Mashed pumpkin continues to prove useful as a lush and flavorful addition to quickbreads and coffeecakes. Mixed with puréed white beans, it's a handy, do-ahead side dish that combines two of New England's favorite ingredients.

Small, sweet sugar pumpkins have the sweetest flesh most appropriate for vegetable dishes and baked goods. You can cut them into quarters, remove the seeds, and bake the pumpkin (at 350°) until it is soft (about one hour). But canned pumpkin is fine, and it saves time. Be sure to buy plain mashed pumpkin rather than "pumpkin pie mix" so you can blend in the spices you like. You can also substitute most winter squashes for pumpkin. If you can find it, try Kuri squash. Kuri is large with deep red-orange flesh, sweet flavor, and a dry texture that is perfect for baked goods.

Kitchen Clue

Nutmeg, an important ingredient for flavoring pumpkin pie, loses its scent and flavor quickly once it's ground. It's worth a few extra dollars to invest in a special grater or mill so you can have fresh nutmeg for pumpkin pie and other recipes. It only takes a few seconds to grate nutmeg, and tinned or boxed varieties can't compare.

When the Puritans made the decision to sweeten pumpkin pulp and season it with fragrant spices imported from Europe, a culinary classic was born. The first pumpkin pies weren't like the ones we know today. The seasoned custard was baked inside the pumpkin, and pieces of pumpkin flesh were scooped out with it for eating. The crust came later.

Modern-day pumpkin pies are made with partially baked pie shells. To bake a pie shell without filling ("blind"), you need to line the dough with foil or parchment paper and weigh down the crust as it bakes. This prevents shrinking and keeps the crust crispy. Pie weights are available in specialty shops. The little pellets are made of aluminum or ceramic.

Pie, All Day Long

When regular flour became cheaper and more available, the colonists prepared the more familiar kind of pie. During the winter, it was a good way to preserve food. The pies were stored in the cellar, packed in snow. Pie wasn't just for dessert then. It was eaten for breakfast, lunch, dinner, and in between. What began as a British specialty quickly became an essential part of American cuisine.

Did You Know …

Pie takes some doing, so it pays to buy pie pans that won't sabotage your effort. Simple glass pans hold heat well, so they are ideal, as are ceramic pans, which are often attractive, too. Dark metal pans are fine; they help the crust to brown well. Nonstick pans may be fine for baking, but the surface gets scratched when you cut slices.

What Is It?

Shortcrust pastry is another name for standard pie dough. For tender crusts, make pie dough at least 30 minutes in advance to give the gluten in the flour a chance to relax. You can freeze pie dough.

Pie can mean several things, of course, and lots of different foods qualify. The necessary elements are filling and crust. Several versions emerged in colonial days. Slumps were so named because the dough slumps into the filling. Grunts refer to the rather indelicate sounds of satisfaction one might make when feasting on this dish. Both are made with seasoned, sweetened fruit topped with biscuit dough. Cobbler and pandowdy contain fruit covered with classic *shortcrust pastry*. To make cobbler or pandowdy you wait for the crust to be done, and then smash into it before serving. The tops look cobbled or dowdy, hence the names.

The colonists used a variety of fruits for pie: pears, blueberries, and so on, but apple pie was always a New England favorite. Tart green apples were, and still are, best for apple pie. They have the most flavor, and the texture holds up well. When green apples aren't available, consider using other varieties of apples and adding acidic ingredients such as rhubarb or cranberries to perk up the taste.

Rhode Island Greenings are the perfect pie apple. However, they aren't easy to find. Other apples that make good pie include Granny Smith, Golden Delicious, Newtown Pippin, Northern Spy, Stayman, Baldwin, Jonagold, Winesap, and Braeburn.

A Sweet Tooth

Maybe it was the austere winters, or maybe the strict religious observances. Whatever the reason, there was a decided yen for sweets in the colonies. White sugar was too expensive for most people, so they settled for maple syrup, made from the sap of maple trees, or molasses, the sweet, thick liquid left over after cane is processed into crystal sugar.

The Natural

The Native Americans showed the settlers how to tap maple trees and boil down the sap to make syrup. For a while, maple was the only sweetener available to glaze ham, enrich baked beans and sweet potatoes, or to sweeten puddings, pies, and other baked goods. Even today, when we have our pick of sweetening agents, maple is a fine choice when you want a delicate and subtle liquid to baste baked apples, glaze poultry, or pour over pancakes or plain yogurt.

Kitchen Clue

Maple syrup is divided into grades, based on color. The lighter varieties are grade A, which are best for serving plain. Darker, more robustly flavored grade B syrups are ideal for use in recipes. Grade B syrup is available in some supermarkets, food specialty stores, and food catalogues.

The Mother of the Revolution

Our second president, John Adams, once said that molasses "was an essential ingredient in American independence." The settlers began importing molasses soon after their arrival. It was their primary sweetener, used for beans and cakes and gingerbread, a particular favorite. Gingerbread was always served on Muster Days, when the men practiced military maneuvers. The molasses was purchased from French, not English, sugarcane processors, because of lower prices. That provoked the British Parliament to pass the Molasses Act, imposing a hefty tax on molasses imported into the colonies. Cries of "taxation without representation" became a rallying cry for war.

Although it may have inspired yearnings for independence, molasses also had an unfortunate impact on American history and culture. It was used to finance the infamous Triangle Trade: Molasses shipped to New England was made into rum that was sold in Africa in exchange for slaves, who were shipped to the West Indies as payment for more molasses to the colonies.

That's the Spirit

Rum, one of the more interesting byproducts of sugarcane production, was the liquor of choice in the colonies. Hot spirited libations such as Toddies, Stones Fences, and Hot Buttered Rum were cheering on cold winter nights. These beverages are unfamiliar now, but rum continues to be popular for drinks and for cooking, used in cakes and frostings, mixed with sweet potatoes, and even used to spike pumpkin pie. Try a spoonful or two of dark rum in homemade whipped cream or on top of sugared strawberries.

A Lobster as Big as the Ritz

Today, when lobster is considered a culinary prize and a lobster dinner can set you back more than a few bucks, it's hard to imagine that these crustaceans were once cheap (a penny a pound) and large (some grew as big as 25 pounds) and plentiful (hundreds crawled along the beaches in colonial times). There were so many lobsters for the taking that colonists grew sick of them and even used them for bait. On the other hand, clever cooks did learn to make some fabulous dishes that endure to this day: lobster stew; lobster pie; and plain lobsters, steamed, boiled, grilled, or pan-roasted.

There are different varieties of lobster. A Maine lobster has two huge claws; rock or spiny lobsters have no claws. Maine lobster has a richer, meatier taste.

Mini-Recipe

Steamed Lobster (4 servings)   In a very large pot, with a rack set on the bottom, bring to a boil a $1/2$" salted water, 2 cups white wine, 2 stalks celery, 2 carrots, and some parsley sprigs. Add 4 live $1^1/_2$-pound lobsters, cover the pot, lower the heat, and cook for about 15 minutes. You can boil lobster, too, by plunging it into boiling water, but steamed lobsters are usually more tender.

Cod, the Fish That Made New England Famous

Well before the first Pilgrims landed at Plymouth, European fishermen braved the Atlantic and faced bitter winters, blinding blizzards, and unfamiliar natives in New

England. It was worth it because codfish was so abundant that it provided a reliable and steady source of income.

The first settlers realized the value in cod, too. In Massachusetts, several families became rich and powerful in the codfish trade. These families formed New England's "Codfish Aristocracy." Boston became an important center of fish commerce, not merely for cod but also for other abundant New England fish and shellfish, such as halibut, mackerel, herring, haddock, bluefish, clams, lobsters, and scallops.

Fein on Food
In 1784, a wooden replica of a codfish, called the Sacred Cod, was put up in the Massachusetts House of Representatives in tribute to the cod's economic and culinary status and importance.

The Many Guises of Codfish

In the early days, codfish was salted and dried so that it could be preserved for year-round use. Salt cod became the standard Sunday dinner in many households, and salt cod cakes became a hallmark New England dish. It's still a favorite, but after refrigeration became available, dishes with fresh cod surpassed it in popularity. Cod is a mild fish that does well when prepared with robust ingredients such as fresh herbs, tomatoes, olives, anchovies, capers, fresh ginger, and curry.

Scrod, the Dish That Made the Parker House Famous

Scrod is a young, filleted cod weighing a pound or two. Early on, it was a featured dish at Boston's Parker House hotel, whose chefs may have invented the name. Broiled Scrod was so well liked that it assured the hotel's fame. The Parker House wooed guests with other well-known dishes, too, most notably Parker House Rolls and Boston Cream Pie.

Mini-Recipe
Broiled Scrod (4 servings)   Preheat the broiler. Brush 4 scrod filets with 2 tablespoons olive oil. Sprinkle with salt and pepper and 2 tablespoons plain, dry bread crumbs. Broil for 6–8 minutes. Sprinkle with some fresh chopped parsley and serve with melted butter and lemon juice.

Happy as a Clam

The Europeans weren't familiar with the mollusks and crustaceans they found in their new home. They approached clams, oysters, and other shellfish with some hesitation at first, but soon understood the value of the catch.

Yes, We Have No Tomatoes

Of all New England's dishes, clam chowder has created the most controversy. Based on the original fish chowders prepared by the Europeans who came for cod, New England chowder took a different turn when the colonists enriched the soup with milk and cream. New England Clam Chowder is white and creamy. New Englanders consider the Manhattan version, which is tomato based, a heresy. (Once, a legislator in Maine introduced a bill that would have outlawed tomatoes in clam chowder. Luckily for lovers of Manhattan Clam Chowder, it didn't pass.) Some food historians believe that Manhattan Clam Chowder began in Rhode Island, whose Portuguese and Italian settlers used tomatoes and other Mediterranean seasonings in their fish chowders.

A Clam for Every Occasion

Native Americans introduced the colonists to yet another enduring tradition: the clambake. Shellfish was placed on hot stones and covered with seaweed. These days, New England clambakes might include grilled hot dogs, sausage, hamburgers, and chicken! Clambakes are large gatherings. For cooking at home, New Englanders have dozens of other clam dishes: hash, stew, and pie; scalloped clams and clam fritters; fried, baked or steamed clams; and clams raw on the half shell.

The Least You Need to Know

- ◆ Succotash can be made with either dried or fresh beans and corn.
- ◆ Recipes for baked beans vary from region to region.
- ◆ Dried beans need soaking before they are cooked.
- ◆ If you use canned pumpkin for recipes, be sure to buy plain pumpkin, not pumpkin pie mix.
- ◆ There are several grades of maple syrup. Grade B is more robust than grade A and is delicious in recipes.
- ◆ Maine lobsters are meaty and have two large claws.

Brandy-Spiked Jellied Cranberry Sauce

If you mold this in cans, everyone will think you're using commercial cranberry sauce—until they taste it! The brandy makes this cranberry sauce extra special.

Prep time: less than 15 minutes • Makes 8 servings

Special equipment: blender or food processor; candy thermometer; molds or washed tin cans

4 cups cranberries (1 lb.)

1²/₃ cups water

1¹/₄ cups sugar

2 TB. orange-flavored brandy such as Gran Marnier

Wash berries and discard any stems that remain. Drain berries and place in a saucepan. Cover berries with water. Bring water to boil over high heat and cook berries for 4–5 minutes or until they pop. Crush berries in a blender or food processor. Strain berries through a sieve into a bowl. Press down to extract as much liquid as possible. There should be 2¹/₄ cups liquid. If not, add some water.

Place liquid in a large saucepan and add sugar. Place a candy thermometer on the rim of the pan. Bring mixture to boil over high heat. Stir only until sugar has dissolved. Cook mixture until it reaches 220° on the candy thermometer. Remove the pan from heat. Stir in brandy. Pour into a 2-cup mold or washed tin cans from canned vegetables or soup. Refrigerate for at least 2 hours. To unmold, use the tip of a small knife to free the edges, and then invert mold and shake slightly.

Hot Tip

If you don't have a candy thermometer, cook liquid until it is very dark. Take a tiny amount of mixture out with a spoon and drop it into a cup of cold water. It should jell at the bottom of the cup. Try these variations:

◆ Substitute ginger brandy or rum for the orange-flavored brandy.

◆ Add small amount of finely chopped pecans or walnuts.

◆ Add 1 tablespoon finely shredded orange peel.

New England Clam Chowder

This is the traditional New England version, the classic, creamy white soup, chock full of juicy clams and bits of crispy salt pork that so pleased Ishmael, the sole survivor of Captain Ahab's relentless pursuit of Moby Dick in Herman Melville's classic novel.

Prep time: less than 30 minutes • Makes 6 servings

2 doz. cherrystone or chowder clams	Ground white pepper, to taste
3 cups water	2 cups half-and-half
4 oz. salt pork, cut into dice	2 TB. butter
2 medium-size onions, chopped	Salt, if desired
4 large all-purpose potatoes, peeled and diced	Paprika

Scrub clams and place unopened in a large saucepan or stockpot. Pour in water. Cover the pot and cook clams over moderate heat for 8–10 minutes, until they have opened. Discard any clams that have not opened. Remove clam meat, discard shells, and mince meat. Set aside.

Strain clam broth through cheesecloth and reserve 4 cups for soup. Cook salt pork in the saucepan over low to moderate heat for 5–6 minutes or until pieces are crispy. Remove pieces and set aside. Discard all but about 2 tablespoons rendered fat. Add onions and cook over moderate heat for 3–4 minutes or until wilted.

Add reserved clam broth and potatoes, cover the pan, and cook for 10–12 minutes or until potatoes are tender. Add clams and cook another 2 minutes. Add ground white pepper, half-and-half, and salt pork. Heat through, but don't let soup come to a boil. Add butter, taste for seasoning, and add salt if desired. Place soup in a tureen and sprinkle with paprika.

Codfish with Olives, Capers, and Tomatoes

Codfish is so mild that it partners well with pungent ingredients. This dish goes nicely with mashed potatoes or steamed white rice and a green vegetable.

Prep time: less than 15 minutes   •   Makes 4 servings

8 plum tomatoes, seeded and chopped

2 cloves garlic, chopped

1 large shallot, chopped

16 pitted green imported olives, cut into pieces

2 TB. capers

2 TB. chopped parsley

2 TB. sherry wine vinegar

3 TB. olive oil

3 sprigs fresh thyme or 1 tsp. dried thyme

2 lbs. codfish filet about 1½" thick

Salt and pepper

Preheat the oven to 450°.

Place tomatoes in a baking dish, and scatter garlic, shallot, olives, capers, and parsley on top. Pour sherry wine vinegar and 2 tablespoons olive oil over vegetables, and place thyme sprigs on top.

Place cod filet on top of vegetables. Coat fish with remaining olive oil. Sprinkle with salt and pepper. Bake for about 15 minutes or until dish is cooked through. Serve fish with the vegetables and pan juices.

Fried Clams with Tartar Sauce

Crunchy, golden-brown fried clams will make you feel transported to a sunny beach, nibbling on succulent delicacies and enjoying the warmth and relaxation.

Prep time: less than 15 minutes   •   Makes 4 servings

Special equipment: cake rack

For the clams:

24 shucked cherrystone or littleneck clams

1/2 cup all-purpose flour

2 eggs, beaten

3/4 cup cracker crumbs

1/2 tsp. salt, or to taste

1/4 tsp. paprika

Freshly ground black pepper to taste

3 cups vegetable oil, approx.

Tartar Sauce (recipe follows)

Pat clams dry on paper towels and dredge them in the flour. Dip floured clams in beaten eggs. Mix cracker crumbs, salt, paprika, and black pepper, and coat clams with this mixture. Set clams aside on a cake rack for about 15 minutes to dry slightly.

Heat 3" vegetable oil in a deep skillet, enough to cover clams completely. When oil reaches about 365°, deep-fat fry clams a few at a time, for about 2 minutes or until nicely browned. Drain on paper towels. Serve with Tartar Sauce.

For the tartar sauce:

1 cup mayonnaise

1/4 cup finely chopped cornichons (small French sour pickles)

1 chopped shallot

2 TB. chopped fresh parsley

1 TB. chopped fresh tarragon

Hot pepper sauce to taste

Mix all ingredients together in a small bowl.

Maine Lobster Pie

This extravagant dish is worthy of special occasions or special company. You can make it a day ahead and rewarm it.

Prep time: less than 30 minutes   •   Makes 4 servings

2 TB. olive oil

1 shallot, chopped

1 lb. cooked lobster meat, cut into chunks

$\frac{1}{4}$ cup sherry

2 TB. butter

2 TB. all-purpose flour

$1\frac{1}{2}$ cups light cream

$\frac{1}{2}$ tsp. salt, or to taste

$\frac{1}{4}$ tsp. paprika

Freshly ground black pepper

$\frac{2}{3}$ cup plain dry bread crumbs

$\frac{1}{2}$ cup finely chopped almonds

3 TB. grated Parmesan cheese

3 TB. melted butter

2 TB. sherry

Paprika

Preheat the oven to 350°.

Heat olive oil in a skillet set over moderate heat. Add shallot and cook for 1 minute or so, or until softened. Add lobster meat, stirring quickly to coat lobster with olive oil, then pour in the $\frac{1}{4}$ cup sherry. Turn heat to high, cook 1 minute, and remove the pan from the heat.

Heat butter in a saucepan over moderate heat. When butter has melted and looks foamy, add flour and cook, stirring occasionally, for about 2 minutes. Gradually add cream and stir for 2–3 minutes or until sauce is thick and smooth. Stir in salt, $\frac{1}{4}$ teaspoon paprika, and pepper. Remove the pan from heat. Stir in lobster mixture. Spoon lobster mixture into a casserole dish.

Combine bread crumbs, almonds, Parmesan cheese, melted butter, and 2 tablespoons sherry, and mix gently. Scatter bread-crumb mixture on top of casserole. Sprinkle with paprika. Bake for 20 minutes or until surface is golden brown.

Hot Tip

Most people use a dry sherry when cooking seafood, but Oloroso sherry, which is sweeter, is a worthy substitute and gives this dish a rich finish. Also try substituting flaked crab or chopped, cooked shrimp for the lobster.

Maple Glazed Chicken

Maple syrup makes a gently sweet glaze for poultry. This simple recipe takes very little preparation and tastes as if you made a big effort.

Prep time: less than 15 minutes • Makes 4 to 6 servings

1 roasting chicken, about 5–6 lbs.

Salt and black pepper, to taste

¼ cup maple syrup

2 TB. port or Madeira

2 TB. butter

1 TB. Dijon mustard

2 tsp. fresh thyme leaves (or ¾ tsp. dried thyme)

Preheat the oven to 400°.

Wash chicken inside and out, removing giblets, liver, and neck. Sprinkle chicken all over with salt and pepper. Place chicken, breast-side down, on a rack in a roasting pan. If you cook the giblets, liver, and neck, place them in the pan with chicken.

Combine maple syrup, port or Madeira, butter, Dijon mustard, and thyme in a small saucepan. Cook over moderate heat, stirring occasionally, for 2–3 minutes or until butter has melted. Brush some of mixture over back of chicken. Place chicken in the oven. Roast for 15 minutes.

Lower heat to 350°. Brush chicken with more maple glaze. Roast another 30 minutes. Turn chicken over and brush with more glaze. Roast for another 30 minutes, then brush with more glaze. Roast another 20 minutes and brush with remaining glaze. Continue to roast chicken until a meat thermometer inserted into thickest part of thigh registers 165 to 180°. Let chicken rest for 15 minutes before carving.

Hot Tip

The USDA recommends cooking chicken to 180° as measured in the thickest part of the thigh, but the meat is juicier when cooked to 165°, and many cooks follow this practice. You must make the decision whether or not to use the more conservative USDA guidelines; I have suggested alternative temperatures. Use a meat thermometer or instant read thermometer to check temperature. In any case, be sure to follow safe food handling basics: Wash hands and wrap, refrigerate, and defrost the meat properly to keep pathogens away.

Red Flannel Hash

This dish was invented as a way to use leftover corned beef. Today, we love it on its own and buy the corned beef just to make the hash. Try this dish with a fried egg on top.

Prep time: less than 30 minutes   •   Makes 4 servings

3 medium all-purpose potatoes

2 TB. butter

1 medium onion, chopped

2 TB. vegetable oil

3 cups diced, cooked corned beef

1 lb. diced, cooked beets (canned is fine)

Black pepper

Freshly grated nutmeg

$^1\!/_2$ cup cream, milk, or stock

Preheat the broiler.

Peel potatoes, cut into chunks, and cook in boiling, lightly salted water for about 12–15 minutes or until tender but still firm. Drain. When cool enough to handle, chop into dice.

Heat butter in a skillet set over moderate heat. When butter has melted and looks foamy, add onion and cook, stirring occasionally, for about 2 minutes or until onion has softened. Add vegetable oil, and heat briefly. Then add meat, potatoes, and beets. Grind fresh black pepper and freshly grated nutmeg over mixture. Pour in cream.

Cook hash for 6–8 minutes, tossing the ingredients occasionally, or until ingredients are somewhat crispy. Place the pan under the broiler for a minute or so to brown the top.

Maple Baked Beans

This version of baked beans is tangy and savory, but it is milder than the classic Boston style because it calls for maple syrup rather than molasses. If you can find it, use grade B syrup, available in some supermarkets, specialty stores, and food catalogues, for the best flavor.

Prep time: less than 15 minutes   •   Makes 6 servings

1 lb. pkg. dried navy or great northern beans	³/₄ cup maple syrup, preferably grade B
6 cups water	2 tsp. powdered mustard
4 oz. slab bacon or salt pork, cut into 1" pieces	1 tsp. salt
1 medium onion, chopped	¹/₂ tsp. powdered ginger
	Boiling water

Place beans in a large saucepan and cover with water. Bring water to boil over high heat. Lower heat and let beans boil gently for 2 minutes. Remove the pan from heat and let beans soak for one hour. Return the pan to the heat and simmer for 45 minutes. Drain beans and put in a casserole dish. Add bacon, onion, maple syrup, mustard, salt, and ginger. Pour in enough boiling water to cover beans by 1". Cover casserole and put in the oven. Set temperature to 300° and cook beans at least 4 hours or until they are tender, stirring occasionally and adding water, if necessary, to keep them moist.

Succotash with Pancetta

This traditional dish dates back to Pilgrim days, but the pancetta gives it a modern touch. Make it with salt pork if you prefer more authenticity.

Prep time: less than 15 minutes   •   Makes 4 to 6 servings

4 oz. pancetta	1 tsp. sugar
2 TB. olive oil	$\frac{1}{3}$ cup water
1 small onion, chopped	$\frac{1}{2}$ cup light cream
1 (10-oz.) pkg. frozen lima beans	Salt and pepper, to taste
1 (10-oz.) pkg. frozen corn niblets	

Chop pancetta into small pieces. Cook in a skillet over moderate heat for 6–8 minutes or until lightly crispy. Remove pancetta and set aside.

Discard fat from the pan. Return the pan to the heat and pour in olive oil. Swirl the pan to coat the bottom with olive oil. Add onion and cook, stirring once or twice, for 2–3 minutes or until onion has softened. Add lima beans, corn, sugar, and water. Stir, cover the pan, and turn heat to low. Cook ingredients for 10 minutes.

Remove the cover, pour in cream, and raise the heat to moderately high. Cook, stirring often, until all but a tablespoon or two of liquid has been absorbed. Add pancetta. Taste succotash and add salt and pepper to taste.

White Bean and Pumpkin Purée

A rich, smooth side dish for roasts or grilled meats, poultry, or fish.

Prep time: less than 30 minutes • Makes 4 servings

Special equipment: food processor or blender

2 TB. olive oil

1 small onion, chopped

1 carrot, chopped

1 small stalk celery, chopped

1 large clove garlic, chopped

$\frac{1}{2}$ tsp. fresh thyme leaves

1 cup cooked white beans

1 cup mashed pumpkin

$\frac{1}{4}$ cup half-and-half

Salt and pepper, to taste

1 beaten egg

1 TB. butter, melted

$\frac{1}{3}$ cup fresh bread crumbs

Preheat the oven to 400°.

Heat olive oil in a skillet. Add onion, carrot, and celery, and cook over moderate heat, stirring occasionally, for 2–3 minutes or until the vegetables have softened. Add garlic and thyme, and cook for another minute.

Hot Tip

You can make your own cooked beans and mashed pumpkin, or you can use canned. Rinse canned white beans and drain them thoroughly. Buy plain mashed pumpkin, not pumpkin pie mix.

Place mixture in the bowl of a food processor (or use a blender). Add white beans and process mixture until smooth purée has formed. Add pumpkin and half-and-half, and process briefly to blend ingredients. Add salt and pepper to taste.

Add egg, and process to blend in. Spoon mixture into a casserole dish. Combine melted butter and bread crumbs in a small bowl. Sprinkle mixture over purée. Bake for about 15 minutes or until bubbling hot.

Pumpkin Raisin Bread

This moist tea bread will come in handy for breakfast or after dinner. You can eat it plain, but it's also delicious spread with butter or cream cheese.

Prep time: less than 15 minutes • Makes 1 loaf

1½ cups all-purpose flour	¼ tsp. ground allspice
1 tsp. baking soda	⅔ cup sugar
1 tsp. baking powder	2 eggs
½ tsp. salt	½ cup vegetable oil
1 tsp. ground cinnamon	1¼ cups mashed pumpkin
½ tsp. ground nutmeg	½ cup golden raisins

Preheat the oven to 350°.

Grease a 9" × 5" × 3" loaf pan. Sift flour, baking soda, baking powder, salt, cinnamon, nutmeg, allspice, and sugar together into a bowl.

In another bowl, combine eggs, vegetable oil, and mashed pumpkin; blend thoroughly. Add dry ingredients to egg mixture, and stir to blend ingredients. Fold in raisins. Pour batter into the prepared pan. Bake for about 1 hour or until a cake tester inserted into the center comes out clean.

Hot Tip _____

If you use canned pumpkin, be sure to buy plain mashed pumpkin, not pumpkin pie mix.

Gingerbread

This is among the oldest, most traditional kinds of cake in New England, served on Muster Days when soldiers would practice military maneuvers for the local militia. It's nice served with a dollop of whipped cream.

Prep time: less than 30 minutes • Makes 1 (8") square cake

Special equipment: cake rack

2¹/₂ cups all-purpose flour

2 tsp. powdered ginger

1 tsp. cinnamon

¹/₂ tsp. ground nutmeg

¹/₄ tsp. ground cloves

¹/₄ tsp. salt

¹/₂ cup butter

¹/₂ cup brown sugar

1 cup molasses

2 tsp. baking soda

1 cup boiling water

2 eggs

Preheat the oven to 350°.

Lightly grease an 8" square cake pan. Sift flour, ginger, cinnamon, nutmeg, cloves, and salt together into a bowl and set aside. Beat butter and brown sugar together with a hand mixer or in an electric mixer set on moderate speed. Beat 2–3 minutes, or until mixture is smooth and creamy. Add molasses and beat it in, blending thoroughly. Scrape down the sides of the bowl occasionally with a rubber spatula to make sure you incorporate each ingredient.

Mix baking soda and water together and add to butter mixture gradually, beating constantly. Add flour mixture and beat mixture 1–2 minutes or until thoroughly blended. Add eggs and beat mixture another minute. Pour batter into the prepared pan. Bake 45–50 minutes or until a cake tester inserted into the center comes out clean. Let cool in the pan for 10 minutes, then invert onto a cake rack to cool completely.

Apple-Cranberry Pie

This variation on classic apple pie adds a cup of cranberries to give the dessert some piquancy and vibrant color.

Prep time: less than 30 minutes   •   Makes 1 (9") pie

Dough for two-crust pie (see Basic Pie Dough, Appendix C)

2¹/₂ lbs. pie apples, peeled, cored, and sliced

1 cup cranberries

1 cup brown sugar

1 TB. lemon juice

1 tsp. freshly grated orange peel, optional

¹/₂ tsp. cinnamon

¹/₄ tsp. nutmeg

2 TB. all-purpose flour

1 TB. butter

Preheat the oven to 400°.

Make the dough (see recipe in Appendix C). On a floured surface, roll out half the dough and fit it into a 9" pie pan.

Mix apples, cranberries, brown sugar, lemon juice, orange peel, cinnamon, nutmeg, and flour in a bowl. Pour mixture into the pie pan. Cut butter into small pieces and place on top of fruit.

Roll remaining dough and place on top of berries. Crimp edges to seal the pie. Bake for 45 minutes or until the crust is crisp and golden brown.

Pumpkin Pie

The traditional fall classic.

Prep time: less than 15 minutes • Makes 1 (9") pie

Half a recipe of pie dough (see Basic Pie Dough, Appendix C)

2 eggs

$^{1}/_{2}$ cup sugar

$^{1}/_{4}$ cup brown sugar

$1^{3}/_{4}$ cups pumpkin, mashed

1 tsp. cinnamon

$^{1}/_{2}$ tsp. ground ginger

$^{1}/_{4}$ tsp. nutmeg

$^{1}/_{4}$ tsp. cloves

$^{1}/_{2}$ tsp. salt

1 (13-oz.) can evaporated milk

Preheat the oven to 400°.

Roll dough on a floured surface and fit inside a 9" pie pan. Cover dough with aluminum foil and place pie weights or dried beans inside. Bake crust for 10 minutes. Remove weights and foil and continue to bake crust for another 3–4 minutes.

Remove partially baked pie from the oven and let cool. Beat eggs, sugar, and brown sugar together until fluffy and well blended. Stir in pumpkin, cinnamon, ginger, nutmeg, cloves, and salt, and blend ingredients thoroughly. Blend in evaporated milk.

Pour mixture into pie pan and bake for 15 minutes. Reduce oven heat to 350°. Bake pie for another 45 minutes, or until top is evenly browned and custard is set.

Boston Cream Pie

This pie actually is a pudding cake of yellow layers stuffed with vanilla custard and glazed with dark chocolate sauce. It was made famous at Boston's Parker House Hotel.

Prep time: less than 1 hour   •   Makes 1 (9") layer cake

Special equipment: cake rack

For the cake:

1½ cups cake flour	⅔ cup sugar
2 tsp. baking powder	2 eggs
¼ tsp. salt	1 tsp. vanilla extract
6 TB. butter	½ cup milk

Preheat the oven to 350°.

Sift cake flour, baking powder, and salt into a bowl. Set aside.

In another bowl, cream butter and sugar with an electric beater at medium speed for 2–3 minutes or until smooth and creamy. Add eggs and vanilla extract and beat them in. Add milk, alternating with flour mixture, and beat for 2–3 minutes until the batter is uniform. Pour batter into 2 greased 9" cake pans.

Bake for 16–18 minutes or until a cake tester inserted into the center of cake comes out clean. Cool in the pans for 10 minutes, then invert onto a cake rack to cool completely.

For the custard:

½ cup sugar	2 eggs, beaten
3 TB. cornstarch	1 TB. butter
⅛ tsp. salt	1½ tsp. vanilla extract
1¼ cups milk	

Mix sugar, cornstarch, and salt together in a saucepan. Place the pan over moderate heat and gradually add milk, cooking and stirring with a whisk for 3–4 minutes, or until mixture is very thick. Gradually add about a cup of hot mixture to beaten eggs.

Return mixture to the pan. Turn heat to low. Cook for about 2 minutes, but do not let mixture come to a boil. Remove from heat and stir in butter. Let mixture cool completely. When cold, stir in vanilla extract. Place one of the cake layers on a cake plate, top with custard, and then the other cake layer.

continues

continued

For the chocolate glaze (makes about 1¹/₄ cups):

¹/₂ cup cream

¹/₂ tsp. instant coffee powder

8 oz. bittersweet chocolate, coarsely chopped

Combine cream and coffee powder in a small saucepan and heat. Stir to dissolve coffee, until liquid comes to a boil. Remove from heat and stir in bittersweet chocolate. Stir until melted and smooth. Place cake on a rack with a large plate beneath. Drizzle glaze over cake and gently spread on top. Let drip down the sides. Catch extra drippings in the plate and drizzle over cake.

Indian Pudding

This is one of the oldest New England specialties, still popular today because it is exquisitely rich, smooth, and tasty. It is well worth waiting the hours it takes to cook.

Prep time: less than 30 minutes • Makes 8 servings

3 cups milk

¹/₃ cup molasses

¹/₃ cup cornmeal

1¹/₂ TB. butter

2 eggs

¹/₄ cup brown sugar

¹/₂ tsp. salt

¹/₈ tsp. baking soda

¹/₂ tsp. ground cinnamon

¹/₂ tsp. ground ginger

Dash or two grated nutmeg

1 cup golden raisins

1 cup cream

Preheat the oven to 300°.

Combine milk, molasses, and cornmeal in a saucepan. Cook over moderate heat for 5–6 minutes, or until mixture has thickened. Add butter and stir until melted.

Combine eggs, brown sugar, salt, baking soda, cinnamon, ginger, and nutmeg in a bowl, using a whisk. Gradually add hot milk mixture to egg mixture and stir to blend thoroughly. Stir in raisins. Pour mixture into a buttered 6-quart baking dish and bake for about 1¹/₂ hours.

Pour cream on top of pudding but do not stir. Bake for another hour, or until the top is golden brown. Serve warm.

Snickerdoodles

Despite their funny name, these cookies are delicious—sweet and fragrant and wonderful for dunking. They freeze well in plastic bags.

Prep time: less than 30 minutes   •   Makes about 60 cookies

1 cup butter	$\frac{1}{2}$ tsp. salt
1$\frac{1}{3}$ cups sugar	1 tsp. vanilla extract
3 eggs	1 cup chopped almonds
3$\frac{1}{4}$ cups all-purpose flour	1 cup raisins
1 tsp. grated nutmeg	2 TB. sugar
1 tsp. baking soda	$\frac{1}{8}$ tsp. cinnamon

Preheat the oven to 350°.

In the bowl of an electric mixer, cream butter and 1$\frac{1}{3}$ cups sugar together for 3–4 minutes on medium speed, or until mixture is well blended and fluffy. Add eggs, one at a time, beating well after each addition. Add flour, nutmeg, baking soda, and salt. Add this to butter mixture and blend ingredients thoroughly. Mix in vanilla extract, almonds, and raisins.

Drop mounds from a teaspoon onto a greased cookie sheet, leaving a 1" space between each cookie. Mix 2 tablespoons sugar with cinnamon. Sprinkle sugar on top of each cookie. Bake 15–16 minutes or until lightly browned.

Peach and Blueberry Grunt with Cinnamon Cream

You'll understand why this dish is called a grunt once you taste it and make those approving sounds with each bite.

Prep time: less than 30 minutes • Makes 6 to 8 servings

For the filling:

5 cups peaches, sliced, peeled

1 cup fresh blueberries

³/₄ cup sugar

3 TB. all-purpose flour

1 TB. lemon juice

¹/₄ tsp. cinnamon

For the biscuit dough:

1 cup all-purpose flour

1 TB. sugar

1¹/₂ tsp. baking powder

¹/₂ tsp. salt

4 TB. butter, cut into chunks

¹/₃ cup milk, approx.

1 egg yolk

For the topping:

1 cup chilled whipping cream

1 TB. sugar

¹/₂ tsp. cinnamon

Preheat the oven to 400°.

Place sliced peaches and blueberries in a bowl. Add sugar, flour, lemon juice, and cinnamon, mix gently, and place mixture in a baking dish.

To make biscuit dough, mix flour, sugar, baking powder, and salt in a bowl. Work butter into dry ingredients with hands or a pastry blender until mixture resembles coarse meal. Mix ¹/₃ cup milk with egg yolk and add this to flour mixture. Stir to make a soft dough, adding a bit more milk if dough seems too dry. Drop dough on top of fruit to form 6 even mounds. Bake for 25–30 minutes, or until crust is puffed and golden brown. Let cool for a while before serving.

Beat cream with sugar and cinnamon until thick but still pourable. Spoon out portions of dessert and pour cinnamon cream on top.

Chapter 2

The Mid-Atlantic

In This Chapter

- ◆ The Dutch cooking adopted by America
- ◆ Two Pennsylvania cuisines: plain and fancy
- ◆ Presidential dining
- ◆ The gardens of New Jersey and Delaware
- ◆ Maryland's slightly southern cooking

New York, Pennsylvania, New Jersey, Delaware, Maryland, and Washington, D.C., make up the mid-Atlantic states. Fertile land, good weather, and a long coastline helped to define this region's cuisine. From the beginning, farms and gardens blossomed with vegetables, and apple orchards flourished in the Hudson Valley. Oysters, clams, crabs, and fish were plentiful.

But ethnic influences are obvious, too. These are the states that first welcomed settlers from Holland, Germany, and Scandinavia. French Huguenots, Roman Catholics, and Quakers left Europe and made their homes here. Each had a lasting impact on American cookery. American cookies, doughnuts, waffles, and coleslaw trace back to the Dutch. German ways with cabbage, pork, and desserts have left their mark particularly in Pennsylvania Dutch cuisine, with its scrapple, corn relish, and pies.

Many of the newcomers were prosperous. They didn't suffer privation or make do with simple, earthy fare. That three places (Philadelphia, New York, and Washington, D.C.) once served as our nation's capital also meant that tables would be set with rich and luxurious foods such as Roast Beef and Roast Long Island Duck.

The Dutch Arrive in New York

In 1609, Hendrik Hudson sailed down the river that now bears his name, and soon after, the Dutch built settlements from the Hudson Valley to the far reaches of Long Island. Peter Minuit bought the island of Manhattan from the Native Americans, and the little village of New Amsterdam was soon a thriving metropolis. Like their New England neighbors, the settlers learned about local produce from Native Americans.

I'll Take Manhattan (and the Bronx, Upstate, Long Island, and Staten Island)

The Dutch newcomers were prosperous and not particularly religious. Many were farmers who were interested in continued success in that area. They were lucky: The weather was good and there were vast expanses of prime, fertile land. Although the Dutch political presence lasted only about 40 years (England took over in 1664 and New Amsterdam became New York), their culinary influence was enormous and everlasting. Many foods we think of as American have their roots in the Dutch settlements of old New York.

Dutch Treats

Doughnuts are big business in the United States. The millions of Americans who eat them for breakfast every morning can thank the Dutch, who called them *oliekocken*. The original recipe called for raised yeast dough, shaped into balls and fried in hot fat. There weren't holes until years later, when Dutch bakers realized that cutting out the middle would eliminate soggy centers.

Yeast doughnuts are pleasantly puffy, with a moist interior and crispy surface. They need about two hours of rising time. Cake doughnuts, which are leavened with baking powder, need no rising time. They are densely textured and are drier than raised doughnuts, which make them great for dunking. Both are fried in hot fat. If you don't have a deep-fryer, use a large pot. Be sure the fat is four inches deep to prevent the doughnuts from burning.

The Dutch were terrific bakers, beyond doughnuts. In fact, they opened the first commercial bakeries in America. They prepared little cakes called *koeckjes*, known to Americans today as cookies. Dutch apple cakes, filled with tender fruit and dusted with sugar and cinnamon, were renowned. And Dutch waffles, prepared in special "irons," became a favorite for breakfast.

Kitchen Clue

Anyone who bakes should invest in a good cookie sheet or two. The sheets usually have one rim and three open sides, so you can lift the cookies easily with a spatula. Some have two or three rims. Look for sturdy models that provide even heating capability. Dark metals and nonstick coatings may bake faster than shiny metal pans, so check cookies carefully during baking to be sure the bottoms don't burn. You may want to line these cookie sheets with parchment paper as a precaution.

From Duck to Coleslaw

There was more to Dutch cooking than dessert. Their Sunday dinners were lavish meals that might have included roasted pork or duck. Plump, rich-tasting ducklings had been cultivated on Long Island since the first ducks were brought there from Peking, China. Because so many Dutch were dairy farmers in the old country, they imported cows to this country and contributed to making cheese an important part of the American diet. They also gave us the recipe for one of our most beloved summer staples: coleslaw, which they called *koolslaa*, or "cabbage salad."

There are dozens of varieties of coleslaw. To the classic cabbage slaw, you can add some red cabbage or carrot shreds for a splash of color. Include scallion or onion if you like your slaw heartier. Add shredded jicama, red peppers, or bean sprouts to provide extra crunch. Like sweet slaw? Stir in some raisins, chopped apple, or pear. Mix the salad with mayo. Or vinaigrette. Coleslaw is one of our most versatile dishes.

Out on Long Island

At one time there was a profusion of hard-shell and soft-shell clams, scallops, and oysters out on Long Island. The Dutch, and later the English, took advantage of the bounty. Oyster Bars became the rage throughout New York. Hard-shell clams and oysters were mostly eaten raw, on the halfshell, but New York developed its own version of clam chowder, which is well seasoned and includes tomatoes. Some other New York specialties were Angels on

Mini-Recipe

Angels on Horseback (makes one dozen)
Preheat the oven to 450°. Cut 6 slices of bacon in half and fry until bacon is lightly browned but still pliable. When cool enough to handle, wrap the half slices around 12 oysters. Secure with toothpicks. Place them in a shallow pan. Bake for several minutes, turning occasionally, until bacon is crisp.

Horseback (oysters wrapped in bacon and cooked until crisp; see the mini-recipe) and Clams Casino (with vegetables and bacon). These recipes still make wonderful hors d'oeuvres.

New York, New York: It's a Wonderful Town

Because of New York City's location, it became a major disembarkation point for immigrants. Italians, Jews, Eastern Europeans, and Chinese flocked to America. Many stayed in the city. The ethnic diversity of New York became quickly apparent in its ever-changing, ever-exciting cuisine. In later years, the trend toward ethnic cuisine continued. Waves of immigrants from the Balkans, Latin America, Korea, Southeast Asia, the Middle East, and other places have had a culinary impact. If you eat in New York, there are lots of different kinds of food to choose from, and an interesting meal is guaranteed. (For more on ethnic foods, see Chapter 9.)

The Fancy Folks of Philadelphia

Philadelphia was once America's capital and most important city. It was established by wealthy Quakers who were fond of good living and refined food. From its earliest days, Philadelphia was known for luxurious cuisine.

The Food Caused No Inconvenience

Because so many important politicos resided in Philadelphia, the city's tables featured upper-class English dishes such as Roast Beef with Yorkshire Pudding and Trifle, as well as French specialties. Future President John Adams complained about Philadelphia's emphasis on rich food and finery. But after tasting some of the fare, he admitted that the food and wine caused him "no inconvenience."

Fein on Food

Philadelphia boasted elegant private dining clubs. The most famous is the Fish House, founded in 1732. Its recipe for punch, which blends rum, brandy, cognac, fruit juice, and sugar, is a historic and potent elixir, still popular at parties.

For extra convenience when you prepare a large roast, be sure to use a large roasting pan that will allow the dry oven heat to crisp the food's surface. (Buy smaller pans for smaller roasts.) Large roasting pans should be two or three inches deep. If they are deeper, the food will steam, rather than roast, and the texture might be soggy rather than properly moist. Because so many roasts—turkey, prime rib, and so on—are heavy, buy sturdy roasting pans with large, well-attached handles. Disposable pans may be convenient, but they are flimsy and difficult to handle.

I Scream, You Scream ...

Historic Philadelphia's connection with important politicians and its love affair with French food was instrumental in making ice cream as popular as it is today. Philadelphia ice cream was once considered a luxury, first served to George Washington by the French envoy to America. Classic Philadelphia ice cream contains no eggs, as opposed to French versions, which begin with an egg-custard base.

Presidential Preferences

Philadelphia's political wining and dining was a harbinger of things to come when Washington, D.C., became the country's capital. Presidential eating habits always make news and have an influence. Thomas Jefferson was the first to employ a French chef at the White House, and French fries became part of America's culinary culture during his administration. Unassuming Harry Truman's taste for simple, typically American fare showed in his loved of Ozark Pudding, which he served to Winston Churchill on the occasion of the famous "Iron Curtain" speech. John F. Kennedy spurred an interest in haute cuisine during the 1960s. His successor, Lyndon Johnson, scoffed at lavish French fare. A true Texan, he enjoyed grassroots dishes such as barbecue and chili con carne. When Jimmy Carter was president, the country showed an interest in southern food. It was during the Reagan era that Americans became familiar with California cuisine.

Not So Fancy

Today, Philadelphia is known not so much for its high-style cuisine as for *scrapple*, cinnamon buns, and cheesesteak. These more plebeian treats pay tribute to the city's democratic roots. Pennsylvania was the first American colony to welcome Europeans other than English. City folk were eager to try scrapple, an invention of the Pennsylvania Dutch, and German cinnamon-scented *schnecken*, forerunner of the city's renowned sticky pastries. Cheesesteaks are street food: shaved beef grilled with onions, topped with melted cheese, and stuffed into a hard roll.

What Is It?

Scrapple is a highly seasoned mixture of pork scraps and cornmeal packed into a compact loaf. It is usually sliced and pan-fried until crispy and served with syrup or alongside eggs. It's also a good filler for omelets and frittatas.

Hearty Food for Hardworking Folk

Waves of German immigrants brought gastronomic goodies to other parts of Pennsylvania. The "Pennsylvania Dutch," a corruption of the word *Deutsch*, meaning "German," were mainly Amish and Mennonites, Protestant sects who sought protection in America from religious persecution. William Penn welcomed them and promised religious freedom and land at 10 cents an acre. They were hardworking farmers who enjoyed plain, filling meals.

Seven Sweets and Sours

The Pennsylvania Dutch kitchen takes advantage of farmland: fresh corn, lima beans, potatoes, and cabbage are mainstays. But much of the vegetable bounty goes into the preparation of the relishes and preserves that make up the famous "7 Sweets and Sours" that are standard on a Pennsylvania Dutch smorgasbord. According to tradition, at least seven sweet and seven pungent dishes should be served at mealtime as a way of showing hospitality. Familiar items include Chow-Chow, which is a mixed vegetable relish; Pepper Relish; Corn Relish; and Apple Butter, a thick, sweet-and-spicy cooked apple reduction used as an accompaniment to meat or as a spread for muffins.

> **Did You Know ...**
> Apple butter is a wonderful ingredient for adding moistness to cakes and quickbreads. Consider it as a replacement for applesauce, puréed pumpkin, or mashed bananas.

A Thing for Pie

The bountiful Pennsylvania Dutch table includes substantial desserts. Dumplings and squiggly funnel cakes (made by squeezing sweet batter through the bottom of a funnel into hot fat, and served dusted with confectioner's sugar or dipped in molasses) are typical, but the prize is pie. There are the familiar ones—apple, lemon meringue, and so on—but specialty pies set their baked goods apart. Shoofly is probably the most well known. Legend has it that this ultra-sweet confection was named because home cooks had to shoo the flies away from the sticky molasses center. Funeral Pie, with a raisin filling, is the traditional dessert served to mourners and their family and friends, but it is sweet and delicious any time.

Not all Pennsylvania Dutch pies are sweet. One standby is Chicken Pot Pie, which is unlike other versions because the filling is topped with noodles, not shortcrust pastry.

Kitchen Clue

Funeral Pie has a meringue crust, made by beating egg whites and sugar. Meringues can be problematic, but here are some tips: Have the whites at room temperature, and beat them just before you make the meringue. For best volume, use an electric mixer with a whisk attachment. Add sugar, salt, or cream of tartar after the whites have been beaten to the foamy stage. Add the sugar gradually during the beating process. Increase mixer speed to high to finish. Beat the whites to stiff peaks, which look glossy and tip over only a tiny bit when you lift the beater.

Our Best-Loved Foods

Some of America's best-loved foods began in Pennsylvania. Consider that the next time you nibble on a pretzel, dip your fries in ketchup, or rhapsodize over a bar of chocolate.

A Little Reward

Legend has it that pretzels were invented during the Middle Ages by a French monk who used soft, sugar-coated yeast twists as a reward, or *pretiola*, for children who were well versed in prayer. The recipe got to Germany, where salt replaced the sugar (it was better for beer drinking). The Germans brought pretzel know-how to America, where, in Lititz, Pennsylvania, the country's first pretzels were made at the Sturgis Pretzel factory. Sturgis also invented hard, dry pretzels.

Thick, Red, and Slow

Ketchup has been around for centuries and once came in a variety of flavors: plum, walnut, and mushroom, for example. Tomato ketchup as we know it was created in the nineteenth century, and after Pittsburgh's H.J. Heinz produced its version, Americans became almost addicted to the stuff. Even though American cooking has become more sophisticated, our devotion to this condiment has remained steadfast. We pour it onto hamburgers, drizzle it over French fries, and use it in a multitude of recipes.

Did You Know ...

You can make a quick shrimp cocktail sauce by mixing ketchup and white horseradish. To make Russian dressing, combine ketchup and mayonnaise.

The Spellbinder

Chocolate has enthralled us since the days when Cortez conquered the Aztecs and brought the recipe for hot chocolate to Europe. The first chocolate factory in America opened in 1765, but chocolate was a luxury too expensive for most folks. Americans can thank Pennsylvania's Milton Hershey, candymaker extraordinaire, for making chocolate accessible to the masses. Hershey gave us the Hershey bar, of course, and lots of other inexpensive chocolate snacks. When chocolate became affordable, Americans used it for making cakes, pies, cookies, and other treats.

When cooking with chocolate, keep in mind that it burns easily. If a recipe calls for melted chocolate, use a double boiler. Break the chocolate into small pieces and put them in the top part. The top part should fit snugly into the bottom one so that steam cannot escape from the lower pan (steam can cause the chocolate to become rock hard). Heat the water in the bottom pan over low heat, and don't let the water boil. The water in the lower pan should be at a near simmer, about 200°.

The Two Garden States

People who don't live in New Jersey picture the state with masses of twisting high-ways and stacks of air-polluting refineries. But it's called the Garden State for a reason. New Jersey grows several of the country's important agricultural products, including tomatoes and blueberries. It is also the birthplace of America's first apple brandy, Applejack, invented by William Laird in 1698. You can use Applejack as a substitute for the more expensive French brandy, Calvados. It makes a luscious basting fluid for pork and poultry.

> **What Is It?**
>
> A **broiler-fryer** chicken weighs two-and-a-half to four pounds and serves three to four people. Broiler-fryers are sold both whole and in parts. They were developed to reduce cooking time. These young birds cook quickly under the intense heat of a broiler or grill or in hot fat.

Delaware is another vast garden. It was first settled by Dutch, German, and Scandinavian farmers who grew vegetables. Eventually, though, this tiny state was the place where the modern *broiler-fryer* chicken industry began in the 1920s.

Somewhat Southern

Maryland's beginnings were unlike the other parts of the mid-Atlantic. Many of the English who settled the area were wealthy, slaveholding tobacco planters. Culturally, the state resembled those in the South, and some of its famous foods—fried chicken and biscuits, baked ham with sweet potatoes, and cornbread—have a southern flavor. But Maryland's geography and its rich citizenry guaranteed it a unique cooking style. Maryland fried chicken, for example, is always served with a cream-based gravy made from the pan drippings.

The state's location on Chesapeake Bay guarantees plenty of fish and shellfish. In the early days, oysters were so abundant they were eaten at practically every meal. They were not only a cheap food for the poor, but served on the plantations, where owners and guests would feast on oyster stew and roasted turkey with oyster stuffing.

Maryland's biggest claim to fame, of course, is the Chesapeake Bay blue crab, which is used in all sorts of recipes, most notably crabcakes. The most succulent wonders, though, are the soft-shell crabs: sautéed, deep-fried, or grilled. Blue crabs molt several times, and soft-shells are the ones that have just shed their shells. Once cleaned of its gills and apron, the entire crab is eaten. The crab's size is an indication of its age. The smaller ones are sweeter and more delicate; the larger ones more meaty and sea-flavored.

Kitchen Clue

You can buy fresh crab-meat in tins. "Lump" crabmeat has larger pieces; "flaked" crab, which is less expensive, is shredded. Always buy live soft-shell crabs to ensure freshness and quality. Have the fishmonger remove the gills and apron. Crabs are perishable, so cook them within 24 hours of purchase.

The Least You Need to Know

- ◆ A high-quality cookie sheet makes cookie baking more successful.
- ◆ Use a large, sturdy roasting pan for turkey, roasts of beef, and other large items.
- ◆ Our presidents have had a great deal of influence on the kinds of food that are popular in the United States.
- ◆ Melt chocolate in a double boiler to prevent scorching.
- ◆ Broiler-fryer chickens are meant to cook quickly in the broiler, grill, or hot fat.
- ◆ Always buy live soft-shell crabs to ensure freshness and quality.

Coleslaw

This is very mild coleslaw. The yogurt cuts down on the fat and gives the salad a bit of tang.

Prep time: less than 15 minutes   •   Makes 6 to 8 servings

Special equipment: food processor (not essential, but it helps you shred the cabbage quickly)

6 cups green cabbage, finely shredded

1 large carrot, finely shredded

$1/4$ cup fresh parsley, chopped

$1/2$ cup mayonnaise

$1/2$ cup plain yogurt

Pinch of sugar

2–3 TB. cider vinegar

Salt and pepper, to taste

Combine shredded cabbage, carrot, and parsley in a large bowl and toss to distribute ingredients evenly.

In another bowl, combine mayonnaise, yogurt, sugar, and 2 tablespoons cider vinegar. Mix thoroughly and pour over cabbage mixture. Taste coleslaw and add remaining vinegar, if desired. Sprinkle with salt and pepper to taste.

Hot Tip

Try these variations:

- Use mayonnaise instead of yogurt.
- Add 24 shredded snow peas or $1/2$ cup green bell pepper and 2 shredded scallions.
- Add 1 small jalapeño pepper, chopped.
- Add $1/4$ cup sweet cream.
- Add 2 teaspoons Dijon mustard.

Manhattan Clam Chowder

This is New York's famous soup, the one that causes arguments with New Englanders about who has the better and more authentic version. Fact is, they're both good! To peel whole tomatoes, drop them in some boiling water for 15–20 seconds, drain under cold water, and pierce the skin near the stem. The skin will peel off easily.

Prep time: less than 30 minutes • Makes 8 servings

2 doz. cherrystone clams	4 large tomatoes, peeled, seeded, and chopped
3 cups water	2 cups tomato purée
3 TB. olive oil, butter, or a mixture of the two	1 bay leaf
2 medium onions, chopped	1½ TB. thyme leaves (or 1½ tsp. dried)
1 carrot, chopped	Salt and black pepper, to taste
1 stalk celery, chopped	2 large all-purpose potatoes, peeled and diced

Scrub clams and place unopened in a large saucepan or stockpot. Pour in water. Cover the pot and cook clams over moderate heat for 8–10 minutes, until opened. Discard any clams that have not opened. Remove clam meat, discard shells, and mince meat. Set aside.

Strain clam broth through cheesecloth, reserving 5 cups broth. Dry the pot. Heat olive oil (or melt butter) in the pot. When oil is hot, or butter has melted and looks foamy, add onions, carrot, and celery. Cook over moderate heat for 3–4 minutes or until softened.

Add reserved clam broth, tomatoes, tomato purée, bay leaf, thyme, and some salt and black pepper. Simmer for 35 minutes. Add potatoes, cover the pot, and cook another 15–20 minutes or until potatoes are tender. Add clams and cook 3–4 minutes. Add salt and pepper to taste.

Hot Tip _____

Try this variation of Manhattan Clam Chowder: Use 4–6 slices of bacon or salt pork. Fry the bacon and use 3 tablespoons of the rendered fat instead of the olive oil or butter. Reserve the meat, crumble it, and add it to the soup at the end.

Broiled Chicken with Garlic Tomatoes

This easy recipe can be made with all breasts or all dark meat. It's nice with a side of polenta or couscous and some fresh asparagus.

Prep time: less than 15 minutes • Makes 4 servings

3–4 lb. broiler-fryer chicken, cut into 8 pieces

3 TB. olive oil

Salt and pepper

10 plum tomatoes, seeded and cut into chunks

1 medium onion, chopped

5 large cloves garlic, minced

1/4 cup fresh basil, minced

3 TB. fresh parsley, minced

1/4 cup balsamic vinegar

Preheat the broiler.

Wash chicken parts and dry thoroughly. Place in a shallow baking dish and rub with 1 tablespoon olive oil. Sprinkle with salt and pepper. Broil chicken about 6" from heat, turning pieces occasionally, for about 25 minutes or until cooked through.

While chicken is cooking, combine tomatoes, onion, garlic, basil, parsley, balsamic vinegar, and remaining olive oil. Add salt and pepper to taste.

When chicken is done, remove the broiler pan from oven and place chicken on a serving platter. Spoon tomato mixture on the broiler pan and place under broiler for 3–4 minutes. Serve chicken topped with tomatoes and pan juices.

Frittata with Scrapple, Potatoes, and Cheese

Most people eat scrapple as a side dish, but it also makes a tasty filling for omelets or frittatas. You can try this brunch dish using bacon, ham, or breakfast sausage instead.

Prep time: less than 15 minutes   •   Makes 4 servings

2 medium all-purpose potatoes, peeled and cut into small dice

3½ TB. butter

4 slices scrapple, cut ½" thick

1 onion, chopped

½ cup grated sharp cheddar cheese

6 eggs

1 TB. milk

Salt and pepper, to taste

Preheat the broiler.

Cook potatoes in lightly salted water for 8–10 minutes or until tender. Drain potatoes and set aside.

Heat 2 teaspoons butter in a skillet over moderate heat. When butter has melted and looks foamy, add scrapple and cook for 5–6 minutes, turning slices once or twice, or until meat is crispy. Break up scrapple as it cooks in the pan. Remove scrapple and set aside.

Add 1 tablespoon plus 1 teaspoon butter to the skillet. When it has melted and looks foamy, add onion and cook for 2 minutes. Add potatoes and cook for 4–5 minutes or until vegetables are lightly browned. Remove from the pan. Toss with grated cheese.

Beat eggs and milk in a bowl. Add the remaining 1½ tablespoons butter to the pan. When melted and foamy, pour egg mixture into the pan and turn heat to low. Sprinkle eggs with salt and pepper. Place scrapple and onion mixture in egg mixture, scattering ingredients evenly. Cook eggs, stirring occasionally, for about 3 minutes or until almost set but still creamy on top. Place the pan under the broiler and cook briefly to set the top. Remove the pan, cut frittata into wedges, and serve.

Crabcakes

There are many variations on Maryland's famous crabcakes. This version is slightly spicy. If you like, serve the cakes with hot salsa.

Prep time: less than 15 minutes   •   Makes 4 servings

1 lb. flaked crabmeat	1 tsp. fresh thyme leaves (or $\frac{1}{4}$ tsp. dried thyme)
1 egg, beaten	2 TB. fresh parsley, minced
1 tsp. powdered mustard (or 1 TB. Dijon mustard)	$\frac{1}{4}$ cup milk
$\frac{1}{2}$ tsp. salt, or to taste	2 TB. cracker crumbs or all-purpose flour
$\frac{1}{4}$ tsp. cayenne pepper	3 TB. vegetable oil, approx.

Combine crabmeat, egg, mustard, salt, cayenne pepper, thyme, and parsley in a medium-size bowl. Stir in milk. Add cracker crumbs or flour and blend thoroughly. Shape mixture into 8 patties about a $\frac{1}{2}$" thick. Heat vegetable oil over moderate heat in a skillet.

Fry crabcakes a few at a time about 3 minutes per side, or until both sides are browned and crispy. Add more oil to the pan, if necessary, to prevent sticking. Drain crabcakes on paper towels.

Hot Tip

If you reheat crabcakes, put them in a preheated oven at 400°, in a single layer on a cookie sheet. For even better results, put them on a rack set inside the cookie sheet. Bake until hot.

Lox and Eggs

This New York City specialty can be found at diners, coffee shops, and the fanciest hotels. It's for breakfast, brunch, or dinner. Although usually made with onions, this version has chives, which gives it some color. My daughter Meredith and son-in-law Greg make this dish often and have created the variations noted after the recipe.

Prep time: less than 15 minutes • Makes 2 servings

$^1/_2$ cup smoked salmon, chopped	$^1/_4$ cup milk
2 TB. fresh chives, chopped	1 TB. butter
4 large eggs	Salt and pepper, to taste

Combine salmon and chives and set aside.

Beat eggs and milk together. Heat butter in a skillet over medium heat. When butter has melted and looks foamy, pour in eggs. Stir occasionally with a rigid spatula (if you like large curds and creamy eggs), or constantly with a large spoon (if you prefer small curds and well-cooked eggs). After eggs set slightly, add smoked salmon and chives, sprinkle with salt and pepper. Cook until eggs have reached the desired consistency.

Hot Tip _____

Try these variations:

- Add 2 tablespoons cut-up cream cheese with smoked salmon.
- Add $^1/_2$ cup cottage cheese, or cottage cheese mixed with dairy sour cream, with smoked salmon.
- Season the dish with a sprinkling of fresh, chopped dill.
- Use a small chopped onion instead of chives.

Roasted Honey-Orange Long Island Duckling

Crispy, roasted duck makes a festive dinner. The sauce is dark and sweet, a harmonious balance for duck's rich meat.

Prep time: less than 30 minutes • Makes 4 servings

1 duck, about 5 lbs.	1 medium onion, peeled
3 TB. orange-flavored brandy	$\frac{1}{4}$ cup honey
Salt and pepper, to taste	$\frac{1}{2}$ cup chicken or duck stock
Garlic powder	1 tsp. cornstarch
4 juice oranges	

Preheat the oven to 450°.

Wash and dry duck. Remove giblets and neck from the cavity. Reserve for other uses, or roast alongside duck. Cut and discard excess fat from duck. Rub surface of duck with 1 tablespoon orange-flavored brandy. Sprinkle with salt, pepper, and garlic powder. Quarter one orange, and place with the onion inside duck cavity.

Tie back duck wings. Place duck breast-side down on a rack in a roasting pan. Cover the pan with aluminum foil. Roast duck for 30 minutes. While duck is roasting, combine juice of one orange with honey and 2 tablespoons orange brandy. Set aside.

When duck has roasted 30 minutes, remove the foil. Prick duck skin in several places with the tines of a fork. Brush duck with honey mixture.

Reduce oven heat to 350°. Roast another 30 minutes. Turn bird breast-side up. Roast another hour, brushing with honey mixture every 20 minutes or until thigh meat registers 180° on a meat thermometer. Remove duck to a carving board but let rest for 15 minutes before carving. Remove and discard the orange and onion from cavity. While waiting to carve duck, prepare sauce. Juice remaining two oranges. Discard pan fat. Put the pan on the stovetop over moderate heat.

Add orange juice and stock, and cook, stirring with a wooden spoon to scrape up any bits at bottom of pan. Simmer for 2–3 minutes to obtain a dark sauce. Mix cornstarch with some of the pan sauce and add to the pan. Stir briefly until slightly thickened. Strain sauce. Carve duck and serve with sauce.

Roast Rib of Beef with Yorkshire Pudding

Rib of beef is impressive; it makes an excellent company dinner. The Yorkshire Pudding is a terrific foil for the rich pan juices.

Prep time: less than 30 minutes   •   Makes 6 to 8 servings

4 tsp. paprika

2 tsp. salt, or to taste

1 tsp. freshly ground black pepper

1–1$\frac{1}{2}$ tsp. garlic powder

1 (3-rib) standing beef roast

Preheat the oven to 450°.

Place paprika, salt, pepper, and garlic powder in a small bowl and add enough water to make a paste. Brush onto meat and bones. Place roast, bones-down, in a roasting pan. Roast beef for 20 minutes.

Lower heat to 350° and cook 15–20 minutes more per pound, depending on whether you like the meat rare, medium, or well done. A meat thermometer inserted into middle of meat will read 120° to 135° for rare, 135° to 145° for medium, and 145 plus° for well done. Let roast beef stand 15 minutes before carving.

For the Yorkshire Pudding:

6 TB. pan drippings from the roast beef

2 eggs

1 cup milk

1 cup all-purpose flour

$\frac{1}{2}$ tsp. salt

Pepper, to taste

Preheat the oven to 450°.

Place 4 tablespoons pan drippings inside a 9" square or 8"×10" baking dish, and swirl to coat bottom. In a bowl, beat eggs with milk and flour until smooth and uniform. Stir in remaining pan drippings, salt, and pepper, to taste. Pour into the baking dish. Bake for 10 minutes. Reduce heat to 350°. Bake about 15 minutes or until golden brown and puffy.

Hot Tip

The meat will be easier to carve if you ask the butcher to cut the meat from the bones and tie it back with kitchen string. When you're ready to carve, cut the strings. Remove the meat from the bones; you will have a boneless roast. Carve the meat. Slice between the bones to separate them and serve them separately.

Sautéed Soft-Shelled Crabs Almondine

Soft-shelled crabs are sweet and delicate. They have a short season, so enjoy them when you can. This is one of the easiest ways to prepare them.

Prep time: less than 15 minutes • Makes 4 servings

3 TB. olive oil

2 TB. butter

¾ cup almonds, chopped

8 large soft-shelled crabs

All-purpose flour for dredging

Salt and pepper

Juice of 1 large lemon

Heat 1 tablespoon olive oil with 1 tablespoon butter in a skillet over medium heat. When butter is melted and foamy, add almonds. Cook for 4–5 minutes or until lightly toasted, stirring occasionally. Remove almonds and set aside.

Rinse crabs and dredge in flour, shaking off excess. Add remaining olive oil and butter to the pan. When butter has melted and looks foamy, add crabs. Sprinkle with salt and pepper. Cook crabs for 3–4 minutes per side or until lightly brown and crispy.

Remove crabs to a platter. Add lemon juice to the pan, whisking ingredients once or twice to blend. Pour liquid over crabs. Top with almonds and serve.

Sweet and Sour Red Cabbage

This is a German and Pennsylvania Dutch specialty. It is especially good with pork. It keeps well, too; you can make it three or four days in advance.

Prep time: less than 30 minutes • Makes 6 servings

Special equipment: food processor (not essential but it helps you to shred the cabbage quickly)

2 TB. vegetable oil	$^1/_3$ cup brown sugar
2 TB. rendered bacon fat or butter	3 cups water
1 medium onion, chopped	$^1/_2$ cup red-wine vinegar
2 tart apples, peeled and chopped	2 TB. lemon juice
1 medium red cabbage, shredded	$^1/_2$ tsp. salt
1 bay leaf	Pinch of ground cloves (or 2 whole cloves)

Heat vegetable oil and bacon fat or butter in a large skillet. Add onion and apples, and cook over moderate heat for 3–4 minutes, stirring occasionally. Add cabbage, bay leaf, brown sugar, water, vinegar, lemon juice, salt, and cloves, and toss to distribute evenly. Cover the pan and cook at a simmer for about one hour, stirring occasionally, or until cabbage is tender. Remove bay leaf and serve.

Corn Relish

This pungent relish is colorful and goes well with grilled meats and poultry. Use it when you barbecue, or take it on a picnic.

Prep time: less than 30 minutes • Makes 1½ quarts

4 cups cooked corn (frozen corn that has been thawed is fine)

¼ medium cabbage, coarsely chopped

1 sweet red pepper, seeded and chopped

3 stalks celery, sliced ¼" thick

1 medium onion, chopped

¼ cup sugar

1 TB. salt

1 TB. dry mustard

¼ tsp. turmeric

Dash cayenne pepper

⅔ cup cider vinegar

½ cup water

1½ tsp. cornstarch, mixed with enough water to make a paste

Combine corn, cabbage, red pepper, celery, and onion in a large saucepan. Mix sugar, salt, mustard, turmeric, cayenne pepper, cider vinegar, and water in a small bowl and pour mixture over vegetables.

Bring liquid to a boil, and then lower the heat and cook about 12 minutes, stirring occasionally. Add cornstarch paste, stir thoroughly, and cook the relish another 3–4 minutes. Refrigerate relish and serve cold or at room temperature.

Apple Cider Cake Doughnuts

You might find people standing around the fryer waiting for these doughnuts to be ready. They fill the entire house with the sweet scent of autumn, and they taste even better than they smell! Doughnuts get stale quickly, but you probably won't have leftovers.

Prep time: less than 30 minutes   •   Makes about 2 dozen

Special equipment: doughnut cutter

3½–4 cups all-purpose flour

⅓ cup sugar

⅓ cup brown sugar

1 tsp. salt

2 tsp. baking powder

½ tsp. baking soda

1 tsp. freshly grated nutmeg

1 tsp. cinnamon

1 cup less 2 TB. apple cider

4 TB. butter, melted and cooled

2 eggs

1 tsp. vanilla extract

Vegetable shortening

Sugar, cinnamon sugar, or confectioner's sugar

Combine 2 cups flour with sugar, brown sugar, salt, baking powder, baking soda, nutmeg, and cinnamon in an electric mixer bowl. Mix cider, cooled melted butter, eggs, and vanilla extract in a bowl and beat to blend. Add liquid to flour mixture and mix ingredients on moderate speed until uniform batter forms, about 2–3 minutes. Add remaining flour by the half-cupful, stirring until soft, sticky dough forms. Remove dough to a floured surface and shape into a soft ball. Put enough vegetable shortening in a deep-fryer or large saucepan to melt to 4" deep. Heat to 365°. Press or roll dough gently on a floured board to a thickness of a ½". Cut out doughnuts (as close together as possible) with a 2½" doughnut cutter. Let doughnuts and holes rest for 15 minutes.

Add doughnuts to the pan, a few at a time. Fry doughnuts, flipping often to keep from over-browning. Cook for about 2 minutes, and then drain on paper towels. Fry holes separately; they will take less than a minute to cook. Let doughnuts cool slightly, and then roll in sugar, cinnamon sugar, or confectioner's sugar.

Funnel Cakes

These fried squiggles of dough are fun to make, and are even better to eat!

Prep time: less than 15 minutes • Makes 6 to 8 servings

Special equipment: funnel

2 eggs	1½ tsp. baking powder
¼ cup sugar	½ tsp. salt
1¼ cups milk	Vegetable oil for deep-fat frying
2 to 2½ cups all-purpose flour	Confectioner's sugar or molasses

Beat eggs and sugar together with an electric beater set at medium high for 2–3 minutes, or until fluffy. Add milk and beat in. Add flour, baking powder, and salt, and blend in thoroughly. Batter should be thick, but liquid enough to run through the bottom of a funnel; add more flour if batter is too runny.

Heat vegetable oil in a deep pot or fryer to 375°. Pour about ½ cup batter into a ½" funnel and hold the bottom closed with your finger. Release your finger to let batter fall into the hot fat as you move the funnel around, so that spirals form in the pan. Fry a portion of batter at a time.

When the bottom of spirals are golden brown (less than 1 minute), turn them to cook on the other side. When brown, remove and drain on paper towels. Proceed with the rest of batter. Sprinkle funnel cakes with confectioner's sugar or serve with molasses for dipping.

Philadelphia Cinnamon Buns

These fragrant, tender buns are wonderful for breakfast and coffee breaks.

Prep time: less than 1 hour   •   Makes 9 buns

$^1/_3$ cup milk

3 TB. sugar

$^1/_2$ tsp. salt

2 TB. butter

1 pkg. active dry yeast

$^1/_4$ cup warm water

1 tsp. finely grated lemon peel

2 cups all-purpose flour, approx.

1 beaten egg

3 TB. melted butter

$^1/_2$ cup sugar

2 tsp. cinnamon

$^1/_2$ cup raisins

1 cup confectioner's sugar

4 tsp. water, approx.

Drops of vanilla

Preheat oven to 350°.

In a saucepan, cook milk over moderate heat until bubbles form around the edges of pan. Stir in 3 tablespoons sugar, salt, and butter. Let mixture cool for 5 minutes. While milk mixture cools, combine yeast and water in a small bowl. Stir and let rest for 5 minutes.

Pour milk mixture into an electric mixer bowl. Add yeast mixture, lemon peel, and 1 cup flour, and mix to blend ingredients. Beat in egg. Add more flour gradually, using as much as needed to form soft ball of dough. Knead in mixer (or by hand on a floured board) until shiny, smooth dough has formed (about 3 minutes in the mixer).

Place dough in a lightly greased bowl. Cover the bowl and let rise in a warm, draft-free place for $1^1/_2$ hours or until doubled in bulk. Roll dough into 9" square. Brush with 2 tablespoons melted butter. Mix $^1/_2$ cup sugar and cinnamon, and sprinkle all but 2 tablespoons over dough. Scatter raisins over the surface.

Roll up jelly-roll style, and pinch seam to seal roll completely. Cut into 9 slices. Place in a greased 9"×9"×2" cake pan. Brush tops with remaining butter, and sprinkle with reserved cinnamon sugar. Let rise 45 minutes.

Bake 20 minutes or until puffed and golden brown. Mix confectioner's sugar with enough water to make a sticky glaze. Stir in a few drops of vanilla. Glaze rolls while still warm.

Ozark Pudding

This dessert was one of President Truman's favorites, and he once served it to Winston Churchill. It's actually from a different part of the United States than the mid-Atlantic, but Washington, D.C., knew about the dish when Truman was president.

Prep time: less than 15 minutes   •   Makes 6 to 8 servings

2 eggs	2½ tsp. baking powder
1¼ cups sugar	¼ tsp. salt
2 tsp. vanilla extract	2 tart apples, peeled and chopped
3 TB. rum	½ cup pecans, finely chopped
⅔ cup all-purpose flour	1 cup heavy whipping cream

Preheat the oven to 325°.

Place eggs and all but 1 teaspoon sugar in an electric mixer bowl. Beat on medium speed for about 3 minutes, scraping the sides of the bowl once or twice or until mixture is light and fluffy. Stir in vanilla extract and 2 tablespoons rum.

Combine flour, baking powder, and salt. Put dry ingredients into the mixing bowl and beat until well blended. Stir in apples and pecans. Spoon mixture into a lightly buttered baking pan large enough that batter comes ⅔ of the way up the sides. Bake for about 30 minutes or until lightly browned and crusty.

While pudding bakes, whip cream with remaining 1 teaspoon sugar and 1 tablespoon rum until it stands in thick peaks. Serve pudding warm with whipped cream.

Dutch Almond Cookies

Better make a double batch of these—they go fast! But if there are leftovers, you can freeze them in plastic bags.

Prep time: less than 15 minutes   •   Makes 30 cookies

1½ cups all-purpose flour

12 TB. butter, cut into chunks

⅓ cup sugar

¼ tsp. salt

½ tsp. vanilla extract

1 egg

1 tsp. milk

1 TB. sugar

3 TB. almonds, sliced

Preheat the oven to 350°.

Place flour, butter chunks, ⅓ cup sugar, salt, and vanilla extract into an electric mixer bowl. Mix ingredients at moderate speed for 1 minute or until a soft dough has formed. Roll dough on a floured surface into a thin rectangle approximately 10"×14".

Gently roll dough around a rolling pin and carefully place dough on a lightly greased cookie sheet bigger than 10"×14". Beat egg and milk together and brush most of mixture on dough. Sprinkle with remaining sugar and scatter almonds evenly on top.

Bake for 18–20 minutes or until dough is golden brown and crispy. Remove the cookie sheet from the oven and immediately cut dough into rectangles. Make five cuts on the long side and four cuts on the short side. Remove cookies to a wire rack to cool.

Chocolate Cake

This moist, dense, and fudgy cake gets its rich flavor from dark, strong coffee. It needs no frosting, but you can sprinkle it with confectioner's sugar or use the chocolate glaze given for Boston Cream Pie (see Chapter 1). The recipe was given to me by my sister-in-law, Eileen Vail, from her mother's collection. Evelyn Silverman always made the cake in a sheet pan and added walnuts; this is a plain version for a bundt cake pan.

Prep time: less than 15 minutes • Makes 1 bundt cake

Special equipment: cake rack

2 cups all-purpose flour	2 cups sugar
1 cup cocoa powder	4 eggs, separated
2^1/$_2$ tsp. baking powder	1 cup cold, strong black coffee
^{1}/$_2$ tsp. salt	1 tsp. vanilla extract
^{1}/$_2$ lb. butter	

Preheat the oven to 350°.

Sift flour, cocoa powder, baking powder, and salt into a bowl and set aside.

Cream butter in an electric mixer bowl set at medium speed (or use a hand mixer). Add sugar and blend in. Add egg yolks one at a time, beating well after each addition.

Add flour mixture alternating with coffee. Beat ingredients for about 2 minutes, or until well blended, scraping the sides of the bowl once or twice. Stir in vanilla extract.

Beat egg whites until stiff but not dry. Add about ^{1}/$_4$ of mixture to chocolate batter and blend thoroughly. Fold remaining whites into batter. Spoon batter into the bundt pan. Bake cake about 70 minutes, or until a cake tester inserted into the center comes out clean. Let cake cool in the pan for 10 minutes, and then invert onto a cake rack to cool completely.

Funeral Pie

Funeral Pie, also called Raisin Pie, is a bit unusual for most of us, but it is popular among the Pennsylvania Dutch. This sweet confection is worth a try. It's pretty, too, with a lovely meringue cap.

Prep time: less than 30 minutes • Makes 1 (9") pie

$^1/_2$ cup sugar

2 TB. + 1 tsp. cornstarch

$^1/_8$ tsp. salt

$1^1/_2$ cups milk

$1^1/_2$ cups seedless raisins

3 egg yolks, beaten

2 TB. lemon juice

1 tsp. grated lemon peel

2 TB. butter

9" fully baked pie shell (see Basic Pie Dough, Appendix C)

3 egg whites

6 TB. sugar

Preheat the oven to 350°.

Mix $^1/_2$ cup sugar, cornstarch, and salt in a bowl and set aside.

Heat milk and raisins in a saucepan set over moderate heat for 6–8 minutes or until the raisins start to plump. Add cornstarch mixture gradually, stirring and cooking until mixture has thickened. Add some hot mixture to egg yolks, and then pour yolk mixture into the pan. Cook for 5–6 minutes or until mixture is as thick as dairy sour cream. Don't let mixture come to boil.

Remove the pan from heat. Stir in lemon juice, lemon peel, and butter. Stir until butter melts. Set aside in the refrigerator to cool. Pour cold mixture into baked pie shell.

Beat egg whites until they stand in soft peaks. Continue beating, gradually adding 6 tablespoons sugar, until whites stand in stiff, glossy peaks. Spread whites over pie, making sure to seal fruit completely. Bake for 15 minutes or until meringue is lightly browned. Let cool and serve.

Chapter 3

The South

In This Chapter

- ◆ Southern specialties: sweet potatoes and grits
- ◆ Southern hospitality and lavish plantation fare
- ◆ Down-home fare and soul food
- ◆ The rice industry takes off
- ◆ The importance of pork
- ◆ Spanish Florida's foods

Classic southern cuisine bespeaks a past of lavish living mingled with humility. Antebellum plantations began a tradition of southern hospitality built on fine service and opulent tables laden with country hams and biscuits, roasted meats, and Mint Juleps. The rich could afford exotic spices and the luscious fruits, nuts, chocolates, and other luxuries that came to port. These translated into recipes for curries, stately coconut cakes, and Black Bottom Pie, among others. Rice producers near the coast feasted on pilafs laden with shrimp and oysters.

But others contributed to the region's cuisine, too: the poor, the pioneers, and the slaves. They created magical recipes with simple foods such as sweet potatoes, catfish, and chicken. They hunted squirrels and raccoons for stew. They distilled corn for moonshine and bourbon. Slaves made do with scraps of meat, and cooked nourishing meals of greens, pork, and "pot likker." They added native African ingredients such as black-eyed peas and okra to recipes, and they perfected the art of barbecue.

Ethnic differences account for some unique southern dishes: the Spanish-based foods of Florida, the English-style roasts, and French fricassees. But some common threads run through southern cuisine. Pork and grits are mainstays. And most southerners, whatever their background, are proud of their region's pies, cornbread, and fried chicken and fish.

Here Come the Europeans

Europeans arrived in Jamestown, Virginia, in 1607 with Captain John Smith. They didn't expect to stay because they came looking for gold. They were adventurers, not farmers, and almost all of them were starved. Like their neighbors in the North, they needed help from Native Americans.

The Lifesaver

Fortunately for the Jamestown men, the Native Americans showed them how to roast sweet potatoes. Sweet potatoes saved their lives. The vegetable became a staple in American southern cuisine.

A Yam or a Sweet Potato?

Many Americans say they prefer yams to sweet potatoes, but regardless of store labels, yams are not grown commercially in the United States. What you see in the market are different varieties of sweet potatoes. They include pale yellow, dry-textured types; rich gourd-orange ones; and some with moist, sweet, deep russet-garnet flesh.

Kitchen Clue

Sweet potatoes are loaded with beta carotene and vitamin A. They are also a good source of vitamin C and folic acid. For best flavor and texture, store sweet potatoes in a cool, dry place, not the refrigerator.

To Candy or Not to Candy

The Native Americans roasted sweet potatoes in ashes. The vegetable is still delicious when roasted in the oven or in a closed outdoor grill. But sweet potato flesh is a natural partner for the likes of brown sugar, maple syrup, and honey. It's no wonder that one of the country's favorite dishes is Candied Sweet Potatoes. Southern cooks also mash sweet potatoes for use in pudding and pie.

A Lavish Lifestyle

By 1610, things started to look up in Jamestown after more settlers came, and Virginia soon became a flourishing colony. Early successes growing tobacco paved the way for a culture unique to the South, one of privilege and luxury for wealthy tobacco, cotton, and other planters, and heartbreak and misery for the slaves used to work their plantations.

Southern Hospitality

Some southern plantations were like little communities, complete with manor house, slave quarters, stables, blacksmith sheds, and other outbuildings for storage, housing livestock, and even one specifically for smoking hams. Visitors from other plantations often had far to travel and would stay for a long time. Thus began a tradition of lavish entertaining and "southern hospitality." Plantation tables were laden with food at every meal. Huge breakfasts began the day and included buffets featuring meats, ham, grits, eggs, potatoes, pastries, and sometimes Mint Juleps. (In Kentucky, where Mint Juleps are always served on Derby Day, folks say you must drink them from a silver goblet. But you can sip this sweet libation from a glass.)

Mini-Recipe
Mint Julep (makes one drink)   Put a sprig of fresh mint in the bottom of a glass. Add 1$^1/_2$ teaspoons sugar and crush the mint and sugar together with the handle of a wooden spoon. Add a bit of water and stir to dissolve the sugar. Fill the glass with crushed ice, and then pour in bourbon.

Grits, a Southern Staple

For plantation owners and everyone else, grits were a staple and could be served at every meal. Grits are coarsely ground dried corn, similar to cornmeal but processed differently. Originally, local Native Americans used ashes and water to remove the hull from kernels of dried corn. Today, a solution of lye and water does the trick. Then the kernel is allowed to dry. When dry, it's called hominy, and when ground, it's called hominy grits (or just plain grits) and may be coarsely, medium, or finely ground.

Whole hominy is served as a side dish, a tasty substitute for potatoes, and can be stewed with meats or vegetables. Grits are cooked like hot breakfast cereal and can be served with cream, sugar, syrup, and so on, or with a dab of butter as a side dish with eggs or meat. Grits may be used in place of regular cornmeal in Indian pudding. Like all cereals, grits are sticky. To save time and effort, use a nonstick saucepan to cook them.

Fresh Corn

Fresh corn has always been important in the South, just as in New England and the mid-Atlantic. Succotash is a staple, only here it may include tomatoes and okra, a vegetable introduced by black slaves from Africa. Corn oysters, which are deep-fat fried fritters studded with fresh kernels, or hushpuppies, which are fried balls of cornmeal dough, are traditional accompaniments to fried fish and chicken.

Corn was also the inspiration for America's native alcoholic beverage—bourbon. As the pioneers moved west through the Shenandoah Valley and settled in Kentucky, they discovered that the region's clear spring water made exceptional-tasting whiskey. Native Americans taught the pioneers how to distill whiskey from corn, and it became the potion of choice, since corn was so abundant. "Moonshine" is corn liquor made without regard to proof or precision. But bourbon is a specific kind of corn whiskey. By law, it must be at least 51 percent corn liquor, and must be aged at least 2 years in charred white oak barrels that can never be reused. Bourbon is never more than 160 proof.

Fein on Food

In the 1780s, the first corn liquor still was set up in Kentucky by Elijah Craig, an intrepid Baptist minister who considered the bourbon business to be "as honorable as any." The drink was named after Bourbon County, the site of the still. Jack Daniel's was the first whiskey distillery registered by the government (1866). But it is not a true bourbon; the spirit is filtered through charcoal, which gives this whiskey a distinctive taste.

More Refined

In the old South, wealthy planters could afford refined wheat flour for fresh breads and pastries. White biscuits with crispy tops and dense, moist interiors became a renowned staple. In the earliest days, southern cooks made beaten biscuits. It would take hours to beat air into the dough for the breads to rise properly. That all ended when leaveners became available.

Southern cooks often make biscuits, cornbread, and pancakes with buttermilk because its lactic-acid content ensures baked goods will be fluffy and tender. Paired with eggs, vanilla, and sugar, buttermilk bakes to a velvety, sweet pie filling, too. And its tangy taste makes it a fine base for marinades.

A Decidedly French Influence

Parts of the deep South were settled by French Huguenots who brought their own style and luxurious cuisine to the plantation and to places like Charleston, Savannah, and Natchez, where they lived in grand mansions. Living near coastal waters and rivers meant there would always be plenty of cold, succulent oysters, shrimp, and finfish for the table. The port cities were also host to ships that brought exotic spices, chocolate, coconuts, fruits, and nuts from Asia, South America, and the Caribbean islands. Slave cooks used these ingredients in specialties such as Ambrosia (a melange of fresh fruit and coconut), Coconut Cake, and Black Bottom Pie, which became hallmarks of southern cuisine. They prepared sophisticated fare that blended French, African, and Caribbean culinary styles.

Georgians insist that their famous dish, Country Captain, had just such beginnings. This chicken dish is seasoned with curry and contains currants and almonds, just the kind of ingredients that would have come to port. It had its origins in the Indian-style curries eaten in England, but Country Captain is a French *fricassee*.

What Is It?

A **fricassee** is somewhat like a stew, but much less liquid is used. The main ingredient (which could be chicken, seafood, meat, or vegetables) is sautéed in butter or vegetable oil to brown the surface. Then liquid is added, and the pan is covered and simmered until the dish is done.

The Role of Rice

Rice production in the South began in the late seventeenth century, when seeds were brought to Charleston harbor. A sea captain gave a sack of rice seeds to a planter, who discovered that the grain flourished in swampy areas in South Carolina. Slaves were brought in to clear the area for growing, and the state's rice became a valued industry. South Carolina's rice industry isn't as considerable as it once was (production has shifted to other states and we import much of our rice) but the love of rice dishes, particularly *pilafs*, remains.

What Is It?

A **pilaf** is a dish made by sautéing rice in butter or vegetable oil, and then adding stock, wine, or another flavorful liquid to moisten and soften the grains. The best pilafs are made with long-grain rice such as basmati, which is aromatic and flavorful.

Living High Off the Hog

Pork and ham have always been mainstays in the South. Pigs are cheaper and easier to raise than cattle or sheep. The expression "living high off the hog" is southern, and pays tribute to the pig's usefulness. Every part has value: skin for leather, bristles for brushes, meat for food. At one time, choice roasts were served to plantation owners and landholders. Slave victuals included leftovers and lesser cuts: pig feet, snout, chitterlings (intestines, which are cleaned, poached, and then fried or used for soup), and ribs.

Native Americans showed the first settlers in Virginia how to smoke meat. Ever since, country hams have been a southern staple and are often served with red-eye gravy, made by mixing coffee with pan drippings. (Red-eye gravy is also used as a sauce for grits.) Country hams are not the same as the cured hams you find in the supermarkets, which undergo a wet cure. Country hams are always dry cured (and not necessarily smoked). They are lean, firm, and well seasoned, similar in style to Italian prosciutto, and usually served in thin slices. Virginia's Smithfield hams are a special type of country ham. At one time, pigs intended for Smithfield hams were fed peanuts, which gave their meat a unique flavor. Today, many are still raised on peanuts, but it is the curing process that accounts for the hams' distinctive taste.

Today's pork is much leaner than it used to be. Certain cuts have less fat and cholesterol than chicken. Because of its lower fat content, pork dries out quickly. It's important not to overcook it. Cook pork until the meat is rosy, 155° on a meat thermometer. It will continue to cook for a few minutes after you remove it from the heat, and will reach the USDA recommended 160°. Trichina, which can cause serious illness by contaminating pork, is killed at 137°.

In the early days and well into the twentieth century, pigs throughout the United States were raised for their fat as well as their meat. Bottled vegetable oils and tinned shortenings were not available, so cooks learned to rely on lard (rendered pig fat) for frying. Most health-conscious cooks don't use lard anymore. Shortening provides a rich flavor for fried foods, but it has more saturated fat than vegetable oil. Most vegetable oils are suitable for deep-fat frying. Some southern cooks still add a tablespoon of lard to the deep-fat fryer to give foods an opulent, meaty taste.

Kitchen Clue

Never use olive oil for deep-fat frying. It smokes too easily at temperatures that are too low to fry chicken and other foods properly. For best results when deep-fat frying, be sure that the cooking fat is hot and stays hot; otherwise the food will be greasy. Always add food to the fat gradually to avoid quick changes in the temperature. If you don't have a deep-fat fryer, use a large cast-iron skillet to fry foods. Cast iron retains heat exceptionally well, a vital factor for keeping fried foods as grease-free as possible.

Not Everyone Was a Plantation Owner

We often think of life in the old South as extravagant and carefree. The fact is, most people were not rich and didn't live the life we see in movies like *Gone with the Wind*. For them, southern food meant something different than it did on the plantation.

Down-Home Food for Down-Home Folks

Georgia began as a debtors' colony. Other parts of the South were settled by immigrants from Germany, Ireland, and Scotland, or by pioneers from northern states. These were hard-working people who looked to stake out new lives in new territory, either on farmland or in the hills. They had no money, and their informal cuisine was the fare of poor folk. Poultry was cheap and easy to raise, so fried chicken became the archetypal dish. Catfish were abundant and available—the rich wouldn't eat them then. Catfish is an ugly animal with tough, leathery skin and a bewhiskered face. But its homeliness belies an inner loveliness. The flesh is sweet and succulent, which is why it has become so popular with people from all economic groups. It is now farmed and has become a fishstore staple. Country cooks filet the fish, coat the surface with seasoned cornmeal, and fry it to a crusty brown.

Down-home foods also included dishes like Kentucky Burgoo and Brunswick stew, made with squirrel, possum, raccoon, or rabbit (cooks today use chicken and lamb). Homegrown vegetables were mostly corn, okra, and Irish potatoes, but one of the hill country's most well-known dishes, still a favorite today, consists of collards, kale, and other leafy vegetables stewed with salt pork, bacon, or a ham hock to make a stewed greens with "pot likker." For dessert, one could almost count on pecan pie, one of the southland's renowned confections.

Did You Know ...

Pecan pie is a type of "transparent" pie, which has a glossy, sweet filling made from corn syrup and eggs. Pecan trees grew so abundantly in the South that cooks used the nuts to give their transparent pie fillings some crunch. In Kentucky, recipes for pecan pie are spiked with bourbon. In southern cities, chocolate is added to the mix. Luscious as they are, you can forego the pecans and make the same pie with cashew nuts.

Soul Food

Clever cooks have a way of making a delicious meal from scraps. That's what happened in the plantation slave quarters. Blacks were given the poorest, toughest pig portions and made the stuff taste good. It was slaves who tended the barbecues that grilled pork ribs a rich, lustrous, tangy-sauced brown. They mashed the sweet potatoes for pie and turned collards, kale, and turnip greens into tasty and nutritious dishes.

Black cooks knew the secrets of cooking smooth grits and frying moist, juicy chicken. They turned native African ingredients into mealtime staples: peanuts in soups and desserts, benne (sesame) seeds in cookies, okra in stews and soups, and black-eyed peas in a dish known as Hoppin' John, which combines the black-eyed peas with rice and salt pork or ham hock. The dish is sometimes accompanied by stewed greens.

Southern barbecues usually feature pork and chicken, as opposed to Texas barbecues, where beef is preferred (see Chapter 6). Barbecue sauces and seasonings vary by region. Some cooks use a dry rub and keep sauce to a minimum. Some brush the grilled ingredients with thick, sugary, tomato-based coating. Carolina barbecued pork is tangy and pungent, with a vinegar base.

The Spanish South

It wasn't the English, the Dutch, or the French who built the first permanent settlements in America. It was the Spanish, who explored Florida in the sixteenth century and founded St. Augustine in 1565. They were looking for fabled treasures, and while they were here, they planted peach trees and citrus trees. Centuries later, peaches thrive in Georgia. Florida produces much of the country's oranges, lemons, grapefruit, and limes. The Spanish also introduced black beans, chorizo sausage, pigeon peas, and garbanzo beans to American cooking.

The Spanish influence is still considerable in Florida, notably in dishes such as Black-Bean Soup, Flan, and Roasted Pork, because of the state's large Cuban population. Florida has an eclectic mix of people, though, including senior citizens who have retired to the state. Whatever their ethnic background and age, home cooks in Florida take advantage of the bountiful supply of the produce and fish and shellfish available: pompano, snapper, mullet, stone crabs, conch, spiny lobsters, and rock shrimp.

The Least You Need to Know

◆ Yams are not grown commercially in the United States; what you see in stores are different varieties of sweet potatoes.

◆ Grits are crushed dried hominy, a specially processed corn, and can often be used like regular dried cornmeal.

◆ Bourbon is 51 percent corn liquor, always aged at least 2 years in new, charred white oak barrels. It is never more than 160 proof.

◆ Country hams are dry-cured, not wet-cured as are canned hams.

◆ Today's pork is very lean and can dry out quickly; the USDA recommends cooking it to 160°.

Barbecued Southern-Style Chicken

You can use an oven broiler to make this recipe. Place the rack 6" below the heat.

Prep time: less than 15 minutes   •   Makes 8 servings

2 broiler-fryer chickens, cut into 8 pieces	2 TB. molasses
Salt and pepper, to taste	1 TB. soy sauce
²/₃ cup ketchup	2 TB. chili powder
¹/₂ cup white vinegar	1 TB. dry mustard powder
¹/₃ cup vegetable oil	2 tsp. freshly minced ginger
¹/₃ cup brown sugar	2 cloves garlic, minced

Preheat an outdoor grill and set the rack about 6" from heat.

Wash and dry chicken parts. Sprinkle with salt and pepper. Combine remaining ingredients in a saucepan, bring to a simmer, and cook for 5 minutes. Brush chicken with sauce and cook over low to medium coals with the cover closed for 8–10 minutes. Brush chicken with more sauce, turn chicken, and cook another 8–10 minutes. Continue this procedure, turning meat every 6–8 minutes and brushing with more sauce, until meat is cooked through (about 35–40 minutes).

Hot Tip

Before you measure the molasses, rub a film of vegetable oil on the spoon (using the tip of your finger to spread the droplets left after measuring the oil for the sauce). This will make the molasses pour more easily, giving a more accurate measure. The spoon will be easier to clean, too.

Fried Chicken

If there ever was a reason to make fried chicken at home, this is it. It's my mom's recipe, prepared and enjoyed countless times. It's crispy and well seasoned. Make sure the oil stays hot and it will be grease-free, too.

Prep time: less than 15 minutes • Makes 4 servings

Special equipment: cake rack

$2\frac{1}{2}$–3 lb.-broiler-fryer chicken, cut into 8 parts

$\frac{2}{3}$ cup all-purpose flour

1 tsp. salt

$\frac{3}{4}$ tsp. paprika

$\frac{1}{2}$ tsp. garlic powder

$\frac{1}{4}$ tsp. black pepper

Shortening or vegetable oil

Wash and dry chicken parts. Combine flour, salt, paprika, garlic powder, and black pepper. Coat chicken pieces with mixture. Place chicken on a cake rack to air dry for 15 minutes.

Heat enough shortening or vegetable oil in a deep cast-iron or heavy skillet to reach halfway up the sides of thickest piece of chicken. When temperature reaches 365° (hot enough to sizzle a bread crumb quickly), add chicken pieces gradually, thighs first. Do not crowd pan. Use two pans, if necessary, or cook chicken a few pieces at a time.

Cover the pan. Cook over moderate heat, turning pieces occasionally, for 15–20 minutes or until all pieces are well browned and cooked through. Remove the cover for the last 3–4 minutes. Drain chicken on paper towels.

Cornmeal-Fried Catfish and Hushpuppies

Catfish are moist and sweet to eat. This old-fashioned southern recipe gives them a crunchy, satisfying crust. According to an old story, the hushpuppies that frequently accompany fried catfish got their names when cooks gave some of the crispy fritters to pet dogs who wandered into the kitchen. The dogs stopped barking because they were too busy feasting.

Prep time: less than 30 minutes   •   Makes 4 servings

Special equipment: cake rack

2 lbs. catfish filets	1 tsp. salt, or to taste
1/2 cup milk	1 1/2 tsp. chopped fresh thyme (or 1/2 tsp. dried)
2/3 cup all-purpose flour	1/2 tsp. cayenne pepper, optional
2 eggs	1/4 tsp. garlic powder, optional
2 tsp. water	Vegetable oil
1 cup cornmeal	Lemon wedges

Place fish in a shallow dish and pour milk over them. Let fish soak for about 15 minutes, turning filets at least once. Cut filets into three smaller pieces.

Place flour in a plate, beat eggs and water together in a bowl, and combine cornmeal, salt, thyme, cayenne pepper, and garlic powder, if used, on a plate. Dredge each piece of fish in flour and shake off excess. Coat floured fish with egg. Coat filets with cornmeal mixture. Place fish on a cake rack and let air dry for 15 minutes.

Heat about 1/2" of vegetable oil in a skillet over moderately high heat. When oil is hot enough to make a bread crumb sizzle, add fish, a few pieces at a time. Cook for about 2 minutes per side or until golden brown on both sides. Drain fish on paper towels. Garnish with lemon wedges.

For the hushpuppies (makes about 3 1/2 dozen):

Vegetable oil for deep-fat frying	1 TB. baking powder
1 1/2 cups cornmeal	1 small onion, chopped
1/2 cup all-purpose flour	2 eggs
1 1/2 tsp. salt, or to taste	3/4 cup milk
1 tsp. sugar	

Heat the vegetable oil to 375° in a deep-fat fryer or skillet.

Sift cornmeal, flour, salt, sugar, and baking powder into a bowl. Mix in onion, eggs, and milk. Drop rounded tablespoons of batter into hot fat, making a few at a time. Cook for about 3 minutes or until golden brown. Drain on paper towels.

Country Captain

This old-time dish from Georgia has its origins in East Indian curries. The recipe is said to have come from a sea captain who took shelter in the port of Savannah.

Prep time: less than 30 minutes • Makes 4 servings

1 broiler-fryer chicken, cut into 8 parts	1½ tsp. curry powder
¼ cup all-purpose flour	1½ tsp. thyme leaves (or use ½ tsp. dried)
2 TB. butter	¾ tsp. salt, or to taste
2 TB. vegetable oil	Black pepper, to taste
1 medium onion, sliced	2 TB. parsley, chopped
½ cup green pepper, chopped	¼ cup currants or raisins
2 cloves garlic, chopped	Cooked white rice
2 large tomatoes, cut into eighths	¼ cup toasted almonds, chopped

Wash chicken and dredge pieces in flour. Heat 1 tablespoon butter with 1 tablespoon vegetable oil in a skillet. When butter has melted and looks foamy, add chicken and cook over moderate heat for about 15 minutes, or until lightly browned, turning pieces occasionally. Remove chicken pieces and set aside on a plate.

Heat remaining butter and vegetable oil in the skillet. Add onion and green pepper and cook over moderate heat for 2–3 minutes, or until vegetables have softened. Add garlic, and cook briefly. Add tomatoes, curry powder, thyme, salt, and pepper, and stir to combine ingredients.

Return chicken to the pan, cover pan, and cook for 20 minutes. Stir in parsley and currants. Cook another 5 minutes or until chicken is cooked through. Serve over cooked white rice. Sprinkle with almonds.

Hoppin' John

No one knows for sure how this dish got its name, but it might be because children were made to hop around the table before they were allowed to eat some! In any case, it's considered good luck to eat Hoppin' John on New Year's Day.

Prep time: less than 15 minutes   •   Makes 6 to 8 servings

$1/2$ lb. black-eyed peas	3 cloves garlic, chopped
$6^1/2$ cups water	2 cups water or chicken stock
1 lb. salt pork	$1^1/2$ cups long-grain white rice (not converted)
1 large onion, chopped	Salt and pepper, to taste

Wash the peas under cold running water, then put in a saucepan. Cover with water and bring to a boil over high heat. Cook for 2 minutes. Cover pan and let stand for 1 hour.

Drain peas but reserve 1 cup liquid. Remove rind from salt pork and discard; cut meat into dice. Fry dice in a large saucepan or skillet over low to moderate heat for 7–8 minutes or until lightly browned and crispy. Remove dice and set aside.

Remove all but 3 tablespoons fat from the pan. Add onion to the pan and cook, stirring occasionally, for 3 minutes or until softened slightly. Add garlic and cook another 1–2 minutes. Add peas and reserved 1 cup cooking liquid. Add 2 cups fresh water or chicken stock. Stir in rice. Sprinkle in salt and pepper. Bring liquid to a boil.

Turn the heat to low, cover the pan, and cook for about 50 minutes, or until rice is tender and all liquid has been absorbed. Stir in salt pork, toss ingredients, and let stand for 5 minutes. Taste for seasoning. Add salt and pepper, to taste.

Pork Chops with Dried Fruits, Thyme, and Honey

Pork is so lean that it can dry out quickly. Pan-searing gives it a golden color, and finishing the meat with plenty of liquid in a covered pan helps keep it moist.

Prep time: less than 15 minutes   •   Makes 4 servings

8 pork loin or rib chops, about 1" thick	1 cup dried apricots, halved
Salt and pepper	1 cup dried apples
1 TB. olive oil	1½ tsp. fresh thyme leaves (or ½ tsp. dried)
1 small onion, chopped	2 TB. honey
1 clove garlic, chopped	Juice of 2 oranges
2 tsp. freshly chopped ginger	

Sprinkle pork chops with salt and pepper. Heat a skillet over high heat and brush surface with olive oil. Quickly sear chops over high heat (about 1–2 minutes per side) only until surfaces have browned. Remove chops and set aside.

Turn heat to low and add onion, garlic, and ginger to the pan. Cook, stirring constantly, for 1–2 minutes. Return chops plus any accumulated juices to the pan. Add apricots and apples. Season ingredients with thyme. Pour in honey and orange juice. Cover the pan and cook for 12–15 minutes, or until meat is barely cooked through and still rosy. Serve meat topped with fruits and pan sauce.

Roasted Pork with Orange and Sherry

The Spanish brought pork, oranges, and sherry to America. They combine beautifully in this savory casserole that pairs well with cooked white rice.

Prep time: less than 15 minutes   •   Makes 6 servings

3 lb. boneless pork loin	1 TB. grated orange peel
1 TB. olive oil	1 cup raisins
Salt and pepper	$^1/_2$ sherry
Pinch cayenne pepper	$^1/_2$ cup orange juice
3 cloves garlic, finely chopped	

Preheat the oven to 450°.

Place pork loin in a small roasting pan and rub top surface with olive oil. Sprinkle with salt, pepper, and cayenne pepper. Scatter garlic and orange peel on top. Roast for 15 minutes.

Reduce heat to 325°. Remove the pan from the oven and place raisins around meat. Pour sherry and orange juice over them. Roast meat another hour or until a meat thermometer registers 155°. During roasting, baste meat a few times with the pan juices. Let roast rest for about 15 minutes before carving.

Hot Tip

The USDA recommends cooking pork to 160°. The meat will continue to cook to 160° after you remove it from the oven when its internal temperature reaches 155°.

Shrimp Pilau

This is a famous Charleston dish, with the Charleston spelling of "pilaf." It is abundant with fresh seafood.

Prep time: less than 15 minutes • Makes 4 servings

2 TB. olive oil

1 TB. butter

1 medium onion, chopped

1 cup long-grain rice

1½ tsp. fresh thyme leaves (or ½ tsp. dried)

Salt and pepper, to taste

1¾ cups fish or vegetable stock or bottled clam juice

1 lb. shrimp, shelled and deveined

1 cup chopped ham

1 cup frozen peas, thawed

Heat olive oil and butter in a large skillet set over moderate heat. When butter has melted and looks foamy, add onion and cook for about 2 minutes, or until softened. Add rice, stirring until grains are coated with cooking fat. Add thyme and some salt and pepper. Then pour in stock or clam juice. Bring to a boil, turn the heat to low, and cover the pan. Simmer for 12 minutes.

Hot Tip
Try substituting white wine for some of the stock or clam juice.

Add shrimp to the pan and cook, covered, 5–6 minutes, or until shrimp are bright pink and rice has absorbed all liquid. Add ham and peas. Keep the pan covered for 2–3 minutes. Remove the pan cover and toss ingredients. Let stand 5–6 minutes before serving.

Stewed Greens with Pot Likker

This yummy dish is healthy, too; full of vitamins and minerals! Be sure to sop up all the pot likker, either by pouring it over the greens or by dunking cornbread.

Prep time: less than 15 minutes   •   Makes 6 servings

3 lbs. mixed greens (collards, mustard, and turnip)

½ lb. slab bacon, salt pork, or pancetta

1 medium onion, chopped

4 whole dried red chili peppers, seeded

2 cups water

Salt and black pepper, to taste

Vinegar, if desired

Wash greens and cut away tough stems. Tear greens into large pieces and set aside. Cut bacon into small pieces and fry in a Dutch oven or deep skillet over moderate heat until crispy. Discard most of the rendered fat, leaving about 2 tablespoons. Add onion and cook for 2 minutes, or until softened. Add chili peppers and cook for 1 minute. Pour in water and add greens.

Cover the pan and cook for 45 minutes, turning greens once or twice, or until very tender. Taste for seasoning. Add salt and pepper to taste. Remove chili peppers. Serve greens with some of the liquid and vinegar, if desired.

Fried Green Tomatoes

Crunchy outside, juicy within, these make great snacks or a side dish for barbecued meat or poultry and are a terrific choice if you have lots of unripened tomatoes in your garden.

Prep time: less than 15 minutes • Makes 4 to 6 servings

4 medium green tomatoes	$^1/_4$ tsp. paprika
$^1/_2$ cup yellow cornmeal	Freshly ground black pepper
$^1/_4$ cup all-purpose flour	2 eggs, beaten
$^1/_2$ tsp. salt, or to taste	Vegetable oil for frying
$^1/_4$ tsp. garlic powder	

Wash and slice tomatoes $^1/_4$-inch thick. Combine cornmeal, flour, salt, garlic powder, paprika, and a few grindings of black pepper in a bowl. Dip tomato slices in egg. Dredge egg-coated tomato slices in flour mixture and place on a cake rack to air dry for about 15 minutes.

Heat $^1/_4$-inch vegetable oil in a skillet over moderately high heat. When oil is hot enough to make a bread crumb sizzle, fry tomato slices a few at a time for about 3 minutes or until golden brown. Drain on paper towels.

Candied Sweet Potatoes

Candied sweets are a natural for Thanksgiving dinner, but many people enjoy them year-round. This version has a refreshing taste of citrus.

Prep time: less than 15 minutes   •   Makes 8 servings

3 or 4 large sweet potatoes	1 tsp. ground ginger
6 TB. butter	1/4 tsp. cinnamon
3/4 cup brown sugar	Pinch freshly ground nutmeg
3/4 cup apricot nectar (or orange juice)	1 1/2 tsp. freshly grated orange peel
1/2 tsp. salt, or to taste	

Peel sweet potatoes and cut into large chunks. Place chunks in a saucepan and cover with lightly salted water. Bring water to a boil, lower the heat, and cook potatoes for about 12–15 minutes or until tender. Drain potatoes and set aside.

Put butter in a large skillet over moderate heat. When butter has melted and looks foamy, add brown sugar and mix into butter with a wooden spoon or whisk. Add apricot nectar, salt, ginger, cinnamon, nutmeg, and orange peel.

Cook, stirring occasionally, for 4–5 minutes, or until pan fluids are thick and syrupy. Add potatoes. Cook for 3–4 minutes, basting occasionally, or until hot and well glazed with syrup.

Okra and Grape-Tomato Succotash

Grape tomatoes are small and attractive, so they make this dish pretty as well as tasty. You can substitute cherry tomatoes, or cut up plum or beefsteak tomatoes.

Prep time: less than 15 minutes • Makes 4 to 6 servings

1 lb. okra	1 cup frozen lima beans, thawed
3 oz. slab bacon, salt pork, or pancetta	1 cup corn kernels (or frozen corn kernels, thawed)
1 medium onion, chopped	$^1/_3$ cup chicken stock or cream
Salt and pepper	
2 cups grape tomatoes	

Wash okra, remove stem and tips, and cut into $^1/_4$-inch slices. Set aside.

Cut bacon into dice. Fry dice in a large saucepan over low to moderate heat for 7–8 minutes or until crispy. Remove dice and set aside.

Remove all but 2 tablespoons fat from the pan. Add onion and cook for 1–2 minutes, stirring occasionally. Add okra, sprinkle with salt and pepper, and cook for 10 minutes. Add tomatoes and cook for 2 minutes. Stir vegetables occasionally during this time. Add lima beans and corn, cover the pan, turn the heat to low, and cook 10 minutes. Add stock, taste for seasoning, and add salt and pepper, to taste.

Grits and Cheese Casserole

This is a wonderful do-ahead dish that could accompany almost any roast or grilled meat or poultry.

Makes 6 servings   •   Prep time: less than 15 minutes

2 cups water	1 small onion, chopped
1 1/2 cups milk	1 tsp. dried sage
1/2 tsp. salt, or to taste	1/2 cup ricotta cheese
3/4 cup regular hominy grits	1 1/2 cups fontina cheese, grated
2 TB. butter	3 TB. Parmesan cheese, grated

Bring water, milk, and salt to a boil in a large saucepan. Gradually pour in grits, stirring constantly with a whisk until mixture begins to boil again. Turn heat to low and cook 18–20 minutes, or until all liquid has been absorbed and grits are thick and fluffy.

Heat butter in a skillet over moderate heat. When butter has melted and looks foamy, add onion and cook for about 3 minutes, or until softened. Add onions and sage to cooked grits. Stir to blend ingredients thoroughly. Spoon mixture into a 13"×9" baking dish. Refrigerate for at least 1 hour, until thoroughly cold.

Preheat the oven to 350°.

Cut cold grits into three smaller rectangles. Place one rectangle into a smaller baking dish and top with ricotta cheese and 1/2 cup fontina cheese. Set another rectangle of grits on the first and top with 1/2 cup fontina cheese. Top with remaining rectangle and fontina cheese. Sprinkle with Parmesan cheese. Bake for about 30 minutes or until hot and beginning to brown.

Baking Powder Biscuits

Everyone loves fresh hot biscuits! The cake flour makes them oh-so-tender. Buttermilk means that they'll be properly flaky. You can substitute a tablespoon or two of fresh lard for the butter for biscuits that are even more tender and delicious.

Prep time: less than 15 minutes • Makes 10 to 12 biscuits

Special equipment: doughnut cutter

$1^1/_2$ cups all-purpose flour

$^1/_2$ cup cake flour

2 tsp. baking powder

$^3/_4$ tsp. salt

$^1/_2$ tsp. baking soda

8 TB. cold butter

$^2/_3$ cup buttermilk

Preheat the oven to 400°.

Lightly grease a cookie sheet. Sift all-purpose flour, cake flour, baking powder, salt, and baking soda into a bowl. Add butter and cut it into dry ingredients with two knives, your fingers, or a pastry blender, until mixture resembles coarse meal. Add buttermilk and quickly work mixture into soft ball.

Place dough on a lightly floured surface and knead about 10 times. Roll or press dough gently to $^1/_2$-inch thickness. Cut with a knife or doughnut cutter. Place pieces 1 inch apart (for darker biscuits) or close together (for fluffier biscuits) on the cookie sheet. Bake for about 20 minutes or lightly browned.

Hot Tip _____

For variety, stir in any of the following into the biscuit mixture before baking:

- ◆ 4 or 5 slices cooked bacon, crumbled
- ◆ $^1/_2$ cup minced ham
- ◆ $^1/_2$ cup grated cheese
- ◆ $1^1/_2$ TB. freshly grated orange peel
- ◆ 2 tsp. freshly grated lemon peel

Black Bottom Pie

This is an old-fashioned southern favorite, with layers of rich, dark chocolate, creamy rum custard, and fluffy, sweet whipped cream.

Prep time: less than 30 minutes • Makes 1 (9") pie

1 envelope unflavored gelatin

¹/₄ cup water

³/₄ cup sugar

1 TB. cornstarch

Pinch salt

2 cups milk

4 egg yolks

2 oz. unsweetened chocolate

1 tsp. vanilla extract

1 fully baked 9" pie shell (see Basic Pie Dough, Appendix C)

3 TB. rum

1¹/₂ cups whipping cream

Chopped pecans, cocoa powder, or shaved chocolate

Mix gelatin and water in a small bowl. Set aside.

Combine ¹/₂ cup sugar, cornstarch, salt, and milk in the top part of a double boiler set over simmering water. Cook, whisking frequently, for 8–10 minutes, or until thickened slightly. Add egg yolks and cook for 2–3 minutes. Don't let mixture come to a boil. Add gelatin mixture. Stir until completely dissolved. Cook mixture for 4–5 minutes, or until thick enough to coat the back of a spoon. Mix 1 cup custard with chocolate and vanilla extract; stir to blend completely. Pour mixture into baked pie shell. Refrigerate.

Add rum to remaining custard and refrigerate mixture until cooled completely. Beat whipping cream with remaining ¹/₄ cup sugar until cream stands in stiff peaks. Mix ¹/₃ whipped cream with rum-custard mixture. Spoon mixture over chocolate layer in pie shell. Spread remaining whipped cream on top of rum custard. Garnish with chopped pecans, or dust with cocoa powder or shaved chocolate.

Buttermilk Pie

You might not be familiar with this pie, an old southern classic. It's rich but also light; a perfect summer dessert.

Prep time: less than 15 minutes • Makes 1 (9") pie

Special equipment: hand mixer

Half a recipe of pie dough (see Basic Pie Dough, Appendix C)

4 eggs

1¹/₂ cups sugar

2 TB. all-purpose flour

6 TB. melted butter

1 tsp. vanilla extract

¹/₄ tsp. salt

1 cup buttermilk

¹/₃ cup sliced almonds

Preheat the oven to 350°.

Lightly flour a pastry board or a clean work surface. Roll pie dough on the floured surface to fit a 9" pie pan. Crimp edges to seal pastry onto the pan. Combine eggs, sugar, flour, melted butter, vanilla extract, and salt in a large bowl. Beat with a whisk or electric mixer at moderate speed for 2–3 minutes, or until smooth and uniform. Add buttermilk and blend in. Pour filling into pie shell. Sprinkle almonds on top. Bake 45 minutes or until surface is golden brown and the center is set.

Bourbon Pecan Pie

The liquor adds some pizzazz to this classic dessert.

Prep time: less than 15 minutes • Makes 1 (9") pie

Half a recipe of pie dough (see Basic Pie Dough, Appendix C)

3 eggs

1 cup sugar

$\frac{1}{2}$ cup dark corn syrup

1 TB. all-purpose flour

$\frac{1}{4}$ cup melted butter

$\frac{1}{4}$ tsp. salt

2 TB. bourbon

$1\frac{1}{4}$ cup pecans, chopped

Preheat the oven to 425°.

Lightly flour a pastry board or a clean work surface. Roll pie dough on the floured surface to fit a 9-inch pie pan. Crimp edges to seal pastry onto the pan. Beat eggs, sugar, corn syrup, and flour with an electric mixer at medium speed for 2 minutes. Add melted butter, salt, and bourbon, and beat for 1 minute. Stir in pecans.

Pour mixture into pie shell. Bake for 10 minutes. Reduce heat to 325° and bake for another 30–35 minutes or until top is golden brown and batter is set.

Coconut Cake

This tall, stately cake is gorgeous. The lemon-curd center deliciously balances the ultra-sweet frosting.

Prep time: less than 30 minutes   •   Makes 1 (9") layer cake

Special equipment: cake rack

For the cake:

2¹/₂ cups cake flour

2¹/₂ tsp. baking powder

¹/₂ tsp. salt

¹/₂ cup butter

1¹/₂ cups sugar

2 eggs

1 tsp. vanilla extract

1 cup milk

1 TB. freshly grated lemon peel

³/₄ cup jarred lemon curd

Frosting (recipe follows)

3 cups shredded coconut

Preheat the oven to 350°.

Grease and flour 2 (9") cake pans. Sift flour with baking powder and salt. Set aside.

Place butter and sugar in an electric mixer bowl. Beat at medium speed for 3–4 minutes, or until light and fluffy, scraping sides of the bowl once or twice. Add eggs and vanilla extract, and blend in. Add milk, alternating with sifted dry ingredients, and blend in thoroughly. Stir in lemon peel. Spoon batter into prepared cake pans.

Bake about 30 minutes or until a cake tester inserted into the center of cake comes out clean. Let cool in pans for 10 minutes, and then invert onto a cake rack to cool completely. Spread lemon curd on one layer and top with second layer. Cover cake with frosting (recipe follows), and press coconut on top and around sides of cake.

For the frosting:

3 egg whites, at room temperature

1¹/₂ cups sugar

¹/₄ tsp. cream of tartar

2 tsp. light corn syrup

¹/₃ cup cold water

1 tsp. vanilla extract

Put egg whites, sugar, cream of tartar, corn syrup, water, and vanilla extract in the top part of a double boiler set over simmering water.

Beat with a hand mixer set on medium high, for 7 minutes or until mixture stands in soft peaks. Remove the pan from the heat.

Beat another 3 minutes or until very thick, standing in stiff peaks.

Lady Baltimore Cake

This delicate white cake, stuffed with raisins, figs, and nuts, laced with liquor, and cloaked with sweet, glossy frosting, is an old South Carolina dessert. It was popularized when it was featured in Owen Wister's 1906 novel, *Lady Baltimore*.

Prep time: less than 30 minutes • Makes 1 (9") layer cake

Special equipment: cake rack

For the cake:

3¹/₂ cups sifted cake flour (sift before measuring)

4 tsp. baking powder

1 tsp. salt

1 cup butter

1¹/₂ tsp. vanilla extract

³/₄ tsp. almond extract

1³/₄ cups sugar

1 cup milk

8 large egg whites

Preheat the oven to 375°.

Grease and flour 3 (9") cake pans. Sift flour a second time with baking powder and salt.

In a large bowl, beat butter and vanilla and almond extracts until smooth and creamy. Gradually add 1¹/₄ cups sugar and beat until very creamy, about 2 minutes at moderate speed. Add flour mixture to butter mixture in parts, alternating with milk. Mix gently after each addition.

In another bowl, beat egg whites until they stand in soft peaks. Gradually add remaining sugar and beat until mixture stands in stiff peaks. Fold beaten egg whites into batter. Pour batter into the prepared pans. Bake about 25 minutes or until a cake tester inserted into center comes out clean. Let cake layers cool in the pans 10 minutes, then remove to a cake rack to cool completely.

For the frosting:

2¹/₄ cups sugar

Dash salt

³/₄ tsp. cream of tartar

¹/₂ cup water

6 egg whites

³/₄ tsp. vanilla extract

Place sugar, salt, cream of tartar, and water in a medium saucepan. Cook over moderate heat, stirring until sugar has dissolved. Continue to cook until mixture reaches 240° (when thin threads drop from a spoon).

In an electric mixer bowl, beat egg whites until soft peaks form. Turn the speed to high and slowly pour in sugar mixture. Add vanilla extract and continue to beat ingredients until stiff peaks form. Reserve 2 cups mixture for filling. Use the rest to frost outside of cake.

continues

For the filling:

1 cup chopped pecans

$^3/_4$ cup raisins

$^3/_4$ cup chopped dried figs

$^1/_2$ cup chopped candied cherries

2 cups frosting

3 or 4 TB. sherry, bourbon, or brandy

Mix all ingredients together. Use as filling between cake layers.

Chapter 4

The Midwest and Great Plains

In This Chapter

- ◆ The two big ones: corn and pork
- ◆ Wild things: persimmons, mushrooms, and rice
- ◆ Apples and cherries galore
- ◆ The breadbasket of America
- ◆ Americanitis: getting Americans to eat right
- ◆ Chicago's bounty

The cooking of the Midwest is grounded in the practical, no-nonsense fare of the early pioneers who first cleared the frontier. It is the food of church suppers and Sunday dinners, of hearty meals for hard-working folk. To many, this is the "real" American cuisine, the kind that evokes nostalgic feelings of the foods and comforts of the "good old days."

It took a lot of backbreaking work in those good old days to tame the plains and the prairies. But today the Midwest is America's breadbasket, abounding with the wheat, oats, barley, and corn that feed a nation. It's a place where giant pastures ensure a steady, substantial dairy industry, and extensive farmland means a plentiful number of hogs. Naturally, sweet corn on the cob and corn chowder, white bread and pancakes, cheddar cheese soup, and roast pork are on the menu here. Breakfast cereals were born in the Midwest, the result of one among many food-reform movements that had their beginnings here.

Midwestern cuisine also reflects many nations. A steady flow of immigrants began coming here early on. Germans settlers gave America beer, potato salad, and sausages, including the wiener, which became our all-American hot dog. Scandinavians gave us our favorite meatballs, Italians our beloved pizza. Chicago is a small universe of various ethnic cuisines that always makes restaurant dining in the city an interesting adventure.

Oh Pioneers!

A vast wilderness bordered the early American colonies. But pioneers braved their way through, clearing the frontier and settling in West Virginia, Ohio, Indiana, Illinois, Missouri, and Michigan. After Congress passed the Homestead Act in 1862, they were joined by other restless easterners and by immigrants from Europe, all eager for land. Many ventured into Minnesota, Iowa, Nebraska, Kansas, the Dakotas, and beyond. They came on foot and by wagon. Their stories have been romanticized in the movies, but, in reality, their lives were harsh and austere. Food was scarce and simple, a culinary routine of cornmeal mush, baked beans, and salt pork supplemented by wild game and foraged vegetation.

The Always Valuable Corn

Like their neighbors in the East, settlers in the midwestern states relied on corn. It was survival food at first, but these days corn is big business, thanks to generations of farming and crossbreeding strains. The Midwest supplies different varieties of corn for animal feed and ethylene alcohol, as well as for food items such as cornstarch, cornflakes, corn syrup, and popcorn. For plain old good eating, though, we buy fresh sweet corn, with yellow, white, or bi-colored kernels. It is among our favorite vegetables and we use it in all sorts of recipes, from fritters to soup, salad, and succotash. You can tuck some kernels into a frittata or add them to a stirfry. Many of us enjoy fresh corn on the cob. If you want the best tasting, sweetest cobs, follow President Thomas Jefferson's advice: Cook them as soon as they are picked, before the natural sugar turns to starch. Some people add a bit of sugar or milk to the boiling water to enhance the corn's natural sweet quality. Don't add salt, though; it toughens the kernels.

 **Kitchen Clue**

Buy the freshest corn possible, preferably from local farm stands, because corn's natural sugar dissipates quickly. Don't buy corn cobs with their husks removed. It may save you time and a mess to do so, but the corn won't taste as fresh or as good.

This Little Piggy

Because pigs are so easy to raise and provide so much nourishment, they were an important part of pioneer life. At one time, Cincinnati was dubbed "Porkopolis" because it was a big pork-packing center. When refrigerated railroad cars made meat shipments safer, hog production moved to other midwestern states, including Illinois and Iowa. Pork dishes are among the mainstays of the region's cuisine, including roast pork loin, stuffed pork chops, grilled spareribs, sausages, and even pork cake.

Wild Thing

A number of delicious foods grew in the wilderness and helped to sustain the first settlers. Three of these continue as favorites in the Midwest and beyond.

A Burst of Sun

Pioneers ate persimmons raw, and the women cooked them into puddings—still the best uses for this fruit. Wild persimmons are rarely seen in U.S. markets, but Asian varieties appear in the fall. There are two main types: Hachiya are large and sunset-orange colored; the flesh is astringent until the fruit ripens and softens, when it becomes sweet and luscious for eating out of hand. Fuyu persimmons look like orange tomatoes; these are crisp and firm when ripe.

Out of the Earth

When the pioneers broke ground in the wilds of Michigan, Minnesota, Wisconsin, and Ohio, one of the treasures they discovered were wild mushrooms. Morels are the jewel in the crown. This large, conical variety has a woodsy, earthy taste, and the crevices in the spongy cap make it particularly good for absorbing sauce, so it is used in dishes with cream sauce or gravy. Morels are expensive, but a little bit goes a long way, and you can mix them with other wild mushrooms in risotto, stirfries, omelets, or pasta dishes. (For more on wild mushrooms, see Chapter 8.)

Mini-Recipe
Sautéed Morels (2 servings)   Rinse and dry 4 ounces morels. Melt 1 tablespoon butter and 1 tablespoon olive oil in a skillet. Add a large chopped shallot and cook for 1 minute to soften it. Then add the mushrooms and cook for 2–3 minutes to soften them. Add 2 tablespoons port wine, sherry, or Madeira, cook 1 minute, and add $1/4$ cup cream. Bring to a simmer, cook briefly, and season with salt and pepper. Serve as a side dish or on top of cooked pasta.

The Most Glamorous Grain

Settlers in Minnesota and Wisconsin watched Native Americans harvest wild rice, a crop so valuable that local tribes waged war over territorial rights to places where the stuff grew. It isn't actually rice, but an aquatic grass. The settlers thought the narrow, tapered shape made it look like rice. (French fur trappers called it "crazy oats.") Wild rice takes longer to cook than white rice, and it retains a chewy texture. It has a smoky, nutty taste, which gives it a heartiness that works well with red meats, roasted poultry, and game. You can also use it for salad: add chopped tomatoes, avocado, and diced shrimp or chicken, and moisten with some mustard-flavored vinaigrette. Wild rice is expensive. To cut costs, you can mix cooked wild rice with cooked white rice for casseroles, stuffings, and salads.

> **Fein on Food**
>
> Crops flourished in the Midwest's rich, fertile soil, but farming was backbreaking work. Two new inventions would revolutionize agriculture: the McCormick reaper (1831), which had horses, not humans, pulling the blades, and John Deere's steel plow (1837), which helped farmers break up the tough prairie sod.

Planting Seeds for the Future

The folks who ventured west brought seeds for fruits and vegetables that would eventually feed a nation. They planted squash, pumpkins, beans, and cabbage. They grew grapes, asparagus, rhubarb, and berries. Immigrants from Germany and Ireland put in potatoes, the Scots brought oats, and the Swedes grew rutabagas.

An Apple a Day

In the early 1800s, folk hero Johnny Appleseed walked west from his home in Massachusetts with a skillet (which he wore on his head), a spade, and a bag of apple seeds. He preached the value of fruit and planted apple trees throughout the Ohio Valley. Within a few years there were thriving orchards in the Midwest, and apples became an essential in pioneer life, used fresh and dried for pie, sauce, and cake, or processed into cider, applejack, and vinegar. Apples are still an American staple. They are available year round, but the best-tasting apples come in the fall when you can buy the ones that haven't been in storage.

You can use a variety of apples for different purposes. The best baked apples are made with York Imperial, Rome Beauty, or Cortland. For pie or cobbler, choose Granny Smith, Rhode Island, Greening, Golden Delicious, Newtown Pippin, Northern Spy, Stayman, Baldwin, Jonagold, Braeburn, Winesap, or Idared. Applesauce is the most versatile: Use any pie apple or McIntosh, Macoun, Jonathan, Winesap, Fuji, or Gravenstein.

Life Is Just a Bowl of Cherries

French settlers planted cherry trees along the shores of Lake Michigan and used the fruit in cobblers, cakes, pies, puddings, and relishes. The trees still thrive, and today Michigan supplies the nation with most of the cherries used in baked goods. These are sour cherries—not the sweet Bings, Lamberts, and Royal Anns we are accustomed to eating out of hand in June and July. Tart, bright red sour cherries with names like Early Richmond and Morello are the best choices for pies and cobbler. You'll need a cherry pitter to remove the stones. Canned pie cherries are available, but quality varies greatly; some are soft and mushy, and it pays to spend a few cents more on a premium brand. (For more on sweet cherries, see Chapter 8.)

Amber Waves of Grain

The grains grown in the Midwest are used for much of the country's bread and also for many of our most prized foods: wheat for pasta, pancakes, piecrust, cake, and biscuits; oats for cereal and cookies; and barley and hops for beer.

As Corny as Kansas in August

Actually, the songwriter got it wrong: Kansas has lots of corn, especially popping corn. But it is primarily a wheat state. Yet, it wasn't until the late 1800s that wheat farming proved successful on the prairie. That's when German Mennonites came to Kansas from the Ukraine and brought seeds of a hard wheat called Turkey Red, which flourished. Hard and soft wheat varieties are also major crops in the Dakotas and Oklahoma. The hardness of the wheat kernel has to do with the amount of protein, or gluten, it contains. Hard and soft varieties serve different purposes:

- Bread flour is made from hard wheat, because breads, particularly crusty, chewy varieties, need gluten to develop properly.
- All-purpose flour is a mixture of hard and soft wheats, making it useful for a variety of foods, including pancakes, piecrusts, cookies, and tender loaves such as white bread.
- Cake flour is a low-protein, soft-wheat variety, designed for tenderness. It is useful for cakes, muffins, quickbreads, and biscuits.
- Semolina flour comes from hard Durum wheat. It is used to make pasta.
- Self-rising flour is either cake flour or an all-purpose type that contains leavening and salt. It is sometimes used for cakes, biscuits, muffins, and quickbreads.

Fein on Food _____

Because Kansas is a leader in wheat-flour production, its breads, muffins, biscuits, and piecrusts are legendary. But nothing beats the pancakes. In the town of Liberal, there's an annual Pancake Race on Shrove Tuesday, a tradition copying an event in Olney, England, that began in the Middle Ages. The women of the town flip pancakes in skillets as they run to the church. After the race, the mayor calls his counterpart in Olney to compare the winners' running times.

An Enduring Contest

America's wheat needed milling into flour, and the water power in Minnesota made that state the likely place for it. In 1871, Charles Pillsbury founded his now-famous company, which came out with its Best XXXX flour a year later and its award-winning Gold Medal brand a few years after that. The Pillsbury Bake-Off, which has become an institution in America, got its start in 1949.

Pancakes Need a Little Something

Pancakes are among Americans' favorite foods. American-style pancakes, unlike crepes and other European types, are thick and puffy because they're made with leavening. We like them served with butter and syrup. Maple syrup was once first choice but it was always expensive. In 1887, a clever Minnesota grocer invented Log Cabin Syrup, a blend of maple (45 percent in those days) and cane syrups, and made pancake topping easier to afford. The original can was shaped and decorated to resemble a log cabin.

Get a Rise Out of This

Americans may always have loved bread, but before there was commercial yeast, much of it wasn't very high quality, and results were always inconsistent. We have Charles Fleischmann to thank for inventing the first commercially manufactured packages of compressed yeast in 1868. It revolutionized bread-baking in this country. Today, we can choose from among a variety of yeasts. Be sure to read manufacturer's suggestions for usage of each type:

◆ Compressed yeast is sold in packaged cubes. It must be kept refrigerated. One cake of compressed yeast is equal to a $1/4$-ounce package of active dry yeast.

◆ Active dry yeast is more popular because it has a longer shelf life and needs no refrigeration. It is available in small packages or larger jars.

◆ Quick-rise dry yeast must be mixed with flour before liquids are added. It is available in packages.

Americanitis

In the mid-nineteenth century, long before fast-food burgers and fries or Tagamet and Nexium, a writer coined the term "Americanitis" to describe a growing population of sedentary city-dwellers and an epidemic of obesity and indigestion everywhere. Sound familiar? Several groups, many of them with origins in the Midwest, decried the American diet and made efforts at reform.

The Shaker Manifesto

The Shakers, a group of Quakers who left England with their leader, Mother Ann Lee, in 1774, established communities in several places, one of the most successful in what is now Shaker Heights, Ohio. Their cuisine was not unlike that advocated by present-day health-conscious Americans. It emphasized using fresh vegetables, cooked tender but still crisp, fresh fruit, and whole grain breads and cereals. For a while, some Shaker communities disallowed meat (and in others, meat-eaters and vegetarians were segregated), but too many members rebelled and the ban was lifted. The Shakers couldn't shake their love of sweets, though, and were known for their sweet meringue pies and for a cake served on their founder's birthday. Mother Ann's Birthday Cake is similar to Lady Baltimore Cake (see Chapter 3) but with peach preserves used for the filling.

> **Mini-Recipes**
> **Shaker Spinach with Rosemary** (4 servings) Wash and dry 12–16 oz. fresh spinach. Heat 2 tablespoons olive oil in a skillet, add a large chopped shallot, and cook for about 1 minute. Add the spinach, 2 tablespoons chopped parsley, 1 teaspoon chopped fresh rosemary, and some salt, and cook, stirring frequently, for about 2 minutes, or until the spinach has wilted.

Too Tempting

Eric Janson left Sweden for America, and set up the town of Bishop Hill, Illinois, in 1840, where he founded a new religion based on asceticism. No alcohol or rich foods were allowed, and the members' diet was the bare minimum needed for subsistence. Unfortunately, as legend goes, he was unable to resist his yearning for his favorite casserole: potatoes, onions, and anchovies cloaked with buttery cream sauce. One night he prepared the dish and was caught by his followers, fork in hand. Whether or not this story is apocryphal, Janson's Temptation is a delicious side dish, and a favorite in Swedish-American communities.

Breakfast Cereal: a Health Food?

It sounds strange today, but breakfast cereals were once touted as health food. The notion began with Sylvester Graham, who inveighed against meats, fats, condiments, and the use of bran-free white flour for bread. One of his followers, a Seventh Day Adventist named Ellen White, set up a sanitarium in Battle Creek, Michigan, and hired John Harvey Kellogg as its director. Kellogg invented his first health food—granola—and then went on to develop corn flakes and a variety of cold cereals that transformed the way Americans eat breakfast. Kellogg and his brother William Keith were marketing geniuses, and word of their products also got some help from Sarah Tyson Rorer, food editor of the *Ladies' Home Journal*. An entire new industry was born. Soon to follow were C.W. Post, who opened his own sanitarium in Battle Creek and created Grape Nuts, and Henry Perky, who invented Shredded Wheat. Some say that Kellogg also invented peanut butter, which was introduced as a health food at the St. Louis World's Fair in 1904.

> **Did You Know ...**
>
> Cold cereals may not be health food, but millions of people eat them. You can use breakfast cereals in numerous other ways. Try pressing crushed cornflakes onto chicken parts for oven-fried chicken; substituting crisped rice cereal for the breadcrumbs on top of baked macaroni and cheese; or topping fruit cobbler with crushed, buttered raisin bran.

Reform Redux

Efforts to reform American eating habits became popular again during the 1960s, and continue to this day. Some people are drawn to vegetarianism. Others object to the use of pesticides, antibiotics, hormones, and additives in foods. Scientific studies have taught us the dangers of dietary fat and cholesterol. An interest in ecology has made us aware of endangered species. Many people have changed the way they eat, making healthier choices, using more fresh fruits and vegetables, and eating less meat and fewer dairy products. In schools, salads and vegetarian meals are offered as alternatives to standard fare. Greenmarkets are burgeoning everywhere, offering an appreciative public fresh produce. Organic foods are widely available. For a while, many top restaurants offered "Spa Cuisine" so that diners could choose low-cal meals. While some still do, the trend now is to offer heart-healthy entrees on many restaurant menus. Unfortunately, according to recent studies, most Americans are still overweight and lead sedentary lives.

Fein on Food _____

Horace Mann, the distinguished nineteenth century American educator, was married to a woman named Mary, who wrote a book called *Christianity in the Kitchen*, in which she warned against eating butter and lard. John Harvey Kellogg's wife also decried the use of butter, and invented the first crumb crusts for pie. Crumb crusts use much less butter than traditional pie crusts (see the Basic Pie Dough and Crumb Crust recipes in Appendix C).

An Ethnic Conglomeration

After the first colonial settlements of Dutch, English, and Spanish in the East, immigrants from all over the world began to make their homes in the United States. In the nineteenth century, when the Midwest was opening up to settlement, there was a huge influx of Europeans. Midwestern cuisine reflects their culinary contributions. Russian, Finnish, and Cornish cooks introduced the pasty, a savory, hand-held small meat pie meant for snacking. From the Scots and Irish came gingersnaps. Poles offered kielbasa, one of Americans' best-loved garlic sausages.

Good, Hearty German Cooking

If it weren't for the German-Americans, the hot dog wouldn't be one of our famous "all-American" foods. The Germans came here with their love and knowledge of sausage-making, and spread the delicious word by way of small shops called delicatessens. Thanks to them, bratwurst, bologna, and liverwurst, to name a few, are everyday eats throughout the United States. German families left their gastronomic mark in other ways, too: potato specialties, such as hot potato salad, potato pancakes, and crispy German-fried potatoes; pork dishes, including pork and sauerkraut; and a variety of hearty foods Americans claim as their own, including meatloaf, noodle casseroles, and coffeecake.

Fein on Food _____

The German wiener came to be called hot dog in 1906 after "Tad" Dorgen, a Chicago cartoonist, drew a picture of a dachshund with a wiener-style body inside a bun.

The Beers That Made Milwaukee Famous

Germans and Bohemians were instrumental in making beer a major industry in the Midwest—at one time the region had thousands of breweries, with Milwaukee claiming the most. Prohibition decimated the business; only a few well-known, well-established firms were able to return when the law changed. It was lager beer that they brewed; before that, Americans drank British-style ale and stout, which are heavier. Beer is particularly delicious with hot dogs and other sausages, and lots of other kinds of food, too, but you can also use it as a cooking ingredient: in stew and pot roast, for example.

Just Like Home

Scandinavian settlers discovered that Minnesota, the Dakotas, and other parts of the Midwest were very much like home in terms of weather and terrain. Wheat crops provided them with flour for coffeecakes and Danish pastries, and the Great Lakes were bountiful with familiar herrings and other fish that were staples in their diet. These settlers continued the tradition of the smorgasbord—a buffet of fish, meats, vegetables, salads, and sandwiches. One of America's treasured recipes is Swedish Meatballs, a dish often found on smorgasbord.

How Cheesy

Before Swiss and Danish settlers arrived in Wisconsin, most people made cheese at home. The first commercial product was Swiss-style cheese. Even now, more than a century later, most cheeses popular in America are reworks of European varieties. One well-known adaptation is Maytag Blue, Iowa's famous Holstein cow cheese, first produced in 1941 by an heir of the Maytag washing-machine fortune. Maytag blue is tangy and creamy. Cheddar, a variation on the traditional English cheese, is the most popular cheese in the United States. (*American cheese* is a type of processed cheddar.)

What Is It?

American cheese is a processed product, not true cheese. It begins as pasteurized cow's milk cheddar, which is milled, shredded, cooked, and colored, and then molded into brick shapes. It is smooth and meltable. It's what you get on a burger or cheese fries. There are yellow and orange varieties, both of which taste the same (the orange kind has added color). The original American cheese was invented by James L. Kraft in the early 1900s. Individually wrapped slices first came to market in 1965. Cheese-food "products" such as Cheez Whiz and Velveeta contain cheese, but also contain other ingredients such as milk, water, gelatin, and corn syrup.

America's original cheeses are these:

◆ Colby, invented in Wisconsin. It is similar to cheddar, but softer and milder. Colby is not aged. Longhorn cheese is the same as Colby but has an elongated shape.

◆ Brick, created in Wisconsin by a man who weighted cheese curds with bricks. It is a firm cheese that can be mild, but is pungent when aged.

◆ Monterey Jack, a California original. It is tender and mild tasting, although sometimes Jack cheese is studded with bits of fiery jalapeño peppers.

Fein on Food

Barbecue isn't a Midwest specialty, except in Kansas City, Missouri, where it's almost a religion. It began with Arthur Bryant, who emigrated from Texas and met a local cook named Henry Perry, owner of three popular barbecue stands in Kansas City. Arthur created a tangy, tomato-based barbecue sauce and soon, with his brother, bought Perry's business. Eventually the restaurant was known as Arthur Bryant's, which Calvin Trillin called the best restaurant in the world.

Chicago, Chicago, That Toddlin' Town

Chicago was once a cowtown; it was the place where cattle came after the long trek from Texas. The animals rested and were fattened up at the stockyards before being shipped east. When refrigerated railroad cars became available, slaughtering began in the city, and that meant Chicago was always a good place for a great steak. But there's much more to Chicago than that. Like New York, this was a place where immigrants came to live, and where there were huge migrations of freed slaves after the Civil War. Chicago is a thriving city where you can feast on steaks and chops and also good, local ethnic foods: Polish, Italian, Middle Eastern, Hispanic, Indian, Jewish, Mexican, and others. One of the city's well-known Italian specialties is deep-dish pizza, created at Pizzeria Uno in 1943. The thick-crusted, tomato-and-cheese-topped pie was virtually unknown to most Americans at the time. Soldiers returning home from Europe after World War II clued everyone in.

The Least You Need to Know

◆ The Midwest provides America's important grains: wheat, oats, hops, barley, and wild rice.

◆ Pork and corn are mainstays of the midwestern diet.

◆ Sour cherries and apples, as well as wild food items such as persimmons, mushrooms, and rice, are important midwestern crops.

◆ Many of America's food reform movements began in the Midwest.

◆ Chicago is famous for its steaks but it is also the home of deep-dish pizza and a host of ethnically diverse cuisines.

Corn Salad

This is a colorful, refreshing salad that is a nice picnic or buffet item. Or you can serve it when you cook food on your outdoor grill. Using thawed, frozen corn and lima beans makes it easy to make.

Prep time: less than 15 minutes plus resting time • Makes 8 servings

1 cup medium pearled barley

1½ cups cooked corn kernels

1½ cups cooked lima beans

½ cup red onion, chopped

½ sweet red pepper, chopped

2 TB. chopped fresh parsley

2 TB. chopped fresh minced basil, or 2 tsp. chopped fresh savory, marjoram, or thyme

½ cup olive oil

3–4 TB. red-wine vinegar

2 tsp. Dijon mustard

Salt and pepper, to taste

Cover barley with water and let rest for 1 hour. Drain barley and place in a saucepan. Add 2 cups water, and bring ingredients to a boil. Lower heat and simmer, covered, for about 30 minutes or until all liquid has been absorbed. Set aside to cool.

In a large bowl, combine the barley, corn, lima beans, red onion, red pepper, parsley, and basil. Toss ingredients. Mix together olive oil, red-wine vinegar, mustard, and some salt and pepper. Pour over salad. Mix thoroughly. Let rest for at least 15 minutes. Serve at room temperature. Taste for seasoning, and add salt and pepper as desired.

Potato Salad

My good friends Janet and Bill Johnson once served this dish to me at a backyard barbecue, and I knew I had to have the recipe. This rich, German-style salad has been made by members of their family for generations.

Prep time: less than 30 minutes • Makes 10 to 12 servings

5 lbs. potatoes, preferably a waxy type, such as Red Bliss

$\frac{1}{2}$ lb. bacon

2 medium onions, thinly sliced

$\frac{1}{2}$ lb. butter

Salt and pepper, to taste

$\frac{1}{3}$ cup vinegar

1 TB. water

Place potatoes in a large saucepan, cover with lightly salted water, and bring to a boil over high heat. Lower heat, and cook potatoes for about 20 minutes, or until fork tender. While potatoes are cooking, fry bacon until crispy. Remove bacon from the pan, crumble the pieces, and set aside.

Drain potatoes, and when cool enough to handle, peel and slice about $\frac{1}{4}$" thick. Put in a large casserole dish. Place onions on top of potatoes in the casserole. Heat butter until melted and browned. Pour browned butter over potatoes and onions. Scatter bacon on top. Sprinkle casserole with salt and pepper. Mix vinegar and water, and pour over all ingredients. Toss ingredients and serve, or let cool to room temperature. Do not serve cold.

Corn Chowder

This colorful, creamy soup is fine in any season. In summer, make it with fresh kernels stripped from the cobs. Other times, use a premium brand of frozen corn.

Prep time: less than 15 minutes • Makes 8 servings

2 strips of bacon

1 TB. butter

1 medium onion, chopped

3 medium all-purpose potatoes, peeled and diced

2 cups water

1 bay leaf

1 tsp. salt, or to taste

$\frac{1}{4}$ tsp. freshly ground black pepper, or to taste

1 tsp. fresh thyme leaves

3 cups milk or half-and-half

3 cups corn kernels

1 cup frozen peas

2 TB. all-purpose flour

Paprika

Fry bacon over moderate heat in a soup pot until strips are crispy. Remove bacon, crumble pieces, and set aside.

Pour off all but 1 tablespoon fat from the pan. Add butter. When butter has melted and looks foamy, add onion, and cook over moderate heat for 2–3 minutes or until softened. Add potatoes and cook about 1 minute. Add water, bay leaf, salt, pepper, and thyme.

Bring soup to a simmer, cover the pan, and cook for 15 minutes or until potatoes are tender. Add milk, corn, and peas, and cook another 2–3 minutes. Add some soup to flour to form a paste. Add paste to soup, and cook soup another 10 minutes. Remove bay leaf. Add bacon, sprinkle with paprika, and serve.

Wisconsin Cheddar Cheese Soup

This is a good, savory opener for any dinner. It has a bit of a bite, thanks to the cayenne pepper. Herb croutons add some textural crunch; you can buy the packaged kind. Use a good, sharp cheddar for this potage.

Prep time: less than 15 minutes • Makes 6 servings

2 TB. vegetable oil	$\frac{1}{8}$ tsp. cayenne pepper
1 TB. butter	1 cup white wine or chicken stock
1 small onion, chopped	1 cup water
1 stalk celery, chopped	1 tsp. Worcestershire sauce
3 TB. all-purpose flour	4 cups milk
1 tsp. salt, or to taste	8 oz. shredded cheddar cheese
$\frac{1}{2}$ tsp. powdered mustard	Herb croutons, optional

Heat vegetable oil and butter in a soup pot over moderate heat. Add onion and celery, and cook for 2 minutes. Stir in flour, salt, mustard, and cayenne pepper, and cook 2 minutes longer, stirring frequently. Gradually add wine or chicken stock, stirring to dissolve flour. Add water and Worcestershire sauce.

Bring soup to a boil, then lower heat, cover the pan, and simmer for 10–12 minutes. Add milk, and bring soup to a simmer. Gradually add cheese, stirring to incorporate it. Let melt before adding more. Serve soup plain or topped with herb croutons.

Beef Stew with Beer

This is a good, hearty stew, perfect for cold weather. The beer gives it a slightly tangy flavor. You can make it a couple of days ahead. It freezes well, too.

Prep time: less than 30 minutes • Makes 4 servings

^{1}/$_3$ cup all-purpose flour

^{1}/$_2$ tsp. salt

^{1}/$_4$ tsp. freshly ground black pepper

^{1}/$_2$ tsp. dried thyme

^{1}/$_2$ tsp. dried oregano

2 lb. beef for stewing, cut into 1^1/$_2$" chunks

4 TB. vegetable oil

2 large onions, sliced

2 cloves garlic, minced

3 TB. freshly minced parsley

12-oz. bottle of beer

^{1}/$_2$ cup beef stock

3 medium all-purpose potatoes

4 carrots

8 oz. fresh mushrooms

Combine flour, salt, pepper, thyme, and oregano in a bowl. Add meat and toss, to coat with mixture. Heat 2 tablespoons vegetable oil in a Dutch oven, large saucepan, or heatproof casserole dish over moderate heat. Brown meat a few pieces at a time. Remove pieces as they brown.

When all meat is browned, heat remaining 2 tablespoons vegetable oil in the pan. Add onion, garlic, and parsley, and cook for 1 minute. Return all meat (plus any accumulated juices) to the pan. Add beer and beef stock. Bring liquid to a boil, and then lower heat, cover the pan, and simmer stew for 1 hour.

Peel and cut potatoes and carrots into chunks, and add to stew. If mushrooms are very large, cut into chunks; otherwise add whole. Cook stew another hour or until meat is very tender.

Bourbon Barbecued Pork Ribs

Slow-cooking and sweet, sticky barbecue sauce make these ribs dark, lush, and tender. Serve with your favorite potato salad and fresh corn on the cob.

Prep time: less than 15 minutes   •   Makes 4 servings

3 TB. olive oil	$\frac{1}{4}$ cup brown sugar
1 large onion, finely chopped	$\frac{1}{4}$ cup orange marmalade
1 stalk celery, finely chopped	2 TB. Worcestershire sauce
2 large cloves garlic, finely chopped	1 tsp. salt, or to taste
1 cup ketchup	$\frac{1}{8}$ tsp. cayenne pepper
$\frac{1}{2}$ cup orange juice	$\frac{1}{8}$ tsp. black pepper
$\frac{1}{4}$ cup bourbon	4–5 lbs. pork spareribs

Heat olive oil in a saucepan over moderate heat. Add onion and celery, and cook for 3 minutes or until vegetables have softened. Add garlic, and cook for another minute. Add remaining ingredients except ribs, and stir to blend. Bring mixture to a boil over high heat. Lower heat and simmer for 15 minutes.

Preheat an outdoor grill or oven broiler. Cut ribs into sections of 3 or 4 ribs. Cook ribs over low to moderate heat, or over indirect moderate heat, for about 50–60 minutes or until cooked through. Turn occasionally and brush with sauce until all sauce has been used.

Cornflake-Baked Chicken

It's amazing what you can do with cornflakes! In this recipe, it gives the chicken a texture that makes it crispy, like fried, but without the fuss and extra calories.

Prep time: less than 15 minutes • Makes 4 servings

1 broiler-fryer chicken, cut into 8 pieces	2 cups crushed cornflakes
2 eggs	3 TB. olive oil
2 TB. milk	Salt, pepper, garlic powder, and paprika

Preheat the oven to 375°.

Wash and dry chicken parts. Beat eggs and milk together in a bowl. Place cornflake crumbs on a plate. Dip chicken pieces into egg mixture, and coat the entire surface. Dip egg-coated chicken in cornflake crumbs, and press firmly.

Place chicken skin-side up on a baking sheet, leaving room between each piece. Drizzle olive oil over chicken, and then sprinkle with salt, pepper, garlic powder, and paprika. Bake for about 50 minutes, or until juices run clear and crust is golden brown.

Hot Tip

Try these variations:

- ◆ Use melted butter instead of olive oil.
- ◆ For Italian-style chicken, eliminate the paprika, and sprinkle some oregano and 3 tablespoons grated Parmesan cheese over the chicken.

Janson's Temptation

According to legend, this dish tempted the leader of a religious community to break his diet. No wonder, with its tender potatoes, tangy anchovies, and rich, creamy sauce.

Prep time: less than 30 minutes • Makes 6 to 8 servings

2 TB. butter

3 TB. plain, dry bread crumbs

2 TB. vegetable oil

2 large onions, sliced thin

6 medium all-purpose potatoes, peeled and sliced thin

2 (2-oz.) cans flat anchovies, drained

Ground white pepper

1³/₄ cups half-and-half

3 TB. butter, cut into bits

Preheat the oven to 375°.

Grease a casserole dish with 1 tablespoon butter. Sprinkle in bread crumbs and tip the dish to coat bottom and sides evenly. Turn casserole over, and shake out excess onto a plate; set plate aside.

Put remaining tablespoon butter and vegetable oil in a skillet set over moderate heat. When butter has melted and looks foamy, add onion, and cook for 4–5 minutes or until softened. Remove the pan from heat and set aside.

Place one third of the potato slices in bottom of casserole. Then top with half the onion and half the anchovies. Sprinkle with ground white pepper. Repeat this layer, ending with a layer of potato slices on top. Pour half-and-half over casserole, and place butter bits evenly on top layer. Sprinkle with reserved bread crumbs. Bake for 50–60 minutes, or until potatoes are tender and liquid is almost completely absorbed.

Pot Roast with Thyme and Mushrooms

This hearty dish can be really welcome during the cold of winter. It's a one-pot meal that you can make a few days ahead, and pop into the oven when you need it.

Prep time: less than 30 minutes • Makes 6 servings

1 pot roast of beef (about 4 lbs.), such as top or bottom round or chuck

Salt and pepper, to taste

2 TB. all-purpose flour

2 TB. olive oil

2 large onions, cut into chunks

2 large cloves garlic, minced

3 large sprigs of thyme (or use 1 tsp. dried thyme)

$^1/_2$ cup red wine or beef stock

8–10 peeled large white onions, cut in half (or 18–20 small white onions)

10 oz. fresh mushrooms, cut into chunks

4 large all-purpose potatoes, peeled and cut into large chunks

1 lb. carrots, peeled and cut into large chunks

Preheat the oven to 300°.

Wash and dry meat, and then sprinkle with salt, pepper, and flour. Heat olive oil in a Dutch oven or braising pan. Brown meat on all sides over moderately high heat for 6–8 minutes, or until all sides of meat are brown. Remove meat from the pan. Add onion chunks to the pan. Cook over moderate heat for 3–4 minutes, or until softened. Add garlic, and cook for another minute.

Return meat to the pan. Sprinkle in thyme, and pour in red wine or beef stock. Cover the pan, and cook in the oven for 2$^1/_2$ hours. Add white onions, mushrooms, potatoes, and carrots, and cook another 2 hours or until meat is tender.

Remove meat and vegetables from the pan. Remove fat from the pan juices, slice meat, and surround meat with vegetables. Pour pan juices over meat and vegetables. If desired, purée some of the vegetables with the pan juices for a thicker gravy.

Roast Pork with Fennel

This is a simple dish, easy to make, and appropriate for dinner anytime. It goes well with a salad and mashed or baked potatoes.

Prep time: less than 15 minutes   •   Makes 4 servings

2¹/₂ to 3 lb. boneless pork roast

¹/₄ cup olive oil

Salt and pepper, to taste

4 large garlic cloves, minced

2 large fennel bulbs, washed, drained, and cut into chunks (use only the bulbs, not the stalks or the frilly fennel leaves)

Several sprigs of fresh rosemary

¹/₂ cup white wine

Preheat the oven to 350°.

Place pork in a roasting pan and pour olive oil over it, letting oil spread to bottom of the pan. Sprinkle meat with salt and pepper, and sprinkle garlic on top of and around meat. Place fennel around pork, and turn to coat with olive oil. Lay rosemary on top of meat and vegetables. Pour in wine.

Roast meat about 1¹/₄ hours, or until a thermometer inserted into thickest part reads 155°. Turn vegetables occasionally during cooking, and baste meat once or twice. Let roast rest for 10–15 minutes before carving.

Hot Tip

Today's pork is much leaner than it used to be and dries out easily, so be careful not to overcook it. Cook pork until the meat is rosy, 155° on a meat thermometer. It will continue to cook for a few minutes after you remove it from the heat, and will reach the USDA-recommended temperature of 160°. Trichina, which can cause serious illness by contaminating pork, is killed at 137°.

Swedish Meatballs

This is a favorite dish at any party. You can make them ahead and freeze them for a month or two.

Prep time: less than 30 minutes plus resting time • Makes about 2½ dozen meatballs

1 cup fresh breadcrumbs	1 egg
1 cup milk	1 tsp. salt
1 lb. ground beef round	½ tsp. freshly grated nutmeg
¼ lb. ground veal	4 TB. butter or margarine
¼ lb. ground pork	2 TB. all-purpose flour
¼ cup onions, minced	½ tsp. instant coffee powder
3 TB. vegetable oil	1¼ cups half-and-half

Combine breadcrumbs and milk in a small bowl, and let soak for 5 minutes. Mix meats together, and add breadcrumb mixture. Heat 1 tablespoon vegetable oil in a small skillet, add onion, and cook over moderate heat for 3–4 minutes, or until softened. Add to meat. Add egg, salt, and nutmeg, and mix well. Place mixture in refrigerator for about 30 minutes.

Shape portions of mixture into balls about 1½ inches in diameter. Heat 2 tablespoons butter with remaining 2 tablespoons vegetable oil. Fry meatballs a few at a time over moderate heat, for about 6–8 minutes or until browned and crispy looking. Turn meatballs occasionally so all surfaces brown. Transfer meatballs to a plate with a slotted spoon.

Hot Tip

If you wish to cut down on saturated fat, substitute olive oil for the butter, ground turkey for the pork, and use whole or 2-percent milk instead of half-and-half.

When all meatballs are cooked, add remaining 2 tablespoons butter to the pan. When melted and foamy, whisk in flour and coffee powder. Cook for 1–2 minutes, stirring constantly. Gradually add half-and-half, stirring constantly. Cook for 2–3 minutes or until thick enough to coat the back of a spoon. Remove pan from heat, and strain sauce. Rinse the skillet and pour sauce into it. Add meatballs, cover the pan, and cook over low heat for 30 minutes, stirring sauce occasionally.

Rutabaga-Potato Casserole

This is a simple, easy, tasty dish that goes well with most entrées. You can make it ahead and reheat it in the oven.

Prep time: less than 15 minutes • Makes 4 servings

2 cups rutabaga, peeled, ½" diced,	½ cup dairy sour cream
2 cups all-purpose potatoes, peeled, ½" diced	¾ tsp. salt
3 TB. butter	Dash of nutmeg

Place rutabaga and potatoes in a saucepan, cover with lightly salted water, and bring to a boil. Lower heat and simmer for about 15 minutes, or until fork-tender. Drain and mash vegetables. Add butter, sour cream, salt, and nutmeg, and stir to blend thoroughly. Serve immediately.

Hot Tip _____

For an interesting variation, place ingredients in a casserole dish and cover with 1 cup fresh breadcrumbs mixed with 2 tablespoons melted butter. Bake in a pre-heated 425° oven for about 10 minutes or until top is golden brown.

Wild Rice-Wild Mushroom Pilaf

This makes a lavish accompaniment to roasts, grilled meats, or poultry.

Prep time: less than 30 minutes • Makes 6 servings

³/₄ cup dried wild mushrooms

2 TB. olive oil

2 TB. butter

1 medium onion, chopped

2 stalks celery, chopped

1 cup wild rice

1¹/₂ tsp. thyme leaves (or ¹/₂ tsp. dried thyme)

1 bay leaf

Salt and pepper, to taste

1³/₄ cups chicken stock

1 cup frozen peas

¹/₂ cup chopped pecans

2 TB. sherry

Place mushrooms in a small bowl, cover with hot water, and let soak for about 15 minutes or until softened. Drain mushrooms, and clean off any debris. Chop mushrooms and set aside.

Heat olive oil and butter in a skillet set over moderate heat. When butter has melted and looks foamy, add onion and celery, and cook for 2 minutes. Add wild rice, and cook another 2 minutes. Stir in mushrooms, thyme, and bay leaf, and sprinkle in salt and pepper. Pour in chicken stock.

Bring liquid to a boil for one minute. Lower heat, cover the pan, and simmer for about 50 minutes or until liquid has been absorbed. Remove bay leaf. Stir in peas, pecans, and sherry. Cook 5 more minutes. Let rest, covered and off heat, for 2–3 minutes. Serve.

American-Style Buttermilk Pancakes with Pecans

These tender flapjacks are puffy, and they absorb syrup delightfully. Use a Grade-B, dark maple syrup for best flavor—but if all you can find is Grade A, pour it on!

Prep time: less than 15 minutes　•　Makes 6 to 8 servings

3 TB. butter

2$^{1}/_{2}$ cups all-purpose flour

2 TB. sugar

1 tsp. baking powder

1 tsp. baking soda

$^{1}/_{2}$ tsp. salt

1 egg

3 cups buttermilk

1$^{1}/_{2}$ cups pecans, chopped

Butter for frying the pancakes

Melt 3 tablespoons butter and set aside to cool.

Sift flour, sugar, baking powder, baking soda, and salt into a bowl. Combine egg, buttermilk, and melted, cooled butter in a second bowl. Beat liquid ingredients to form a uniformly colored mixture. Add liquid ingredients to dry ones, and stir only until all flour is moist. Fold in pecans.

Preheat a griddle or large skillet over moderate heat. Lightly butter the pan before making each batch of pancakes. Pour out enough batter to make circles in the pan, leaving space between each one. Make circles silver-dollar size, or 3" in diameter, or pan size. Cook pancakes 1–2 minutes or until tiny bubbles begin to appear on surface. Flip pancakes with a rigid spatula and cook another 30 seconds or until bottom side looks golden brown.

Homestyle White Bread

This is a firm white bread, terrific when sliced and spread with butter, but also wonderful for sandwiches and French Toast.

Prep time: less than 15 minutes, plus rising time • Makes 2 ($8^{1}/_{2}$" × $4^{1}/_{2}$") loaves

1 cup milk	2 pkgs. active dry yeast
$^{1}/_{3}$ cup sugar	$^{1}/_{3}$ cup warm water
1 tsp. salt	$4^{1}/_{2}$–5 cups bread or all-purpose flour
3 TB. shortening	2 eggs, beaten
3 TB. butter	

Preheat the oven to 375°.

In a small saucepan, heat milk until bubbles form around the edges of the pan. Add sugar, salt, shortening, and butter. Stir to dissolve ingredients. Remove the pan from heat, and let mixture cool to about 85° (lukewarm).

Combine yeast and warm water, stir, and let rest for 5 minutes. Pour milk mixture into an electric mixer bowl, add yeast mixture, and stir to combine ingredients. Add 2 cups flour and blend in. Then add eggs and blend in. Continue to add flour, mixing continuously, until a soft, non-sticky dough forms.

Knead with a dough hook, or by hand, on a floured surface until dough is smooth, uniform, and elastic (about 4 minutes by machine, 10 minutes by hand). (You may use a food processor; kneading will take about 1 minute.) Place dough in a lightly oiled bowl, cover, and put in a warm place for $1^{1}/_{2}$ hours or until dough has doubled in bulk.

Punch dough down and let rest for 10 minutes. Cut dough in half and place in two lightly greased $8^{1}/_{2}$" × $4^{1}/_{2}$" loaf pans. Let rise for 20 minutes. Bake for 30 minutes. Loaf should sound hollow when tapped on bottom. Turn the bread out of the pans and cool on wire racks. Do not slice until completely cool.

Oat Bran Muffins

These muffins were hot stuff when scientists said oat bran could lower blood-cholesterol levels. But the best reason to eat them is the flavor. Oats are sweet and nutty-tasting. These are great for breakfast. You can freeze them for months in freezer-safe plastic bags.

Prep time: less than 15 minutes   •   Makes 10 to 12 muffins

1 cup oat bran	$^1/_2$ tsp. ground cinnamon or grated lemon peel
1 cup all-purpose flour	2 TB. vegetable oil
$^3/_4$ tsp. salt	2 eggs
$1^1/_2$ tsp. baking powder	1 cup buttermilk
$^1/_2$ tsp. baking soda	$^1/_2$ cup chopped apple, optional
3 TB. sugar	

Preheat the oven to 400°.

Lightly grease 10–12 muffin tins. In a bowl, combine oat bran, flour, salt, baking powder, baking soda, sugar, and cinnamon or lemon peel.

In another bowl, mix vegetable oil, eggs, and buttermilk until well blended. Pour liquid into flour mixture and stir only to blend ingredients. Do not overmix. Fold in chopped apple, if used.

Spoon batter into the muffin tins. The tins should be $^2/_3$ full. Bake for 22–25 minutes or until puffed and golden brown.

Pumpkin Sour-Cream Coffeecake

This lovely, pale-orange cake is delightfully tender and has a satisfyingly crunchy top. It's good for breakfast, coffee breaks, and even dessert. It freezes well, too.

Prep time: less than 30 minutes • Makes 1 (8") cake

Special equipment: cake rack

⅓ cup sugar	1½ cups all-purpose flour
¼ cup butter	1 TB. baking powder
½ cup mashed pumpkin (canned is fine)	½ tsp. baking soda
⅓ cup sour cream	¼ tsp. nutmeg
1 egg, beaten	¼ tsp. salt
2 TB. freshly grated orange peel	⅓ cup milk

For the streusel topping:

¼ brown sugar	¼ tsp. salt
3 TB. cold butter	⅓ cup chopped nuts
4 TB. all-purpose flour	

Preheat the oven to 375°.

Lightly grease an 8" square cake pan. Beat sugar and butter together with a hand mixer or electric mixer, set at moderate speed, for 1–2 minutes or until smooth and creamy. Add pumpkin, sour cream, egg, and orange peel, and beat ingredients for 1–2 minutes or until smooth.

Sift flour, baking powder, baking soda, nutmeg, and salt into a bowl. Add half the dry ingredients to butter mixture, and beat until blended. Add half the milk, and beat until well blended. Repeat until all flour and milk have been used up. Pour batter into the prepared pan. Combine streusel topping ingredients and mix with your fingers, with a pastry blender, or with 2 knives, until the mixture resembles coarse crumbs. Sprinkle streusel over batter.

Bake for 30 minutes, or until a cake tester inserted into middle of cake comes out clean. Let cake cool in the pan 10 minutes. Then carefully invert cake twice onto a cake rack to cool completely. (The first time you invert the cake, the crumbs will be on bottom. Turn cake right-side up to cool completely.)

Cherry Cobbler

Fresh sour cherries would be best here, but you can substitute good-quality canned cherries. This sweet, cheerful dessert is best served warm with a scoop of vanilla ice cream.

Prep time: less than 30 minutes   •   Makes 4 servings

Special equipment: cherry pitter

4 cups pitted sour red cherries or 2 (16-oz.) cans, drained

1 cup sugar

2 TB. minute tapioca

1 TB. lemon juice

$^1/_2$ tsp. ground cinnamon or $^1/_4$ tsp. almond extract

6 TB. butter

$1^1/_2$ cups all-purpose flour

2 tsp. baking powder

$^1/_2$ tsp. salt

1 egg

$^1/_3$ cup milk

Preheat the oven to 400°.

In a bowl, mix cherries, $^3/_4$ cup sugar, tapioca, lemon juice, and cinnamon or almond extract. Let mixture stand for 10 minutes.

Place cherries in a baking dish. Cut 2 tablespoons butter into small pieces and place over cherries. Mix flour, remaining sugar, baking powder, and salt in a bowl. Add remaining butter in chunks. Cut into dry ingredients until mixture is crumbly. Beat egg and milk together. Add to dry ingredients and mix until a soft dough has formed.

Roll dough out on a floured surface to a thickness of $^1/_2$". Cut out circles on a floured surface with a cookie cutter or the rim of a glass. Cover cherries with the circles of dough. Bake for 25 minutes or until dough is golden brown.

Louisiana

In This Chapter

- The difference between Creole and Cajun
- How gumbo and jambalaya came to be
- Hot stuff: peppers and blackened fish
- Louisiana's sweet tooth
- Some famous sandwiches

Louisiana's unique cuisine came about as a confluence of several cultures. From its earliest days, it was a kind of French-and-Spanish-gone-local with the help of Native American, Black African, and West Indian culinary traditions. Gumbos have their origins in French bouillabaisse. Jambalayas began as paella. This rich mix of people was the core of America's first culinary "melting pot."

New Orleans was once home to aristocratic French and Spanish plantation owners who expected the kind of luxurious, sophisticated Creole fare that prevails in the city to this day. In the country bayous, settled by French Canadians, home cooks developed spicy, robust Cajun specialties. Today, these cooking styles have blended somewhat. Both make plentiful use of fish and shellfish, rice, and hot peppers. Louisiana is the place to feast on Crawfish or Shrimp Etouffee, Blackened Fish, Dirty Rice, and sweet puffs of rice-stuffed Calas. Dessert is appreciated here, too, particularly fragrant Bread Pudding served with a spirited Bourbon Sauce.

The Big Bargain

In what may have been the savviest real-estate deal in American history, President Thomas Jefferson purchased the territory of Louisiana from the French in 1803 for about three cents an acre. The parcel wasn't just present-day Louisiana. It also included most of America's Midwest and Great Plains states and parts of Texas. Most important, the United States secured New Orleans, a thriving port city. France and Spain each had owned the territory, and New Orleans was home to a heterogeneous mix of people: French and Spanish, Native Americans, and Blacks from Africa and the West Indies. Early on came immigrants from England, Ireland, Italy, and Germany. Out of this confluence of cultures a unique cuisine emerged, the oldest true "melting-pot" cooking in America.

Creole and Cajun Cuisine

Creoles are the descendants of the original aristocratic and wealthy French and Spanish who came to New Orleans. Many were plantation owners. Their cooking style is lavish and sophisticated. It is based in the French classics but uses local ingredients and the tastes of other cultures: Spanish peppers, Italian tomatoes, African okra, West Indian fruits and vegetables, and Native American *file powder*.

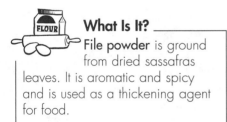

What Is It?

File powder is ground from dried sassafras leaves. It is aromatic and spicy and is used as a thickening agent for food.

Cajuns are the descendants of the French-Canadians who left Acadia, now Nova Scotia, when Canada was taken over by the British in 1755. (The word Cajun is a corruption of Acadian.) They had been fishermen, so it was natural that when they came to Louisiana, they settled in the state's swamplands and bayous. Cajun cooking is plainer and less luxurious than Creole. It relies heavily on fish, shellfish, and rice. Cajun cookery also adopted the seasonings of other cuisines and tends to be hot and spicy, with lots of chili peppers.

Cajuns are famous for their hospitality and will always give something extra: lagniappe. That means an extra cookie at the bakery and mention of a special technique or other tip in a recipe.

How Bouillabaisse Got to Be Gumbo

Both Creole and Cajun cooks are famous for Gumbo, which is a cross between a soup and a stew. It is always served over rice. The dish has its origins in French bouillabaisse, but when the French came to Louisiana, they had to substitute local fish such as red snapper and pompano, and shellfish such as crab, oysters, and Gulf shrimp, for the familiar Mediterranean seafood species. Spanish cooks added bell peppers. Sometimes tomatoes were included. And that's how Gumbo developed. There are now many varieties, some with chicken and andouille sausage, some with only vegetables and herbs: Gumbo Z'herbes, a Good Friday specialty. But there are only two basic types of Gumbo, and they are distinguished by how they are thickened.

File Gumbo

The Choctaw Indians showed the Europeans how to use file powder to thicken food. File also has a distinctive, if light, flavor that is reminiscent of thyme. It is always sprinkled into Gumbo at the last minute. Once it is added, take care not to boil the soup or the file powder will become stringy.

Kingumbo

The term Gumbo is from an African word for okra. African slaves brought okra seeds to America. The vegetable is a green, tapered pod with ridged skin. It is usually two to three inches long, but may grow much bigger. Okra provides an earthy flavor and its white seeds become gelatinous when cooked, thereby thickening the food.

Kitchen Clue
Don't use both okra and file powder when making Gumbo. The soup could become too thick and the flavors confusing.

It Used to Be French

Gumbos begin with a mixture called a roux. A classic French roux is a blend of flour and butter, used for enrichment and thickening. It takes a couple of minutes to cook and must never darken—if it does, the cook throws it out. Roux evolved into something quite different in Louisiana, where it is usually made with vegetable oil. The mixture is slow cooked to tan or even dark brown, depending on how it will be used. Tan roux is best in gravies and sauces for robust meats such as game, beef, and duck; darker roux is preferred for Gumbos and dishes made with chicken, pork, and shellfish. Roux provides a nutty perfume and flavor to foods.

Mini-Recipe
Roux (makes about 1 cup)   Combine 1 cup flour and 1 cup vegetable oil in a cast-iron or other heavy skillet set over low to moderate heat. Whisk constantly and cook the dish from 12 to 20 minutes, depending on the color desired. If the mixture begins to darken too quickly, remove the pan from the heat momentarily.

Something to Sing About

Hank Williams immortalized one of Louisiana's most well-known specialties in his song, "Jambalaya." The dish is an extravagant rice pilaf that probably has its roots in Spanish Paella. The word derives from the French jambon (ham) and African ya (rice). Jambalaya usually contains andouille sausage (a peppery Cajun pork and garlic sausage that has been smoked over sugar cane and pecan wood) or ham (if you can find it, use Tasso ham, a spicy Cajun ham available in some gourmet specialty stores; otherwise, use smoked ham). Jambalaya may contain other meats and fish such as chicken, pork, shrimp, crab, crawfish, and oysters. Crawfish look like tiny lobsters and their meat is white, sweet, and lobster-like. Most of the meat is in the tail; experts know how to suck out the claw portions.

Rice Is Nice

Louisiana is a major U.S. rice-producing state. Rice is important in both Cajun and Creole cookery. In addition to Gumbo and Jambalaya, other Louisiana rice specialties include the following:

♦ Dirty Rice, so-called because of the tiny speckles of chicken liver and giblets that make the dish look dusty. It is old-fashioned, down-home food, but well known in New Orleans where it may be served as a meal or side dish.

Kitchen Clue

The best all-purpose rice for Jambalaya, Dirty Rice, Red Beans and Rice, and Calas is long-grain, which cooks to fluffy, separate grains. Varieties include regular, basmati, texmati, jasmine, wehani, and pecan.

♦ Red Beans and Rice, traditionally served on Monday because, according to most tales, it was always made with the bone from Sunday's ham. Red kidney beans are simmered with ham, bacon, or salt pork, and onions in a spicy sauce and served over rice.

♦ Calas, which are sweet, crispy rice puffs sprinkled with confectioner's sugar. They are a splendid accompaniment to Café au Lait.

The Other Sacred Trio

In most other parts of the country, Native Americans and early settlers depended on corn, beans, and squash for their survival. In Louisiana, there was another important trio of ingredients: onions, celery, and peppers. Perhaps these weren't critical for survival, but they formed the basis for many of the unique and beloved foods of the region.

Ouch! That's Hot!

The early Spanish brought hot peppers to Louisiana. Today, fresh and dried peppers are staples in Creole and Cajun cookery. But the state's most famous pepper product is Tabasco sauce, which is made from dried, ripe red peppers that are ground, fermented, and mixed with vinegar. It is the best-known hot sauce in the world. Tabasco sauce gives more than heat to food. It also provides flavor and balance to other ingredients in a dish.

Fein on Food _____

Tabasco sauce comes from the seeds of hot peppers that were brought to Louisiana from Mexico in 1848, when the Mexican War ended. They flourished on Avery Island, home of the McIlhenny family. The McIlhennys fled the island during the Civil War and when they returned in 1868, their plantation was in ruins, except for the peppers. Edmund McIlhenny, once a banker, crushed the peppers and invented a piquant hot sauce. It was an immediate commercial success. Today, there are several varieties of Tabasco, including a blistering hot Habanero sauce.

Basic Black

A generation ago, Paul Prudhomme, a New Orleans chef, gained national fame with a new dish: Blackened Redfish. No one in any other part of the country had ever heard of redfish, but this recipe was such an amazing success that professional and home cooks throughout America started making this dish, and redfish became scarce. "Blackened redfish" is coated with butter and a mixture of spices, and then pan-fried over very high heat. Its warmth and exquisite flavor helped create a yen for hot and spicy foods in America. Today, people make blackened fish using halibut, snapper, pompano, grouper, and other varieties, as well as blackened meat and poultry.

Blackening spices are available in bottles, but you can make your own blend and keep it in a tightly covered jar with your other spices. Double the spice mix suggested in the recipe for Blackened Fish (later in this chapter).

You'll need a cast-iron skillet if you want to make classic blackened fish. Cast iron holds heat exceptionally well and it must be ash-white hot before you put the fish in. Smoke alarms may go off! You can make a reasonable facsimile of blackened fish, without all the fuss, in your oven broiler.

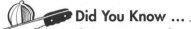

Did You Know ...

Cane syrup is a by-product of sugar cane production, made by boiling the juices extracted from the sugarcane plant. It is very sweet, thick, and dark brown, and tastes somewhat like molasses. It is used like maple syrup: over pancakes and waffles and so on. If you can't find any, you can make a reasonable substitute by mixing some dark corn syrup with molasses.

A Sweet Tooth

Centuries ago, a French confectioner invented a candy made with sugar and almonds and called it a praline. When the French came to New Orleans, they were as inventive with this recipe as they were with others; they understood that pecans, which grow abundantly in Louisiana, might work even better than almonds. The state had an abundance of sugar, too, because cane was an agricultural crop. Pecans are soft and sweet, and they partner perfectly with sugar to make one of Louisiana's best-loved treats: pecan pralines.

Time for a Coffee Break

Coffee is a big deal in New Orleans. In the French Quarter, people stop by for coffee and a beignet (doughnut) or pecan praline or hot Calas. Sometimes the coffee includes dried, ground chicory root. Chicory, which provides a vaguely bitter flavor, was used during the Civil War to stretch the coffee. Nowadays it may be in the brew for the sheer love of the stuff. Even when there's no chicory, Louisiana coffee is full-bodied and strong, using a dark-roasted bean. People might drink plain coffee, but more often than not, they are apt to sip one of the other coffee specialties:

- Café au Lait, New Orleans' favorite. It is a mixture of equal quantities of strong, dark coffee and steamed milk.
- Café Brulot, a warm, aromatic blend of coffee, spices, and brandy. A bit of theatrics accompanies this brew: You heat the brandy and set it aflame as you serve it.
- Café Diable, a sophisticated mix of coffee, brandy, and lemon peel.

Well Bread

In New Orleans, cooks rely on bread for some of the city's most famous foods. First are the big, overstuffed sandwiches similar to heroes or subs. Then there are two popular sweets, both made with leftovers.

Po' Boys and Muffulettas: That's a Mouthful

Hero sandwiches meet a need for casual eating and for satisfying food that stops short of a commitment to a full, sit-down dinner. In Louisiana they are known as Po' Boys. Some say the name came about in the nineteenth century, when out-of-work laborers calling themselves po' boys asked for free sandwiches. But this dish may have had earlier origins. In the Catholic convents, nuns would slit bread loaves and fill them with whatever ingredients were left over in the larder. Whenever a young waif would knock on the door asking for a handout (*pourboire* in French), the sister would offer a sandwich. Their origin as a vehicle for leftovers is probably the reason for the varied and unusual fillings. Po' Boys can contain fried catfish or shrimp, meatballs, cooked potatoes and onions, and *chaurice*, *boudin*, or other kind of sausage.

What Is It?

Chaurice is a hard, spicy pork sausage similar to Spanish chorizo. **Boudin** is softer but also spicy, made with pork, rice, chicken, and vegetables.

One of the tastiest and more interesting Po' Boys is called La Mediatrice, or The Peacemaker. According to local legend, a married couple quarreled about the husband's flirtations. One night he felt guilty about spending too much time in New Orleans' French Quarter and brought home a fried oyster hero: crispy oysters and juicy tomatoes moistened with tangy Creole Mayonnaise (a combination of regular mayo and Creole mustard) on toasted French bread. His wife took one bite and all was forgiven. The sandwich continues to be a favorite in New Orleans.

New Orleans Muffulettas are the prize of a grocery store. In 1910, the Italian proprietors of the Central Grocery created these sandwiches by stuffing cheese and deli meats inside Italian bread. What makes these different than most hero sandwiches is the bread, which is a round loaf, and the olive salad, which caps the meat.

Waste Not, Want Not

Leftover bread is too good to throw out, so Louisiana cooks came up with two signature dishes: Bread Pudding and Pain Perdu. Both are based on stale French bread. Louisiana Bread pudding isn't at all like the bland nursery fare most people associate with the dish; it's sugary sweet and rich with eggs, and best of all, it's drizzled with boozy bourbon sauce. Pain Perdu is like French Toast, but more stylish. It's made with stale French bread soaked in milk, eggs, sugar, and rum or brandy. Some may eat it at breakfast, but it's more like a dessert or brunch food.

The Least You Need to Know

- Louisiana cuisine is a blend of French, Spanish, Native American, Black, and West Indian cooking traditions and makes plentiful use of fish, shellfish, rice, and hot peppers.

- Creole cuisine is based on the French classics but uses local ingredients; Cajun cuisine, which is spicier and more robust, derives from country French-Canadian cooking.

- Gumbo, a cross between a soup and a stew, and Jambalaya, an elaborate rice pilaf, are two of Louisiana's most notable dishes.

- Long-grain rice is a basic ingredient in dishes such as Jambalaya, Calas, and Dirty Rice.

- Louisiana is famous for its dessert coffees and sweet desserts such as bread pudding and pralines.

Calas

Crispy outside, tender within, these rice puffs are delicious with coffee and even as an hors d'oeuvre.

Prep time: less than 30 minutes • Makes 12 puffs

$1^1/_3$ cups all-purpose flour

$1^1/_2$ tsp. baking powder

$^1/_2$ tsp. nutmeg

$^1/_4$ tsp. salt

$^1/_2$ tsp. freshly grated lemon peel

2 eggs

$^1/_4$ cup sugar

2 cups cooked white rice, cooled

Confectioner's sugar or cinnamon sugar

Mix flour, baking powder, nutmeg, and salt. Stir in lemon peel. Set aside.

Beat eggs and sugar for 2–3 minutes or until light and fluffy. Stir cooked rice into egg mixture. Gradually add flour mixture, stirring to blend ingredients thoroughly. Shape mixture into 12 balls.

Heat vegetable oil in a deep fat fryer or a deep skillet to 360°. Drop balls a few at a time into hot fat and fry for 4 minutes, or until golden brown. Drain on paper towels. Sprinkle with confectioner's sugar or cinnamon sugar.

Hot Tip

It's helpful to dampen your hands with cool water before forming the rice balls to keep them from sticking. Rubbing a little flour on your hands helps, too.

Chicken and Sausage Gumbo

This is a thick, hearty dish that can be dinner or a first course.

Prep time: less than 30 minutes • Makes 8 to 10 servings

Special equipment: Dutch oven or flameproof casserole

$1/2$ cup vegetable oil	1 onion, chopped
$1/2$ cup all-purpose flour	1 green pepper, chopped
$1/2$ lb. dry smoked sausage, chopped	2 celery stalks, chopped
1 broiler chicken, cut into 8 pieces	1 large clove garlic, chopped
$1/2$ cup all-purpose flour	8 cups chicken stock
1 tsp. salt, or to taste	$1/2$ tsp. hot pepper sauce
$1/4$ tsp. paprika	1 cup oysters, optional
$1/4$ tsp. cayenne pepper	1 TB. file powder

Make the roux:

Heat vegetable oil and $1/2$ cup flour in a Dutch oven or large, flameproof casserole, and cook over low to medium heat, whisking constantly, for about 15 minutes, or until mixture turns dark tan. Remove from heat and pour into a bowl. Cut sausage into bite-size pieces and fry in the pan set over low heat for 4–6 minutes or until they have rendered some fat. Raise heat to moderate and fry meat about 2 minutes, or until lightly browned. Remove meat with a slotted spoon and set aside.

Wash and dry chicken pieces. Combine the $1/2$ cup flour, salt, paprika, and cayenne pepper in a bowl, mix thoroughly, and dredge chicken pieces in mixture. Add chicken to the pan and cook about 15 minutes or until lightly browned. Remove chicken pieces and set aside.

Wipe the pan clean with paper towels. Return roux to the pan and place the pan over moderate heat. Add onion, green pepper, celery, and garlic, and cook for 3–4 minutes, or until vegetables have softened. Add stock and hot pepper sauce. Bring to a boil, lower the heat, and add sausage and chicken. Cover the pan and set heat to low. Cook for 1 hour.

Hot Tip
Roux separates easily, so give it a stir before you use it.

Remove chicken pieces and let cool slightly. When cool, remove chicken meat from bones and cut into bite-size pieces. Return chicken meat to the gumbo. Taste soup for seasoning and add salt to taste. Add oysters, if used, and cook for 1 minute. Stir in file powder, cook 1 minute, and then serve.

Blackened Fish

Paul Prudhomme made blackened fish famous all over America. It involves frying well-seasoned fish in a hot pan. I suggest broiling the fish but have also given you instructions in case you want to make the dish using the authentic Paul Prudhomme method.

Prep time: less than 15 minutes • Makes 6 servings

2 tsp. paprika

1 tsp. salt

1 tsp. onion powder

1 tsp. garlic powder

$^1\!/_2$ tsp. cayenne pepper

$^1\!/_2$ tsp. black pepper

$^1\!/_2$ tsp. dried oregano

$^1\!/_4$ tsp. dried basil

$^1\!/_4$ tsp. dried thyme

12 TB. butter

6 $^1\!/_2$-inch thick pompano, grouper, or red snapper filets, about 8 oz. each

Preheat the broiler.

Combine paprika, salt, onion powder, garlic powder, cayenne pepper, black pepper, oregano, basil, and thyme in a shallow dish and mix thoroughly. Melt butter. Dip fish in melted butter, and then dredge in herb and spice mixture. Drizzle a few drops of melted butter on top of filets. Broil about 6 minutes, or until just cooked through.

Alternatively, heat a cast-iron skillet over high heat for about 10 minutes, until the bottom begins to turn gray-white. Cook filets 2 or 3 at a time in the skillet. Cook about 3 minutes per side. Reduce heat, if necessary, to avoid burning crust. Repeat with remaining filets.

Hot Tip

Be sure to use an exhaust fan when cooking this dish in the skillet or you may find your kitchen filled with smoke and your smoke alarm clanging!

Crab Remoulade

A lovely warm-weather dish; you can use the sauce with any cooked seafood.

Prep time: less than 15 minutes • Makes 6 servings

Lettuce leaves, rinsed, and patted dry

4 cups lump crabmeat

1½ cups mayonnaise

1½ tsp. Creole or Dijon mustard

2 TB. gherkin pickles, chopped

2 TB. capers, rinsed, and drained

2 TB. fresh parsley, chopped

2 TB. fresh tarragon, chopped

1 anchovy filet, mashed, or ¼ tsp. anchovy paste, optional

1 hard-cooked egg, grated

Place lettuce leaves on each of the 6 plates. Top each with crabmeat. Combine mayonnaise, mustard, pickles, capers, parsley, tarragon, and anchovy in a bowl and mix thoroughly. Place some dressing on top of crabmeat. Garnish salad with grated hard-cooked egg.

Crawfish or Shrimp Etouffee

Etouffee means "smothered," and refers to dishes cloaked with a thick sauce and served over rice. This special dish is suitable for company. You can make the sauce ahead, reheat, and proceed with adding the shellfish.

Prep time: less than 30 minutes • Makes 4 to 6 servings

6 TB. butter

6 TB. all-purpose flour

1 medium onion, chopped

2 scallions, chopped

2 stalks celery, chopped

$^1/_2$ cup green bell pepper, chopped

2 large cloves garlic, chopped

1 tsp. salt, or to taste

Black pepper, to taste

$^1/_4$ tsp. thyme leaves

$^1/_4$ tsp. cayenne pepper

1 TB. lemon juice

$2^1/_4$ cups fish stock, vegetable stock, water, or bottled clam juice

1 lb. shrimp, shelled and deveined, or 1 lb. peeled crawfish tails

2 TB. chopped fresh parsley

3 cups cooked white rice

Heat butter in a large skillet over low to moderate heat. When butter has melted and looks foamy, add flour and cook ingredients, stirring constantly with a whisk, for 9–10 minutes, or until mixture turns dark tan.

Add onion, scallions, celery, and bell pepper, and cook for 4–5 minutes or until vegetables have softened. Add garlic and cook 1 minute. Add salt, black pepper, thyme, cayenne pepper, lemon juice, and fish stock. Simmer ingredients for 15 minutes. Add shrimp and cook another 2–3 minutes.

Hot Tip
This recipe calls for a butter roux, which gives the dish a rich flavor. You can substitute vegetable oil if you prefer.

Remove the pan from heat, cover, and let ingredients rest for 15 minutes. Place ingredients on a serving platter, sprinkle with parsley, and serve over cooked white rice.

Jambalaya

This is one of Louisiana's most famous dishes and deservedly so. You can use scallops, lobster, clams, or mussels in place of or in addition to the shrimp, if you wish.

Prep time: less than 45 minutes   •   Makes 6 servings

4 medium tomatoes

1 TB. olive oil

$^1/_2$ lb. baked ham, diced

$^1/_2$ lb. andouille or similar sausage, diced

2 medium onions, chopped

1 medium green bell pepper, chopped

2 stalks celery, chopped

3 cloves garlic, chopped

2 TB. parsley, chopped

$1^1/_2$ tsp. thyme leaves (or $^1/_2$ tsp. dried)

1 tsp. salt, or to taste

$^1/_2$ tsp. cayenne pepper

$^1/_8$ tsp. ground cloves (or use 1 whole clove)

Black pepper, to taste

$1^1/_2$ cups long-grain rice

3 cups fish, vegetable, or chicken stock, or water

2 TB. tomato paste

1 lb. shrimp, shelled and deveined

Cut tomatoes in half, crosswise, and squeeze out seeds. Chop tomatoes coarsely and set aside.

Heat olive oil in a deep skillet over moderate heat. Fry ham and sausage, stirring occasionally, for 5–6 minutes or until browned and crispy. Remove meat and reserve.

Add onion, bell pepper, and celery to the pan and cook for 3–4 minutes, or until softened. Add garlic and cook briefly. Add tomatoes, the reserved meat, parsley, thyme, salt, cayenne pepper, cloves, and black pepper. Stir ingredients. Add rice and cook, stirring, for 1 minute. Add stock and tomato paste. Stir to combine ingredients.

Bring liquid to a boil, turn heat to low, cover the pan, and simmer for 20–22 minutes. Add shrimp, stir, cover the pan, and cook for about 5 minutes or until shrimp are pink and all liquid has been absorbed. Let stand covered for 5 minutes before serving.

The Peacemaker

This is a dish of which legends are made: An errant husband supposedly gave one of these sandwiches to his wife, who, after one taste, forgave his shenanigans.

Prep time: less than 30 minutes • Makes 2 to 4 servings

24 shucked oysters

$^{1}/_{2}$ cup all-purpose flour

$^{1}/_{2}$ tsp. salt

$^{1}/_{4}$ tsp. cayenne pepper

2 eggs

1 TB. water

1 cup cornmeal

$^{1}/_{2}$ cup plain breadcrumbs

Vegetable oil for deep-fat frying

1 loaf French bread, about 18" long

4 TB. softened butter

Creole mayonnaise (recipe follows)

Leaves of soft lettuce (such as Bibb or Boston), rinsed and patted dry

2 tomatoes, sliced

Preheat the oven to 400°.

Wipe oysters dry. Mix flour, salt, and cayenne pepper in a bowl. Dredge oysters in flour mixture. Beat eggs and water in a bowl and coat floured oysters with egg. Combine cornmeal and breadcrumbs in a bowl and dredge egg-coated oysters in mixture. Set oysters on a cake rack to air dry.

While oysters are resting, heat about 3" of vegetable oil in a deep-fat fryer or deep skillet to a temperature of 365°. Slice bread in half, lengthwise, and scoop some of soft bread from the centers (discard or save for bread crumbs). Spread butter lightly over bread surface. Bake for 5–6 minutes or until lightly browned and crispy. Remove from the oven.

Fry oysters a few at a time in the hot fat for about 2 minutes or until crispy and golden brown. Drain on paper towels. When all oysters have been fried, spread Creole mayonnaise on bread. Place a few lettuce leaves on bottom slice, top with tomato slices and oysters. Cover with top half of bread. Cut into 2 or 3 pieces.

For the Creole mayonnaise (makes about $^{1}/_{3}$ cup):

$^{1}/_{3}$ cup mayonnaise

2 tsp. Creole or Dijon mustard

1 tsp. lemon juice

Few drops of hot pepper sauce

Blend all ingredients thoroughly.

Dirty Rice

This is an unusual dish for folks who don't live in Louisiana. It has spice and tang and looks interesting. A real treat!

Prep time: less than 30 minutes • Makes 4 servings

Special equipment: food processor

½ lb. chicken gizzards

¼ lb. boneless pork

2 TB. vegetable oil

1 medium onion, chopped

1 medium green bell pepper, chopped

1 stalk celery, chopped

2 cloves garlic, chopped

1½ tsp. salt, or to taste

1 tsp. paprika

¼ tsp. cayenne pepper

¼ tsp. black pepper

1 tsp. thyme leaves (or ½ tsp. dried)

1 cup long-grain rice

2 cups chicken stock, water, or a combination

½ lb. raw chicken livers, chopped

Cut gizzards and pork into small pieces and place in the food processor workbowl. Process on pulse until finely chopped. Heat vegetable oil in a skillet over moderate heat. Add gizzards and pork and cook for 3–4 minutes, or until lightly browned.

Add onion, bell pepper, celery, garlic, salt, paprika, cayenne pepper, black pepper, and thyme leaves. Cook, stirring occasionally, for 3–4 minutes, or until vegetables have softened. Add rice, stir for 1 minute, and add stock. Bring to a boil, stir, turn the heat to low, and cover the pan. Simmer for 10 minutes.

Stir in chicken livers. Cover and cook for another 15 minutes or until rice is tender and all liquid has been absorbed. Let stand for 5 minutes before serving.

Pain Perdu

This is the New Orleans' version of French Toast. The name means "lost bread." The dish was invented to use up stale bread.

Prep time: less than 15 minutes • Makes 4 servings

3 large eggs

¹/₂ cup milk

3 TB. sifted confectioner's sugar

2 TB. dark rum

1 tsp. finely grated lemon peel

8 (1" thick) slices of French or Italian bread

Butter for frying

Beat eggs, milk, confectioner's sugar, rum, and lemon peel with an electric beater, or whisk, for 1–2 minutes or until thick and foamy. Pour mixture into a shallow dish or a pan big enough to hold bread slices. Add bread slices and let soak 4–5 minutes or until thoroughly soaked, turning occasionally.

Preheat a griddle or large skillet over moderate heat. Add about 2 teaspoons butter before you make each batch of bread. When butter has melted and looks foamy, add soaked bread slices and cook 2–3 minutes or until bottoms are golden brown. Turn bread with a rigid spatula and cook slices another 2–3 minutes or until bottoms are golden brown.

Serve warm with cane or maple syrup, confectioner's sugar, or fruit preserves.

Café Brulot

A fine after-dinner treat.

Prep time: less than 15 minutes • Makes 4 servings

3-inch piece of cinnamon stick

6 whole cloves

1¹/₂ TB. sugar

Peel of half an orange

Peel of half a lemon

¹/₂ cup orange-flavored brandy

¹/₄ cup cognac

2 cups brewed dark-roast coffee

Place cinnamon stick, cloves, sugar, orange peel, and lemon peel in a chafing dish pan and light flame. Pour in orange-flavored brandy and cognac. Stir to dissolve sugar. When alcohol is hot, ignite with a match. Pour coffee in gradually, stirring until flames die down. Ladle into cups and serve.

Bread Pudding with Bourbon Sauce

The best use of stale bread you'll ever eat, and be sure to lick the bourbon sauce bowl. You won't want to waste any!

Prep time: less than 30 minutes   •   Makes 8 servings

1-day-old French bread, about 10 oz.	¹/₂ cup raisins
3 cups whole milk	1 tsp. freshly grated orange peel
3 eggs	1 TB. vanilla extract
1¹/₃ cups sugar	

Preheat the oven to 350°.

Break bread into pieces and put in a bowl. Pour milk over bread and let soak, mixing a few times, for several minutes or until most liquid has been absorbed.

In a separate bowl, beat eggs and sugar together with an electric mixer set at high speed for 2 minutes or until thick and pale. Stir in raisins, orange peel, and vanilla extract. Mix well and pour into bread mixture. Stir. Pour bread mixture into a buttered deep baking dish. Place dish into a larger pan filled with enough water to come 1" up sides of the baking dish.

Bake for 1 hour. Let cool but serve warm with ice cream, whipped cream, or Bourbon Sauce (recipe follows).

For the Bourbon Sauce (makes 1¹/₂ cups):

¹/₂ cup butter	1 cup confectioner's sugar
1 egg	6–8 TB. bourbon

Melt butter and keep hot over low heat. Beat egg and sugar together in the top part of a double boiler set over barely simmering water for 2–3 minutes, or until thick and pale. Gradually add melted butter and blend ingredients thoroughly. Cook for 1 minute, stirring, but don't let mixture come to a boil.

Remove the top pan from heat. Let cool slightly and stir in bourbon.

Chapter**6**

The Southwest

In This Chapter

- ◆ A Spanish influence
- ◆ Tortillas in all guises
- ◆ Bean cuisine
- ◆ Feel the heat: fresh and dried chili peppers
- ◆ Big beef and barbecue

The foods of the Southwest have become everyday fare throughout the United States. Chili Con Carne is a culinary icon, and the popularity of dishes such as Fajitas and Nachos, Guacamole, and Salsa is powerful proof of an enthusiastic acceptance of these once local specialties.

Southwestern cuisine has its roots in the sixteenth-century Spanish conquest, when conquistadors came in search of gold and silver. They clashed politically, militarily, and culturally with Native Americans, but exchanged culinary ideas. The Spanish were taught by the natives how to use corn, beans, and squash, and to eat tortillas and piñons. The Native Americans learned from the Spanish to eat beef and pork, eggs, cheese, and foods brought north from Mexico: chili peppers, avocados, and tomatoes. Today, these ingredients form the core of the region's best-known foods.

Barbecue became standard fare in the Southwest centuries ago. The Spanish learned the Native American technique of cooking foods on grids over an open fire and used this method for cooking their beef and pork.

Because of the region's natural beauty and relaxed pace, artists and retirees have flocked to the Southwest in recent years. They brought with them an awareness of innovative and sophisticated American cooking, and so the cuisine continues to modernize and adapt.

The Arrival of the Conquistadors

Driven by a lust for riches, sixteenth-century Spanish conquistadors set out in search of El Dorado, the legendary kingdom of silver and gold. What they found was the American continent, with its vast expanses of land. They came upon highly cultured native civilizations and unsophisticated nomadic tribesmen. They found a wealth of new foods. As with people elsewhere, natives and Europeans exchanged ideas about ingredients and cooking styles. What evolved was the cuisine of the American Southwest.

A Blending of Cuisines

Native tribes in the Southwest lived in structures called pueblos and had developed an early system of irrigation that allowed life-sustaining corn, beans, and squash to flourish. They ate buffalo, venison, wild turkey, and rabbit, *piñons*, and cactus fruit.

What Is It?

Piñons are the tiny nuts of the piñon tree, similar to pignoli nuts. The Native Americans ground the nuts and added them to stews to thicken them. Piñons also add flavor and crunch to salads and vegetable dishes. You can enhance their flavor by lightly toasting the nuts.

The Spanish brought over horses, which made hunting easier, and foods from Europe including cattle, pigs, sheep, and chickens. Domesticated animals broadened the meat supply and made eggs, milk, and cheese important parts of the larder. Peaches, apricots, figs, and grapes were planted, and wheat, garbanzo beans, lentils, and anise were introduced. The Spanish had lived for so long in Mexico that when they came to the American Southwest, they also brought with them some south-of-the-border staples: avocados, tomatoes, chocolate, jicama, and a variety of bell peppers and chili peppers.

Corn Is King

Corn has been growing in the Southwest for thousands of years. It was a life-sustaining crop for the Native Americans and remains important in southwest-style cookery.

The natives dried whole corn kernels and soaked them in ash to remove the outer hull (today, lye or slaked lime is used). These whole grains, or hominy, go into many dishes, most notably Posole, a pork stew with chili peppers and garlic. Posole is a traditional Christmas and New Year's dish in New Mexico. Hominy is available dry or in cans.

Dried corn was also ground and used to make flat breads similar to the early jonnycakes of the eastern Native Americans and colonists. But in the Southwest, the flatbreads, called tortillas, endured, and are among the most distinctive foods of the region. You can make your own tortillas by mixing masa harina (corn flour) with water and pressing the dough flat with a rolling pin between pieces of waxed paper, or with a special tortilla press sold in cookware specialty stores. Packaged tortillas are available in most supermarkets.

Cornmeal can be made from corn that has yellow, white, or blue kernels. Blue cornmeal has an earthy, nutty flavor and is a favorite in southwest cookery.

Tortillas are used in a number of ways:

♦ *Tostaditas* are tortillas that have been cut into wedges and fried in hot fat—what we know as corn chips. They are eaten plain and are the scoopers of choice for guacamole (avocado dip), salsa (a condiment), and chili con queso (a melted cheese dip).

♦ *Tostadas* are flat, whole fried tortillas, usually covered with savory ingredients.

♦ *Tacos* are grilled or fried and then folded and filled, usually with meat and salsa.

♦ *Enchiladas* are soft tortillas, filled, folded, baked, and served with a sauce. Sometimes enchiladas are stacked, rather than rolled around the filling.

♦ *Quesadillas* are soft, filled tortillas that are folded and either pan-fried or grilled.

♦ *Huevos Rancheros* are "ranch-style eggs" made with flat, soft tortillas topped with fried or scrambled eggs and covered with salsa and cheese. They are usually served with refried beans.

Mini-Recipe

Guacamole (makes about 2 cups)   Peel 2 avocados and mash the flesh in a bowl. Stir in 2 tablespoons lime juice. Mix in 1 chopped tomato; 1 small, chopped onion; 2 tablespoons chopped cilantro; 1 seeded, chopped jalapeño pepper; and some salt.

◆ *Nachos* are fried tortilla chips (tostaditas) smothered with melted cheese and chopped jalapeño peppers. Today, most people make nachos with packaged corn chips and top them with a variety of ingredients such as refried beans, salsa, sour cream, guacamole, chopped olives, and tomatoes.

◆ *Flautas* are tightly rolled, flute-like tortillas that are filled and fried.

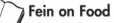

Did You Know ...

Although the word *salsa* means "sauce," there is a distinction: A sauce is usually cooked, and is an integral part of a dish or is served together with the food. Salsas are usually uncooked and are served as condiments to accompany food. The most common salsas are made with tomatoes and chili peppers, but most any fruit or vegetable can be used to make salsa.

The Power of Wheat

After wheat flour became available, a new kind of tortilla, the burrito, was invented. Burritos are usually larger than tortillas and are made with wheat flour instead of cornmeal. They are served folded, with traditional fillings of beef, pork, chicken, and/or beans, or more contemporary items such as grilled vegetables, and even with sweet fillings of fruit or chocolate. When they are filled, folded, and fried, they are called chimichangas.

In recent years, fajitas have become immensely popular throughout the United States. Fajitas are burrito-wrapped sandwiches stuffed with quickly grilled ingredients. The name means "little skirts" and refers to the strips of skirt steak used as a filling for steak fajitas. But even though steak fajitas are delicious, no one limits the dish to beef. You can make fajitas with all sorts of grilled items such as chicken, fish, and vegetables. You can also enrich the sandwich with guacamole, cheese, salsa, tomatoes, and sour cream.

Fein on Food

After the Spanish introduced pigs to the Southwest, an entire culinary culture changed. Pork was a new meat, but lard, the rendered fat, had even more impact. The natives were able to fry foods for the first time. That's how now-classic foods such as tostadas and Navajo Fry Bread came about.

The availability of wheat was an inspiration for cooks of the Southwest. Besides the burrito, there is Navajo Fry Bread, a tender but crunchy flatbread, and sopapaillas, which are similar to yeast-risen doughnuts. Both may be eaten as a savory with beef, cheese, chili, or beans but are just as good when served as a sweet, drizzled with honey or sprinkled with confectioner's sugar.

Beans to You

Because they are packed with high-quality protein, dried beans have been an important source of nourishment since prehistoric times. They were certainly a mainstay among the Native Americans of the Southwest and continue as a staple of the region's cuisine.

There are dozens of varieties of beans, but the ones most familiar to southwest cooking are the following:

◆ Black beans (also called turtle beans) are small, black, and kidney-shaped with an earthy taste and somewhat mealy texture.

◆ Pinto beans are kidney-shaped and rose-colored, with pink-brown flecks. They have a full-bodied flavor and a mealy texture.

◆ Anasazi beans are small, kidney-shaped, reddish-brown beans with white markings. They fade to a uniform dark pink when cooked.

◆ Jacob's cattle beans, brought to the region with German settlers, have red-brown speckles.

Dried beans need soaking before you cook them. You can cover them with water and let them rest for about 8 hours, but here's a quicker method: Place beans in a large saucepan and cover with water. Bring water to boil over high heat. Lower the heat and let the beans boil gently for 2 minutes. Remove the pan from heat and let beans soak for an hour.

Southwest cookery has its own version of baked beans using pinto beans, tomatoes, and chili peppers, but the ubiquitous regional dish is *frijoles refritos*, or Refried Beans. It takes a while to make this recipe. You have to poach the beans first, and then fry them. But the result is a rich, earthy, flavorful dish. Refried beans are eaten with tostadas, stuffed into tortillas, or served as a side dish for grilled meats, nachos, and Huevos Rancheros.

Kitchen Clue

Cooked beans can cause flatulence. Some experts say you can avoid this problem by changing the soaking water a few times or discarding the soaking water and cooking the beans in fresh water. Others suggest adding herbs to the pot. If flatulence is a problem for you, you can try Beano, a product that breaks down the gas-causing compounds. Or try eating beans more often to build a tolerance for them.

Hot, Hot, Hot!

You can't cook southwestern style without knowing about chili peppers. The natives had used small chilies, called *chiltepins*, but other varieties were brought from Mexico by the Spanish. Actually, the word pepper, as applied to bell or chili pepper, is a culinary misnomer. When Columbus and his men landed in the New World and tasted these vegetables, they noticed the heat and sting. The explorers were looking for black peppercorns; they might have thought chili peppers were related. In those days, anything labeled pepper was sure to make money. Whether or not Columbus was fooled or tried to put one over on an unsuspecting public, fresh peppers (really capsicums) were an immediate success in Europe.

Chili peppers can be mild or hot. Be very careful when handling them. Wear disposable gloves if possible. Wash your hands thoroughly with soap and warm water after working with chilies, and don't touch your face or eyes, or clean your contact lenses and put them back in your eyes.

In 1912, Wilbur S. Scoville, a pharmacist, invented a heat index for food such as chili peppers, which can range from zero or negligible units to over 800,000 units. Most of the heat is in the pepper's ribs and seeds, which are discarded. The flesh has the least heat.

Fein on Food

The Aztecs brewed hot chocolate thousands of years ago. It was a prized beverage for royalty and aristocrats. Cortez, the Spanish conquistador, knew a good thing when he tasted it and brought the recipe back to Europe. But the Aztecs steeped the brew with chili peppers. It took years before folks figured out that hot chocolate tastes even better when sweetened! The Spanish added sugar, and sweetened hot chocolate became the standard throughout Europe.

As Fresh as Can Be

There are many varieties of fresh chili peppers in varying colors of green, yellow, orange, and red. They include the following:

- Anaheim, California, or New Mexico, mild with bright green or red skin; about six inches long.
- Habanero, the hottest variety; small and stubby, it may be orange, yellow, green, or vibrant red.

◆ Jalapeño, medium-hot, short, and tapered with dark green or red skin.

◆ Pequin, the cultivated form of the chiltepin; small, round, very hot.

◆ Poblano, medium-hot, triangular-shaped, dark green; a smoky flavor when roasted.

◆ Serrano, medium-sized with pointy ends, dark green or bright red, a little hotter than a jalapeño.

You can use chili peppers such as jalapeños to give heat to many familiar foods such as potato salad, cornbread, scrambled eggs, fish chowders, and barbecue sauce. Jellies made with chili peppers make a lively accompaniment to meat, a perky spread on cornbread, or a special quick hors d'oeuvre on top of cream cheese and crackers.

Kitchen Clue

Roasting gives peppers a smoky taste and helps in removing the skin, which can be bitter and difficult to digest. To roast a pepper, place it in a covered barbecue grill or under the broiler. Char the skin on all sides, and then put the pepper in a paper or plastic bag. Let it cool, peel the skin, and pull off the stem. Discard the ribs and seeds.

The Dried Kinds Are Special, Too

Certain recipes call for dried, rather than fresh, chili peppers. The most familiar are these:

◆ Ancho, a dried poblano, mild and vaguely sweet.

◆ Cayenne, small, slim, and red, with pointy ends; fiery hot.

◆ Chipotle, a dried, smoked jalapeño pepper. It has a complex, smoke-and-fire flavor and medium heat.

◆ Cascabel, bulbous, dark, medium hot.

◆ Chile de Arbol, small, red, almost as hot as a cayenne.

What Exactly Is Chili Con Carne?

Of all the dishes of the Southwest, Chili Con Carne is the most well known, and has become as American a dish as pizza, French fries, and apple pie. There are chili cook-offs, chili-lover's societies and chili festivals. One thing is certain: People will have chili-hot arguments about what exactly the dish is. In its simplest terms, Chili Con Carne means meat cooked with hot peppers. What else is added is up to the cook.

Native Americans undoubtedly ate buffalo meat with chili peppers, but Texans claim to have invented Chili Con Carne as we know it. In the late nineteenth century, "Chili Queens" sold bowls of the stuff on the streets of San Antonio. Original versions of Texas chili were made with chunks of beef or venison, chili peppers, garlic, and cumin. Tomatoes and onions were later additions. These days, even in Texas, many cooks use ground beef for their homemade "bowl of red" and opt for *chili powder* rather than using dried chili peppers.

> **What Is It?**
>
> **Chili powder** is a blend of spices including dried, powdered chili peppers, garlic, oregano, and cumin. Powdered chili is the pure, ground form of a particular dried chili pepper; no other herbs or spices are added.

Many Texans will tell you that beans are a side dish and don't belong in an authentic Chili Con Carne. President and native Texan Lyndon Johnson was adamant on this point. Elsewhere, cooks consider beans an essential ingredient. As with all culinary debates, taste matters most. Make the dish to please yourself.

You can make Chili Con Carne with ground or minced pork, lamb, chicken, or turkey. You can add red bell peppers. You can make it searingly hot or mild; it all depends on the amount of chili peppers or ground chili powder you use. You can also make meatless chili (of course, that would not be "con carne") using garbanzo and pinto beans.

A Beef Culture

Beef is a big deal in the Southwest, especially in Texas. Not just for Chili Con Carne, but for big, juicy grilled steaks and for barbecue. The Spanish brought cattle to Mexico, and over the years, the herds moved northward to graze. Franciscan monks established missions in the Southwest and domesticated cattle, sheep, and chickens. This was the beginning of a meat culture in the region. After the Mexican War ended in 1848, the area became U.S. territory and it attracted pioneers from the East, and new settlers from England, Ireland, and Germany. These beef-loving Anglos settled along the Rio Grande River and brought new breeds of cattle. They made beef big business.

All-American Barbecue?

Spanish explorers learned barbecue from the Native Americans, who cooked game and fish on racks of green wood over an open fire. In the Southwest, some of the Native Americans cooked buffalo using this method. The Spanish used the word *barbacoa* for the grids that held the food. When the Spanish decided to use the same cooking technique for the pigs and cattle they brought from Europe, barbecue became big time.

Today, grilled and barbecued foods have reached cult status in this country. Most homeowners have grills in their backyards and city dwellers keep them on terraces. Picnic-goers grill food in the park. For most Americans, this kind of cooking used to be a summertime thing, but now many people enjoy grill-seared foods all year. In the Southwest and parts of the South that enjoy a mild climate, barbecue is always a year-round, integral part of the culture.

Old-fashioned barbecuing is not the same thing as grilling. Barbecue refers to slow-cooking of meats in a closed pit or other structure (frequently with mesquite, hickory, or pecan wood for fuel). Grilling involves quicker cooking. We can use our outdoor grills for both grilling of quickly cooked items and for small-scale barbecuing: Use indirect or low heat for foods that require long, slow cooking.

Kitchen Clue

You can cook almost any food on an outdoor grill. Hamburgers, hot dogs, fish, chicken, and steak are popular, but vegetables, bread, and even some fruits also taste delicious when grilled.

The Big Barbecue

Texas barbecues are big, casual affairs that harken back to political rallies of the nineteenth century, when politicians invited would-be voters to enjoy free food. They are still popular social events in Texas today. But whether it's a party for many or dinner for the family, beef is frequently the feature—steaks, roasts, burgers, and so on. On the other hand, there might be pork and chicken and, of course, lots of the same side dishes that accompany barbecue everywhere else in the States: corn on the cob, coleslaw, beans, and potato salad.

Fein on Food

Barbecue made all the difference in the race for the presidency in 1840. The incumbent Martin Van Buren had a taste for fancy French food. His opponent, William Henry Harrison, was characterized as a "man of the people." Harrison threw the biggest barbecue on record. Tons of food were served, and memories of sizzling steaks and chops carried over to the voting booth. He won.

The best meats for grilling are the tender cuts: beef sirloin, strip, T-bone, porterhouse, rib, Delmonico (also called club steak), and tenderloin steaks; lamb rib, loin, and butterflied leg; pork tenderloin, veal rib, and loin chops. Beef skirt steaks and hanger steaks, while less tender, are still terrific when grilled. Flank steaks are fine when grilled, too, but be sure to cut them across the grain when you serve them. The best cuts for barbecuing are those that become tender and succulent with long, slow cooking: pork ribs, beef pot roasts (chuck, brisket, round) and rib roast, whole chicken or turkey, and leg of lamb.

It's All in the Sauce

Barbecue sauce means different things to different people in different parts of the country. In the South, tangy vinegar-based sauces are popular. In the Southwest, meat may take a dry rub of sugar and herbs to enhance flavor. In Texas, barbecue sauces are generally tomato or ketchup-based, and tend to be spicy with fresh chili peppers or chili powder; sometimes they are served on the side, rather than basted on the meat while grilling.

The Latest Pioneers

Over the last couple of generations, there has been an influx of yet another wave of settlers to the Southwest: artists and retirees who appreciate the weather and the laid-back lifestyle. It's a more cosmopolitan crowd, and the food has become more sophisticated. Like other regions across the country, home cooks no longer feel bound to traditional ways. People still enjoy old-fashioned Posole or Refried Beans, but also favor such items as Roasted Red Pepper Soup or Lime Marinated Turkey Cutlets with Fruit Salsa.

The Least You Need to Know

- Southwest-style cuisine has had an enormous impact on the United States; the region's foods, primarily a mix of Native American and Spanish, are eaten regularly all over the country.
- The early Spanish brought pork and cattle from Europe and chili peppers, avocados, and tomatoes from Mexico—all of which are an integral part of the cooking of the Southwest.
- Tortillas, a corn-based Native American flatbread, are staples in the Southwest.
- Beans have always been a mainstay in the diets of Native Americans of the Southwest and maintain their importance in the region's cooking.
- Chili peppers, which can range from mild to very hot, are used frequently in southwestern dishes.
- Barbecue, with an emphasis on beef, is a southwestern staple.

Chili Con Queso

This hors d'oeuvre is a big favorite everywhere; it's great for parties. Serve with cut-up fresh vegetables or corn chips.

Prep time: less than 15 minutes • Makes 3½ cups

2 TB. olive oil

1 small onion, chopped

2 jalapeño peppers, seeded and chopped

2 cloves garlic, chopped

4 plum tomatoes, peeled, seeded, and chopped

2 cups Monterey Jack cheese, shredded

2 cups cheddar cheese, shredded

½ cup light cream or half-and-half

Salt and pepper, to taste

Heat olive oil in a skillet over moderate heat. Add onion and jalapeño peppers and cook, stirring occasionally, for 3–4 minutes, or until softened. Add garlic and cook for half a minute. Add tomatoes and cook 4–5 minutes, or until softened.

Add cheeses and stir for 2–3 minutes, or until melted. Stir in light cream, blend in thoroughly, and cook for 2 minutes. Taste for seasoning and add salt and pepper to taste. Transfer mixture to a chafing dish to keep warm.

Everything Nachos

The all-American favorite snack, and not just for football games. Make plenty; these go fast!

Prep time: less than 15 minutes • Makes 4 servings

4 oz. corn chips (tostaditas)

2 cups Refried Beans (see recipe later later in this chapter)

1 small onion, chopped

1 large jalapeño pepper, seeded and chopped

1 cup cheddar cheese, shredded

1 cup Monterey Jack cheese, shredded

For garnish: dairy sour cream, chopped tomatoes or salsa, guacamole, mashed avocado

Preheat the oven to 450°.

Arrange corn chips in a baking dish. Place refried beans, onions, and jalapeño pepper in between and on top of chips. Sprinkle with cheeses. Bake for 6–8 minutes, or until cheese melts and is bubbly. Serve with garnishes to spoon on top of nachos.

Black Bean and Avocado Salad

Refreshing and colorful; a wonderful side dish for grilled entrées. It's also a lovely buffet dish.

Prep time: less than 30 minutes • Makes 6 servings

1 lb. dried black beans

1 small onion, chopped

1 stalk celery, sliced

1 bay leaf

1 tsp. dried oregano

Salt and pepper, to taste

$\frac{1}{4}$ cup olive oil

2 TB. soy sauce

$1\frac{1}{2}$ TB. red-wine vinegar

$\frac{1}{2}$ tsp. Dijon mustard

1 small red onion, chopped

1 large tomato, peeled, seeded, and chopped

1 small avocado, peeled, pitted, and cut into pieces

3 TB. fresh cilantro, chopped

Orange slices for garnish, optional

Cover beans with water, bring to a boil and let cook 2 minutes. Remove from heat and set aside, covered, for 1 hour.

Drain beans. Cover again with water and add onion, celery, bay leaf, oregano, salt, and pepper. Bring to a boil, lower heat, and simmer for 50–60 minutes or until tender. Drain and set aside.

Blend olive oil, soy sauce, red-wine vinegar, and Dijon mustard in a bowl. Set aside.

Mix together beans, red onion, tomato, avocado, and cilantro. Pour dressing over ingredients and toss gently. Taste for seasoning, and add salt and pepper to taste. Place mixture on a serving plate or bowl, garnished with orange slices, if desired.

Roasted Red Pepper Soup

This soup is a delicate orange-pink and makes a lovely first course at dinner. You can prepare it a couple of days ahead of serving.

Prep time: less than 30 minutes   •   Makes 6 servings

Special equipment: food processor or blender

5 or 6 red bell peppers	5 cups chicken or vegetable stock
2 TB. olive oil	1 cup cream
1 small onion, chopped	1½ tsp. salt, or to taste
1 carrot, chopped	Freshly ground black pepper
1 stalk celery, chopped	6 TB. dairy sour cream
1 TB. fresh parsley, minced	Chipotle powder
2 TB. all-purpose flour	

Preheat the broiler.

Place peppers under the broiler, about 4–6 inches away from heat. Broil for 2–3 minutes, or until skin has blistered. Turn peppers, and repeat this process until entire surface is blistered and lightly charred. Remove peppers and place in paper bags. Close the bags. Let peppers rest at least 10 minutes.

Remove peppers and pull out stems, cut open peppers, and remove seeds. Peel off skin. Cut peppers into smaller pieces.

Heat olive oil in a large saucepan and add onion, carrot, celery, and parsley. Cook over moderate heat, stirring occasionally for 3–4 minutes, or until vegetables have softened. Add flour and blend in. Cook 1 minute. Stir in red pepper and stock. Bring mixture to a boil, and then lower heat and simmer soup for 25 minutes. Purée soup in a food processor or blender.

Clean the saucepan. Return soup to the pan. Stir in cream. Cook over moderate heat for 2–3 minutes or until soup is hot. Taste for seasoning, and add salt and pepper to taste. Ladle soup into serving bowls. Top each portion with tablespoon of sour cream. Dust surface of soup lightly with chipotle powder, if desired.

Hot Tip

Chipotle powder is available in many markets in the dried-spice section.

Beef Ribs with Mango Barbecue Sauce

Mango adds an interesting flavor to these tangy ribs. Substitute peaches if you wish.

Prep time: less than 15 minutes • Makes 6 servings

Special equipment: food processor

1 large ripe mango	¼ tsp. cayenne pepper
1 TB. vegetable oil	¼ cup orange juice
1 small onion, chopped	¼ cup molasses
1 large clove garlic, minced	1 TB. soy sauce
12-oz. bottle chili sauce	6 lbs. beef ribs

Peel mango and cut flesh into small pieces. Put pieces in a food processor workbowl. Purée flesh. Heat vegetable oil in a saucepan over moderate heat. Add onion and cook for 1 minute. Add garlic and cook briefly. Add mango purée, chili sauce, cayenne pepper, orange juice, molasses, and soy sauce. Stir thoroughly to blend ingredients. Turn heat to low and simmer for 15 minutes.

Preheat an outdoor grill or oven broiler and set the rack about 6" from heat. Brush some of sauce on ribs and grill or broil, turning every 5 minutes and brushing with more sauce, for 25–30 minutes.

Chili Con Carne

There may be as many recipes for Chili Con Carne as there are cooks! This one is moderately hot.

Prep time: less than 30 minutes • Makes 8 servings

3 TB. olive oil

2 large onions, chopped

3 large cloves garlic, chopped

2$^1\!/_2$ lbs. beef, such as chuck or round, either ground or chopped into bite-size pieces

2 (28-oz.) cans Italian-style whole tomatoes, drained and coarsely chopped

1 (12-oz.) can tomato paste

Salt, to taste

$^1\!/_4$ cup pure chili powder, preferably hot

3 bay leaves

1$^1\!/_2$ TB. oregano

1 TB. ground cumin

1$^1\!/_2$ tsp. crushed red pepper flakes

$^1\!/_2$ tsp. ground black pepper

3 cups beef broth

3 cups cooked kidney beans (if using canned beans, drain before using)

Heat olive oil in a large, deep skillet. Add onion and cook over moderate heat for 3–4 minutes, or until softened. Add garlic and cook for 1 minute. Add beef and cook over moderately high heat until meat has browned.

Drain all but 2–3 tablespoons of the pan fat. Add all remaining ingredients except beans. Stir, bring to a boil, and lower the heat. Simmer about 40 minutes. Add beans. Simmer another 15–20 minutes, or until chili is thick and most liquid has been absorbed.

Southwest-Style Turkey Breast

This dish is gently spicy, and the hearty flavorings bring out the best in turkey's mild meat. You can make this recipe with a whole turkey breast, or, if you can find one, a breast that has been cut in half. You can also use a small whole turkey.

Prep time: less than 15 minutes • Makes 4 to 8 servings

Turkey breast, 3–6 lbs.

3 TB. olive oil

2 cloves garlic, mashed

1 tsp. chili powder

1 tsp. oregano

$^1/_2$ tsp. ground cumin

$^1/_4$ tsp. cayenne pepper

Salt

2 TB. cornmeal, optional

Preheat the oven to 400°.

Place turkey, skin-side up, in a roasting pan. Combine all remaining ingredients except cornmeal, and brush turkey skin with mixture.

Roast, basting occasionally, or until a meat thermometer stuck into thickest part of breast registers 170°. Start checking the temperature after 1$^1/_2$ hours. If desired, sprinkle cornmeal on top of breast for the last 15 minutes of cooking.

Hot Tip _____

The USDA recommends cooking turkey to 180° as measured in the thickest part of the thigh or 170° in the breast, but the meat is juicier when cooked to 165° (160° breast), and many cooks follow this practice. You must decide whether or not to use the more conservative USDA guidelines; I have suggested alternative temperatures. Use a meat thermometer or instant read thermometer to check temperature. Be sure to follow safe food-handling basics: Wash hands and defrost, wrap, and refrigerate the meat properly to keep pathogens away. Refrigerate cooked turkey no more than an hour after you serve it.

Fajitas

People everywhere love fajitas! Steak fajitas are the original, but be sure to see the substitution suggestions at the end of the recipe.

Prep time: less than 30 minutes   •   Makes 4 servings

16 to 20 oz. skirt steak

Juice of 2 limes

1 TB. olive oil

1 large clove garlic, finely chopped

1 tsp. ground cumin

$1/2$ tsp. red pepper flakes

Salt and pepper, to taste

8 flour tortillas

$1^{1}/_{2}$ TB. olive oil

1 small purple onion, peeled and sliced

1 medium red bell pepper, cut into $1/2$" strips

1 medium yellow bell pepper, cut into $1/2$" strips

Tomato Salsa (see recipe in Appendix C)

Guacamole, optional (see Mini-Recipe earlier in this chapter)

Place the meat in a ceramic, stainless-steel, or other nonreactive dish. In a bowl, combine lime juice, 1 tablespoon olive oil, garlic, cumin, red pepper flakes, and salt and pepper to taste, mix well, and pour over meat. Let rest, covered, in the refrigerator for 1 hour.

Preheat an outdoor grill or oven broiler.

Remove meat from marinade, and grill or broil meat for 3–4 minutes per side, depending on degree of doneness desired. Remove to a carving board and let rest for 5 minutes before carving into strips.

Preheat the oven to 250°.

Wrap tortillas in aluminum foil and place in the oven to warm. Heat olive oil in a skillet over medium-high heat. Add onion and peppers, sprinkle with salt and pepper, and cook, turning occasionally, until tender, about 4–5 minutes.

Place salsa and guacamole, if used, in bowls. Place meat and vegetables on separate plates. Serve tortillas, and let each person take meat and vegetables to wrap inside tortillas. Include salsa and guacamole as desired.

Hot Tip

Try these substitutions for the steak:

◆ Use 1 lb. skinless, boneless chicken breast.

◆ Use 1 lb. shrimp, scallops, or swordfish.

Huevos Rancheros

This is a good choice for Sunday brunch, but you can have this dish for dinner, too. Serve it with Refried Beans (see recipe later in this chapter) and Tomato Salsa (see Appendix C).

Prep time: less than 30 minutes • Makes 4 servings

4 TB. olive oil	$^1/_2$ tsp. salt, or to taste
1 large onion, chopped	Freshly ground black pepper, to taste
2 jalapeño peppers, seeded and chopped	8 tortillas
2 large cloves garlic, chopped	$1^1/_2$ TB. butter
3 large tomatoes, peeled and chopped	8 eggs, well beaten
2 tsp. fresh cilantro, chopped	1 cup Monterey Jack cheese, shredded

Preheat the oven to 140° (warm).

Heat 2 tablespoons olive oil in a skillet over moderate heat. Add onion and peppers, and cook for 2 minutes, stirring occasionally. Add garlic, and cook for 1 minute. Add tomatoes, cilantro, salt, and pepper, and turn heat to low. Simmer, stirring occasionally, for 15 minutes, or until soft. Remove pan from heat but keep warm in the oven.

Heat remaining olive oil in another skillet. Dip tortillas one at a time into the pan for about 10 seconds, or until softened. Place tortillas in a baking dish, overlapping each other, to cover the bottom and lower sides of the dish. Keep warm in the oven.

Put butter into the skillet used for tortillas, and set over moderate heat. When butter has melted and looks foamy, pour in eggs. Cook eggs, mixing in the pan until cooked to desired scrambled-egg consistency. Spoon eggs over tortillas. Spoon sauce over eggs. Sprinkle with cheese. Preheat the broiler. Place dish under the broiler for a minute or so to melt cheese.

Lime-Marinated Turkey Cutlets with Fruit Salsa

A beautiful and refreshing entrée, perfect for family or company.

Prep time: less than 30 minutes • Makes 4 servings

2 lbs. turkey cutlets	¹/₄ cup fresh lime juice
Salt and cayenne pepper, to taste	2 TB. olive oil

Place cutlets in a glass, ceramic, or stainless-steel dish. Sprinkle meat with salt and cayenne pepper, lime juice, and 2 tablespoons olive oil. Marinate in the refrigerator for 45–60 minutes.

Preheat the grill or oven broiler. Grill cutlets for 2 minutes per side or until cooked through. Serve with Fruit Salsa.

For the Fruit Salsa:

1 TB. olive oil	2 TB. fresh cilantro, chopped
2 mangoes, peeled and diced	¹/₂ tsp. grated lime peel
1 avocado, peeled, pitted, and diced	1 clove garlic, minced
1 jalapeño pepper, seeded and chopped	3 TB. lime juice
¹/₃ cup purple onion, chopped	

In a bowl, combine the 1 tablespoon olive oil, mangoes, avocado, jalapeño pepper, purple onion, cilantro, lime peel, garlic, and lime juice. Let rest for 30 minutes.

Posole

This dish is a special Christmas dinner in parts of the Southwest. If you like your food extra spicy, add 1–2 more dried chili peppers.

Prep time: less than 30 minutes • Makes 6 servings

2 TB. olive oil

2 lb. boneless pork butt, cut into 1½" chunks

2 medium onions, coarsely chopped

4 large cloves garlic, chopped

4 dried red chili peppers, seeded

2 tsp. dried oregano

1 tsp. ground cumin

3 cups beef or chicken stock

2 (15-oz.) cans hominy, rinsed and drained

1 large tomato, cut into small chunks

Salt and pepper, to taste

Sliced radishes and shredded scallions as garnish, optional

Heat olive oil in a large saucepan or Dutch oven over medium heat. Add meat a few pieces at a time, and cook until lightly browned. Remove meat. Add onions and cook for 2–3 minutes. Add garlic, chili peppers, oregano, and cumin. Stir ingredients.

Return meat to the pan. Pour in stock. Bring to a boil over high heat, and then reduce the heat, cover the pan, and simmer for 1 hour.

Add hominy, tomato, and some salt and pepper. Cover the pan and simmer for another 30 minutes. Skim fat. Discard chili peppers. Serve with sliced radishes and shredded scallions if desired.

Vegetables with Piñons

A wonderful side dish for any grilled meat, poultry, or fish. If you want to spice it up, use a hot chili pepper instead of the Anaheim chili pepper.

Prep time: less than 15 minutes   •   Makes 6 servings

6 TB. piñons

1 lb. fresh green beans

$^1/_4$ cup olive oil

1 large onion, sliced

1 Anaheim chili pepper, seeded and cut into strips

2 cloves garlic, chopped

1 yellow squash, cut into matchstick strips

Salt and pepper, to taste

$^1/_3$ cup Monterey Jack cheese, grated

Cook piñons lightly in an unoiled skillet over moderate heat for 4–5 minutes, or until lightly brown. Set aside.

Cook green beans in lightly salted water for 5–6 minutes, or until barely tender. Drain under cold water and set aside.

Heat olive oil in the skillet. Add onion and Anaheim chili pepper. Cook for 2 minutes, or until softened. Add garlic and green beans, and cook briefly to coat ingredients with cooking oil. Add squash, sprinkle with salt and pepper, and cook for 2 minutes, or until ingredients are hot. Add piñons and toss ingredients. Sprinkle with cheese.

Refried Beans

A classic! This dish is an all-purpose one. Eat the beans as is, or stuff them into a sandwich. Or serve them with eggs or nachos. And on and on … the uses are almost endless.

Prep time: less than 15 minutes • Makes 8 servings

1 lb. dried pinto beans	8 oz. salt pork, chopped
6 cups water	1 tsp. salt, or to taste
1 large onion, chopped	¼ cup lard
1 large clove garlic, chopped	2 TB. tomato paste
½ cup canned tomato purée	

In a saucepan, cover beans with the water and bring to a boil over high heat. Cook for 2 minutes. Remove the pan from heat and cover. Let rest for 1 hour.

Preheat the oven to 300°.

Place beans and cooking water in a deep casserole. Add onion, garlic, tomato purée, salt pork, and salt. Cover casserole and bake for about 4 hours, or until beans are tender and all but about ½ cup of liquid is absorbed. Check beans occasionally for moisture. If beans dry out before tender, add some more water to casserole. Remove beans from the oven and drain, but reserve liquid.

Hot Tip

If you prefer, you can use vegetable oil or olive oil instead of the lard, but the beans won't taste as rich.

Heat lard in a large skillet set over moderately high heat. When lard has melted, add beans, and press down on them with a wooden spoon or spatula to crush slightly. Add tomato paste and stir beans to blend tomato paste in thoroughly. Add reserved liquid and continue to fry beans for about 10 minutes, or until hot and creamy.

Cheese-Filled Cornbread with Jalapeño Pepper Jam

Naturally, you can serve this cornbread without the jam. Or make it without the cheese. The jam is also a handy hors d'oeuvre item served with cream cheese and crackers. Be sure to use a stainless-steel, enamel, or other nonreactive pan; the vinegar reacts with other metals (such as aluminum), giving the jelly an off-taste.

Prep time: less than 15 minutes   •   Makes 12 servings

Special equipment: cake rack

4 TB. unsalted butter	$1/2$ tsp. baking soda
3 TB. honey	$3/4$ tsp. salt
1 cup cornmeal	2 eggs
1 cup all-purpose flour	$1 1/2$ cups buttermilk
1 TB. baking powder	$1/2$ cup Monterey Jack cheese, shredded

Preheat the oven to 425°.

Lightly grease an 8" or 9" square baking pan. Melt unsalted butter and honey together and set aside to cool.

In a large bowl, sift cornmeal, flour, baking powder, baking soda, and salt. In another bowl, beat eggs and buttermilk together. Stir in cooled butter mixture. Add liquid ingredients to dry ones and stir to combine. Fold in cheese.

Pour batter into the prepared pan. Bake for 25 minutes, or until bread is golden brown. Remove from the oven and let cool in the pan for 10 minutes. Then invert onto a cake rack to cool completely. Serve plain or with Jalapeño Pepper Jam (recipe follows).

For the Jalapeño Pepper Jam (makes just under 2 quarts):

4 mixed green, red, and yellow bell peppers	$1 1/2$ cups cider vinegar
4 large jalapeño peppers, seeded and chopped	6 oz. pectin
$6 1/2$ cups sugar	

Prepare jelly jars in accordance with manufacturer's suggestions for washing them.

Combine peppers, sugar, and cider vinegar in a large stainless-steel or enamel pan. Bring mixture to a full rolling boil, stirring constantly. Cook for 5 minutes, stirring occasionally, adjusting heat as necessary to avoid ingredients boiling over. Raise heat. Add pectin. Boil 1 minute, stirring constantly.

continues

continued

Remove the pan from heat. Skim surface of any foam. Scoop jam into prepared jelly jars. Process in a water bath according to manufacturer's suggestions. If you don't want to bother with processing jam in a water bath, spoon jam into jars, let cool, and keep refrigerated up to 3 months unopened, 2 weeks opened.

Hot Tip

Pectin is a natural substance that forms a jelly when combined with sugar and acid. Commercially packaged pectin, made from apple or citrus pectin, is available in supermarkets.

Navajo Fry Bread

These hot, crunchy breads are wonderful with meats and cheeses, but also terrific served sweet with coffee—just sprinkle them with confectioner's sugar.

Prep time: less than 30 minutes • Makes 8 breads

2 cups all-purpose flour	2 TB. lard or vegetable shortening, cut into chunks
6 TB. powdered dry milk	$^3/_4$ cup cold water
2 tsp. baking powder	Lard or vegetable oil for deep-fat frying
$^1/_2$ tsp. salt	Confectioner's sugar, optional

Combine flour, dry milk, baking powder, and salt in a bowl. Add lard and cut into dry ingredients with 2 knives, with your fingers, or with a pastry blender, until mixture resembles coarse meal. Add cold water all at once and quickly work mixture into soft ball.

Place dough on a lightly floured surface and knead a few times. Shape dough into ball, cover ball with plastic wrap, and let rest for at least 30 minutes. Cut dough into 8 equal portions. Roll each into a circle about 8" in diameter. Prick dough in 2 or 3 places with the tines of a fork.

Heat enough lard or vegetable oil in a 10" skillet to create a depth of $1^1/_2$". Heat to 360°, hot enough to sizzle a bread crumb quickly. Fry breads one at a time, for about 2 minutes per side, or until puffed and golden brown. Turn breads with kitchen tongs. Drain on paper towels. Dust with sifted confectioner's sugar if desired.

Cinnamon-Scented Hot Chocolate

The cinnamon brings warmth to this American favorite.

Prep time: less than 15 minutes • Makes 2 servings

2 TB. unsweetened cocoa powder	3 TB. boiling water
2 TB. sugar	2 cups milk
1/2 tsp. ground cinnamon	3/4 tsp. vanilla extract
Dash of salt	

Mix unsweetened cocoa powder, sugar, cinnamon, and salt in a saucepan. Add boiling water and stir to make a smooth paste. Stir in milk. Bring to a simmer over moderate heat, stirring occasionally.

Remove the pan from heat. Add vanilla extract. Stir, or place liquid in a blender and process until frothy.

Chocolate Chimichangas

It's amazing how far you can take a burrito! These sweets ooze with melted chocolate and are a great ending to any kind of meal.

Prep time: less than 15 minutes • Makes 6 servings

6 burritos (flour tortillas), 6" in diameter	Vegetable oil for frying
6 oz. semisweet chocolate, chopped	Confectioner's sugar
Cinnamon	Ice cream, optional

Heat burritos in an unoiled pan for 20–30 seconds per side to soften. Wrap in aluminum foil to keep warm.

Place equal amounts of chocolate in center of each burrito. Sprinkle lightly with cinnamon. Fold burrito, envelope style (bottom part over the chocolate, 2 sides next, then last flap down). Set aside, seam side down.

Heat 1/2" vegetable oil in skillet until hot (enough to sizzle a bread crumb quickly). Immerse burritos, seam side down, a few at a time, in skillet and cook for about 1 minute, turning occasionally, until crust is browned and crispy. Drain on paper towels. Sprinkle with confectioner's sugar. Serve plain or with ice cream.

Chapter 7

The Great West

In This Chapter

- ◆ Cowboy grub lives!
- ◆ Big-time beef and lamb
- ◆ A profusion of potatoes
- ◆ The evolution of California cuisine
- ◆ The Hawaiian paradise

The cuisine of the West is an eclectic mix. It brings together rustic chow from cowboy days and the plain, humble fare of hard-working pioneers. It offers variety from the traditions of the many ethnic groups that settled in this vast region, including the Spanish missionaries; the Basques, who came as sheep-herders; the Chinese and Mexicans, who built the nation's railroads; and the Asian-Polynesian-Caucasian peoples, who settled in Hawaii.

Western cuisine also attests to the bounty of meat, fish, and fresh fruits and vegetables that flourish here. California's fabulous weather and rich soil have made it a paradise of produce, while mountainous areas have been ideal for raising cattle and sheep, and for growing barley, hops, and lentils. Thanks to volcanic ash that enriches the soil in Idaho, Americans have more than enough potatoes for their beloved French fries.

Many of our country's mainstay dishes—such as beef stew, pot roast, potato salad, and Shepherd's Pie—are western classics. The West is a place where people like food fresh, simple, and unpretentious: a steak or pan-fried trout and baked potato, a big salad, a bowl of hearty lentil or pea soup, a slice of plain angel-food cake. Yet, this is also where a culinary revolution took root and made goat cheese a pantry staple and innovation a catchword for modern cooking.

American History 101

When it comes to the American West, fact and fiction blend. Movies give us images of grazing buffalo, and cowboys and natives exchanging gunfire and arrows. We've seen bad guys robbing railroad trains and sheriffs in shoot-'em-ups in saloons. No one knows how much is real, but one thing is certain: It accounts for only a moment in our history. The story of the buffalo is brief and sad. And the big cattle drives from Texas to the railroads were also short-lived, only about 20 years or so after the Civil War.

Give Me a Home Where the Buffalo Roam ...

After the Louisiana Purchase in 1803, President Jefferson sent Lewis and Clark to explore the new land. With the help of a female Native American guide, Sacajawea, they crossed the Continental Divide, worked their way through the Rockies, and spent three years eating roots, berries, wild game, and buffalo. At that time, a bounty of beaver inhabited the forests, and countless herds of buffalo roamed the plains.

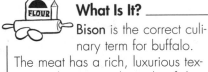

What Is It?

Bison is the correct culinary term for buffalo. The meat has a rich, luxurious texture and tastes similar to beef, but contains less fat and cholesterol.

Westward migration, the building of railroads, and Lewis and Clark's report, which attracted large numbers of fur trappers, all played a part in the near-extinction of the buffalo. When only a few hundred buffalo were left at the end of the nineteenth century, the government passed protective laws. Buffalo are now being farm-raised in the West. The meat is available from *bison* ranches and at specialty butcher shops.

Come and Get It

At one time, cattle drives were needed to get meat to market. Herds moved north from Texas to Chicago and points east. Eventually, railroad stops in Abilene, Kansas, and other small "cowtowns," like Dodge City, made the trip shorter. The cattle could be sent to slaughterhouses by train. Still, trail work was long and difficult, and three big meals a day were required. The "cookie" prepared the food for the trailboss and cowboys. All the supplies were carried in a chuck wagon, and everything from meats, beans, biscuits, and pie was cooked in a big cast-iron Dutch oven.

One of the West's unique culinary features is the no-nonsense cowboy grub of the chuck wagon era: beef stew, braised beef short ribs, and pot roast. Chicken Fried Steak, with its crispy brown coating and creamy gravy, is still an enduring menu item today, even with prime, juicy steaks available.

Dishes such as stew and pot roast are all made with tough cuts of meat such as bottom round, chuck, brisket, short-ribs, and cross-rib. These require long, slow cooking and moisture to make them tender. Pounding is another way to soften meat fibers to tenderness. In the old days, cooks pounded tough meat for Chicken Fried Steak. Today you can avoid that hassle; prepare the dish with thin, tender sirloins, round steak, or cube steak.

Kitchen Clue

Dutch ovens or other deep, large, dome-topped skillets are the best utensils for stew and braised foods. The pan must have room enough for adequate liquid and for other ingredients such as tomatoes and potatoes. The dome shape helps keep the meat succulent; steam droplets from the simmering stew collect under the cover and fall back into the pan.

There's Gold in Them Thar Hills

The discovery of gold at Sutter's Mill in California in 1848 lured many prospectors out west. They came from other states and from Europe in hopes of getting rich quick. Because so many people came from so many places, a mixed cuisine developed in the region.

Mining towns cropped up wherever there was even a whisper of gold, silver, or copper. Most towns were rough, and people subsisted on crude staples. Prices for food and whiskey were sky high. In Hangtown, California, a man who struck paydirt came into the town's hotel with a handful of gold nuggets and demanded the most expensive meal on the menu. The cook whipped up a dish of eggs and oysters. But even that wasn't enough for the guy, who asked for a side order of bacon. Hangtown Fry, a symbol of wealth, is still a popular dish in California, especially near Placerville, the town's more recent name.

It Didn't Pan Out

Most pioneers made their living on the land, not from panning for gold. They had come in Conestoga wagons, braving arid deserts, sprawling plains, and hostile Native

Americans. More came after 1862, enticed by land promised under the Homestead Act. They brought seeds and plantings. They dug cellars to store potatoes and root vegetables. For years they depended on wild game to supplement their rustic corn-meal and salt-pork diet. Today, the pioneering spirit still prevails in the west where venison and game birds such as pheasant and quail may be part of a home cook's repertoire.

Living High

By the second half of the nineteenth century, everyday fare was as varied in western kitchens as it was elsewhere. But pioneers who lived in high-altitude areas in the mountain states found that recipes for cakes failed, until they learned to adapt them for high-altitude cooking. For a good explanation of high-altitude baking and some suggestions, check out *CookWise* by Shirley O. Corriher (see Appendix B).

From the Mountains to the Prairies ...

When the Gold Rush was over, some settlers headed into the mountains. These areas in Idaho, Montana, Wyoming, Colorado, and Nevada were inhospitable to agriculture, at least at first, before irrigation. But the land provided prime grazing for cattle and sheep. Ruthless range wars were fought between cattle ranchers and sheepherders. In the end there was room for both, and today these states provide much of the beef and lamb for the rest of the country.

A Contribution from the Basques

When raising sheep became big business, Basque sheepherders, whose home is the mountainous region in the Pyrenees between France and Spain, came to work in the West. They brought new foods and a unique cooking style that became part of western cuisine. Basque foods are similar to Spanish in the use of bold seasonings such as garlic and peppers, spicy *chorizo* sausages, tomatoes, cured ham, and fresh and salted cod. Codfish balls and Paella are favorites. Naturally, there is a good deal of lamb, either grilled over an open fire or made into stew.

> **What Is It?**
> **Chorizo** is a firm, spicy, paprika-laden sausage usually made of pork. It is available at Spanish-American groceries and in many supermarkets.

The best cuts of lamb for grilling are the tender rib or loin chops. For kebabs, use boneless chunks from the leg. Boneless breast and shoulder portions and bone-in shanks are fine choices for slow-braised dishes such as stew.

One Nation

The Basques were not the only group to emigrate to the West. People from Slavic and Scandinavian countries farmed wheat. The Welsh and Italians came as miners. Mexicans and Chinese were railroad workers. American descendants of German and Scottish settlers made their way west, too. Many found farming to be more suitable than mining or day work on railroad crews. These pioneers began the west's wheat, barley, hops, sugar beet, bean, and lentil industries. Italians fared well as cooks, boarding house owners, and restaurateurs. All these groups influenced western cuisine, and their impact endures today in dishes such as *piroshki*, which are Slavic-style meat pies, and Scandinavian cold fruit soups. Some say that Denver's famous Western Omelet evolved from Chinese Egg Fu Yung.

Kitchen Clue

You'll find several varieties of lentils in the market. Common green or brown lentils are earthy-tasting and wonderful for soups and salads. Red lentils are soft, and they cook quickly. Use these for side dishes with roasts and grilled foods. Green French lentils are the most delicately flavored, ideal for soup, salad, or side dishes. Black lentils are less common and are among the most flavorful all-purpose variety. Lentils don't require soaking, and they cook more quickly than most other dried legumes. Like beans, they contain small amounts of lectins, which can cause stomach cramps. To destroy these toxins, boil the lentils for one minute before using them.

Hot Potatoes

Pioneers who made their homes in mountainous regions knew that the terrain was not promising farmland—it took years and a system of irrigation to make the land flourish with agricultural crops. But they realized immediately that the volcanic soil and cool evenings were terrific for growing potatoes.

When potatoes proved a successful crop, growers sold the spuds to pioneers heading west in wagon trains, and to hungry miners panning for gold. By 1872, horticulturist Luther Burbank had perfected a long, oval-shaped potato called a Russet. It has deep brown,

Fein on Food

The first documented potato planter was a Presbyterian missionary named Henry Spalding. When he observed the decreasing supply of buffalo, he began cultivating the tubers in 1836, in an effort to teach the local Native Americans how to grow food rather than to hunt for it.

resilient skin, and a dry, white flesh. We know it as the "Idaho" potato. The Russet was such a taste sensation that by the 1890s, baked Idahoes were a special feature in railroad dining cars. The managements of the Northern Pacific and Great Northern railroads both claimed to serve the biggest baked potatoes.

Russet potatoes have a low moisture content, which makes them perfect for frying. In fact, over half the crop is processed for packaged and commercial use as French fries. The dry flesh also means that the potatoes are splendidly fluffy when baked; it is the perfect foil for rich dairy items such as butter, sour cream, yogurt, melted cheese, and toppings like crumbled bacon.

Mini-Recipe

Baked Potatoes (4 servings)   Preheat the oven to 400°. Scrub 4 Idaho Russet potatoes. Do not rub with vegetable oil and do not wrap the potatoes in aluminum foil. Pierce the potato with the tip of a sharp knife in two places. Bake for about 45 minutes or until tender.

Kitchen Clue

Store potatoes in a cool, dark place. It's best not to refrigerate them because the natural starches may turn to sugar, causing the potatoes to taste too sweet.

Idaho Russets are still the favorites for baked potatoes, French fries, and potato pancakes. But other varieties are available in American markets:

- **Round Whites (all-purpose)**   Low starch and moist, for mashed potatoes
- **Round Reds (such as Bliss)**   Crisp and low starch, excellent when steamed or made into salad
- **New Potatoes (not really a variety)**   Thin-skinned, young potatoes, for salad
- **Yukon Gold**   Creamy, yellow flesh, for mashed potatoes
- **Long Whites (Californias)**   Thin-skinned and light, for mashed, boiled, or baked potatoes
- **Fingerlings (such as Purple Peruvian and Banana)**   Thin-skinned and shaped like stubby fingers, for salad and stews, or steamed, topped with butter

A Bounty of Fish

The potato was not the only treasure of the mountains. The clear, fresh water of the region's lakes and streams has always supported a variety of fish. Trout is of special importance. Native Americans relied on it for survival. Today, sport fishermen catch the fish, though much of it is farm raised. There are several varieties, but most markets carry rainbow trout, which is rich, sweet, and delicate. Steelhead (salmon trout), brook, and cutthroat trouts may also be available.

The Land No One Else Wanted

During pioneer times, when others searched for gold or land, the Mormons came west fleeing religious persecution. They migrated to several states before settling in Utah's Salt Lake Valley, a region so barren and hostile to farming that no one else wanted it. They spent years clearing fields, irrigating land, and planting crops. Food shortages taught them frugality. Today, leftovers are still used or put up as preserves. The Mormons derive from several ethnic groups, so no particular food style prevails; however, the fare tends to be wholesome and old-fashioned, with a hint of German and Scandinavian in the use of pea soups and beef stews, cabbage dishes, and raisin pies. The religion forbids the use of alcohol, coffee, tea, or tobacco, but Mormons are known to enjoy sweets, dried fruit candies, and caramel corn.

California, Here I Come!

Soon after California became U.S. territory in 1848, only a few Americans settled there. A year later, after gold was discovered, swarms of people came from every-where. California has never been the same. The land of surfers and movie stars, trendy cuisine, and fabulous wines started out as a quiet place.

The first Europeans to settle in California were Franciscan friars in the late eighteenth century. They built missions from San Diego to Sonoma, in hopes of converting the Native Americans. The friars planted the first of California's invaluable crops: oranges, lemons, grapes, apricots, olives, figs, and nuts. They brought foods that the Spanish had cultivated in Mexico: chocolate, chili peppers, cattle, and sheep. From the earliest days, Spanish-Mexican style cookery has been an integral part of California cuisine.

Kitchen Clue

There are several types of orange: thick-skinned navels are easy to peel and best for eating out of hand; thin-skinned varieties such as Valencia and Temple are best for juicing. Blood oranges, with their russet-colored skin and ruby flesh, are a low-acid type, superb for cooking, baking into tarts, and juicing.

Great Grapes

California's wine industry began in 1769 when the friars planted grapes to make wine for sacramental purposes. Local landowners had other uses in mind and soon planted vineyards. European and American settlers brought new grape varieties that flour-ished in California's obliging soil. The first commercial winery was established in 1833. European oenophiles who first sneered at California wines have changed their tune. Today, even some famous French vintners have wine-making operations in California. The industry took a big hit during Prohibition, but made its way back after the 1970s, thanks to a resurgence in interest in American food and wine.

The Best Weather on Earth

Some say California has the best weather on earth. It certainly has helped make the state a paradise of produce. When the mining era ended, settlers began irrigating the valleys. Even desert areas proved fruitful, so much so that the canning industry got an early start in California, making fruits and vegetables available throughout the country. With quick, easy transport, fresh California produce now feeds the nation with many of the fruits and vegetables we use every day, including the following:

- Citrus fruits such as lemons, grapefruit, oranges, limes, kumquats, and tangerines
- Apricots, fresh and dried
- Figs, dates, raisins, and prunes
- Avocados
- Fruit such as melons, peaches, kiwi, and strawberries
- Lettuce
- Vegetables such as tomatoes, asparagus, carrots, cabbage, artichokes, fava beans, eggplant, and broccoli
- Nuts, including almonds, walnuts, and pistachios
- Olives

Mini-Recipe

Broiled Brandied Grapefruit (6 servings)   Cut 3 large grapefruits into halves and cut the flesh into sections within the skin. Place in a broiling dish. Combine 3 tablespoons butter, 3 tablespoons sugar, and $1/3$ cup Grand Marnier in a small saucepan. Cook until butter melts and sugar dissolves. Pour over the grapefruit. Let rest 1 hour. Just before serving, broil for a few minutes until the surface is bubbly.

Salad Days

Because California grows several types of lettuce, salad is important. Three of the state's best-known salads are these (for more on salads, see Chapter 10):

◆ Cobb   Chopped lettuce, avocado, tomato, crispy bacon, chicken breast, and hard-cooked eggs with blue-cheese dressing

◆ Caesar   Romaine lettuce, lemon juice vinaigrette, Parmesan cheese, anchovies, coddled egg, and croutons

◆ Green Goddess   Romaine lettuce and tarragon-mayonnaise dressing

Balboa Knew a Good Thing

The conquistador Vasco Balboa knew a good thing when he saw it: He discovered the Pacific in 1513 and claimed the entirety of it for Spain. And he had never tasted a Dungeness Crab, one of ocean's prize crustaceans. California waters offer a variety of fish and shellfish including tuna, sole, and abalone. Seafood dishes abound, but a favorite is Cioppino, a hearty chowder said to have been invented by an Italian settler in San Francisco.

Did You Know ...
Cioppino usually calls for Dungeness crab, but, like all chowders, you can substitute seafood such as soft-shell crab, mussels, shrimp, clams, oysters, or any firm-fleshed fish.

The New California Cuisine

California cuisine is the result of abundance: a bounty of local fresh fruits and vegetables and a steady influx of immigrants from everywhere. Foods and cooking styles have been ever changing, and innovative chefs are always willing to experiment with new ingredients. It was something the rest of the country didn't appreciate until the early 1970s, when Alice Waters opened her restaurant, Chez Panisse. Her efforts there helped create a new nationwide culinary movement that focused on fresh local ingredients, fresh herbs, and local wine.

The new California cuisine, inspired by France's Nouvelle Cuisine, endeavored to simplify the French classics and to focus on light, fresh, uncomplicated foods. It championed grilled and steamed foods rather than the heavier fried and sautéed fare that had been standard in America. It urged undercooking vegetables to discover their natural, fresh flavors. It was refreshing, without heavy-handed

Fein on Food
Goat cheese, or chevre, was virtually unknown in the United States before the 1970s, when inventive California chefs began using it in new, California-style interpretations of the French classics. Goat cheese is now integral to California cuisine.

sauces. It has changed the way our country eats. California cuisine became the New American Cuisine. (For more on Alice Waters and Chez Panisse, see Chapter 10.)

Aloha!

When U.S. journalist Horace Greeley said "Go west, young man," he probably didn't envision Hawaii. But this state, 2,000 miles west of the mainland, has much to offer: good weather, gorgeous scenery, fabulous beaches … and wonderful food.

Hawaii was uninhabited before Polynesians from Samoa and the East Indies arrived in the sixth century. These settlers were of mixed ethnicity so from the very beginning, Hawaiian cuisine embraced several cultures. As centuries went by, other groups came to live on the islands. Hawaiian cuisine became famous as chefs on the mainland "invented" fusion cuisine (mixing ingredients, seasonings, and cooking styles of two or more cultures).

The Polynesians brought taro, banana, coconuts, breadfruit, yams, and sugar cane to the islands. They grew no grains. Poi, a thick, pudding-like mixture made from taro root, became the most important starch. Poi still figures importantly in cooking today, often as a side dish at *luaus*.

What Is It?

A **luau** is Hawaii's answer to the New England Clambake and Texas Big Barbecue. It is a big event, with the main feature a pit-roasted pig. The succulent pork is served with salted salmon and poi, among other dishes. Dessert might include pineapple chunks soaked in rum, or bananas with rum and coconut.

In the eighteenth century, Spanish and Portuguese trading ships stopped at Hawaii, bringing new foods that soon became staples: pineapple, ginger, guava, and papaya. New England missionaries brought a love of beef and recipes for salted fish, chowders, and stews. Filipinos came with sausages, East Indians with curries. Japanese settlers added soy sauce, sashimi, and noodles. Hawaii's famous Pu-Pu platters (a selection of hors d'oeuvres, usually presented on a hibachi grill) reflect the ethnic mix, featuring specialties such as salted salmon, spareribs, chicken teriyaki, egg rolls, rumaki, and wontons.

Hawaii's nutrient-rich soil and good weather have been ideal for pineapples. Pineapples are available from many countries, but Hawaiian varieties are the sweetest, juiciest, and most fragrant. James Dole developed the first successful commercial pineapple business by the turn of the twentieth century. In those days, pineapple, which is fragile, would spoil by the time it reached markets on the mainland. Today, quick airline transport means we can find fresh Hawaiian pineapples locally, but most of the crop is used for juice and canned fruit.

Many other crops have flourished in Hawaii's volcanic soil and are important to the state's economy and cuisine, including the following:

- Sugar cane, first planted in 1835. Hawaii furnishes about 25 percent of our country's supply.
- Coffee, first grown in the nineteenth century. Hawaii is the only U.S. state with the right climate for growing the beans.
- Macadamia nuts, first brought from Australia. Hawaii is the world's largest exporter of these nuts.

The Least You Need to Know

- Western cuisine is an eclectic mix of the ethnic fare of the region's diverse settlers, including Native Americans, Europeans, and Asians.
- Famous western dishes include the old-fashioned cowboy grub popular during the days of the cattle drives.
- Much of our nation's supply of beef and lamb comes from the West.
- Potatoes thrive in the rich soils of Idaho, California, and other western states.
- California cuisine reflects the state's bounty of produce, an output of fabulous wine, and a willingness to innovate in the kitchen.
- Hawaiian foods have always been a mix of ethnic cultures, embracing Polynesian, Asian, and European influences.

Rosemary-Mascarpone Potato Pancakes

A modern take on traditional potato pancakes. Terrific as a snack, hors d'oeuvre, or side dish.

Prep time: less than 30 minutes • Makes 6 to 8 servings

3 cups russet potatoes, shredded

1 leek, shredded

2 eggs

1/4 cup cornstarch

1 tsp. salt

1/2 tsp. freshly ground black pepper

Dash of nutmeg

1 TB. fresh rosemary, chopped

1 TB. fresh lemon juice

1/2 cup mascarpone cheese

Vegetable oil for frying

Mix shredded potatoes and leeks together, and squeeze out as much liquid as possible from vegetables. Place shreds in a large bowl. Add eggs, and blend in thoroughly. Stir in cornstarch, salt, pepper, nutmeg, rosemary, lemon juice, and mascarpone cheese.

Heat about 1/8" vegetable oil in a skillet. When oil is hot, drop batter into the pan to make pancakes about 2" in diameter. Fry pancakes for a minute or so over moderate heat, or until browned on the bottom. Turn pancakes over and fry another 2 minutes, or until browned. Drain on paper towels.

Hot Tip

You can make the Potato Pancakes ahead and reheat them. Fried foods need to be reheated at hot temperatures: 400°. Put the pancakes on a rack on a baking sheet, in a single layer. Make sure there is plenty of room between the pancakes.

Goat Cheese and Walnut Salad with Balsamic Vinaigrette

This beautiful, fresh salad makes a superb start to an elegant dinner.

Prep time: less than 30 minutes   •   Makes 4 servings

6 TB. broken walnut pieces

1 bunch arugula

1 endive

1 head radicchio

$^1\!/_2$ head oakleaf lettuce

8 oz. log of firm, Montrachet-type chevre cheese

12 TB. olive oil

$^1\!/_2$ cup plain dry breadcrumbs

$^1\!/_2$ tsp. thyme leaves, chopped

1/2 tsp. fresh rosemary, chopped

3 TB. balsamic vinegar

$^1\!/_2$ tsp. Dijon mustard

Salt and pepper, to taste

$^1\!/_4$ cup red onion, chopped

Preheat the oven to 350°.

Place walnuts on a cookie sheet and roast for 5 minutes, or until lightly toasted. Remove from the oven and set aside.

Wash and dry arugula, endive, radicchio, and lettuce. Discard arugula stems. Cut endive into bite-size pieces. Tear radicchio and lettuce into bite-size pieces. Toss salad ingredients in a bowl and set aside.

Cut cheese into 8 slices. Brush cheese with 2 tablespoons olive oil. Combine breadcrumbs, thyme, and rosemary, and coat cheese with this mixture. Heat 2 tablespoons olive oil in a skillet over moderate heat. Add cheese and cook for 2–3 minutes, or until lightly browned. Turn cheese over, and cook for 2–3 minutes on second side. Remove cheese to paper towels.

Combine remaining olive oil, balsamic vinegar, mustard, and salt and pepper to taste. Mix until well combined. Pour dressing over greens. Toss lightly. Place greens in 4 serving dishes. Scatter red onion on top. Place 2 pieces of fried cheese on each salad. Garnish with walnuts.

Potato Salad

There are a gazillion recipes for Potato Salad. This one is unadorned and goes with almost any grilled or roasted meat, poultry, or fish you can think of. A great picnic item, too.

Prep time: less than 30 minutes • Makes 6 servings

2 lbs. new white or red bliss potatoes

6 TB. white wine or chicken stock

1 large shallot, chopped

2 TB. fresh parsley, chopped

$^1/_3$ cup olive oil

2–3 TB. white-wine vinegar

1 tsp. Dijon mustard

Salt and pepper, to taste

Boil potatoes in lightly salted water for about 15 minutes or until fork-tender. Drain under cold water and peel. Cut potatoes into bite-size pieces and place in a bowl. Add wine, shallot, and parsley and toss ingredients.

In a small bowl, combine olive oil, white-wine vinegar, and mustard. Pour over potatoes. Toss, taste for seasoning, and add salt and pepper to taste.

Dried Yellow Pea Soup with Dumplings

This hearty soup is perfect on a cold winter day. The yellow peas give it a soothing color; the allspice adds a hint of sweetness and warmth.

Prep time: less than 15 minutes   •   Makes 8 to 10 servings

1 lb. dried yellow peas	2 stalks celery, chopped
2 quarts water	2 carrots, chopped
4 ham hocks or ½ lb. smoked ham or corned beef	¼ cup parsley, minced
2 onions, chopped	½ tsp. ground allspice
	Salt and black pepper, to taste

For the dumplings:

½ cup milk	½ tsp. salt
1 TB. butter	2 eggs
1 cup all-purpose flour	

Place all soup ingredients in a soup pot and bring liquid to a boil. Reduce heat and cover the pan. Simmer for 2 hours. Remove ham hocks or meat. Either purée soup in a blender or plan to serve chunky. If puréed, return soup to the pot.

Remove meat from ham hocks (or ham or corned beef) and cut into tiny pieces. Add pieces to soup. Heat soup through. Taste for seasoning, and add more salt and black pepper if needed.

To make dumplings, bring milk and butter to a boil in a small saucepan. Add flour and salt all at once. Mix ingredients with a wooden spoon until dough is smooth and uniform. Remove mixture from heat. Add eggs one at a time, and incorporate thoroughly. Drop mixture by the tablespoon into soup. Cover the pot and cook for 10 minutes.

Lentil Soup

This soup is chock-full of tomatoes and vegetables. If you like, add broccoli crowns, corn kernels, and lima beans. Best made with common green or brown lentils.

Prep time: less than 30 minutes • Makes 8 servings

2 TB. olive oil

1 medium onion, chopped

2 carrots, chopped

2 medium leeks, white part only, chopped

2 cloves garlic, chopped

1 large stalk celery, chopped

6 cups vegetable or chicken stock

1 (28-oz.) can Italian-style tomatoes in thick purée, chopped but undrained

1 cup lentils

$^1/_4$ cup fresh parsley, chopped

Salt and black pepper, to taste

$^1/_2$ cup ditalini or other small pasta

Heat olive oil in a soup pot. Add onion and cook over moderate heat for 2 minutes. Add carrots, leeks, garlic, and celery, and cook another 4 minutes, stirring occasionally. Add stock, tomatoes, lentils, parsley, and salt and pepper.

Bring to a boil, cooking for 1 minute. Reduce the heat, cover the pan, and simmer for 45 minutes. Add pasta and simmer another 15–20 minutes. Season to taste with salt and pepper.

Hot Tip _____

It's less messy and less work if you crush the tomatoes using a sturdy wooden spoon while they're inside the pot.

Cioppino

This hearty, Mediterranean-style stew is a favorite in San Francisco. Often it is made with Dungeness Crab, which may be difficult to find in parts of the country. When soft-shell crabs are in season, you can substitute them for the lump crabmeat (add it with the scallops).

Prep time: less than 30 minutes   •   Makes 6 servings

$\frac{1}{4}$ cup olive oil

1 large onion, chopped

1 red bell pepper, seeded and chopped

4 large cloves garlic, chopped

1 medium carrot, finely chopped

1 (28-oz.) can Italian-style tomatoes in thick purée

2 TB. tomato paste

2 cups dry white wine

$\frac{1}{4}$ cup chopped fresh parsley

1 bay leaf

1 TB. chopped fresh oregano (or 1 tsp. dried)

1 TB. thyme leaves (or 1 tsp. dried)

$\frac{1}{8}$ to $\frac{1}{4}$ tsp. cayenne pepper, to taste

Salt and black pepper, to taste

16 clams

16 mussels

$\frac{1}{2}$ cup bottled clam juice or fish stock

1 lb. firm-fleshed fish such as bass, snapper, swordfish, or halibut, cut into chunks

1 lb. extra large shrimp, shelled and deveined

$\frac{1}{2}$ lb. sea scallops

12 oz. lump crabmeat

Heat olive oil in a soup pot. Add onion and bell pepper. Cook over moderate heat for 3 minutes, or until vegetables have softened. Add garlic, and cook another minute. Add carrot, tomatoes with purée, tomato paste, and wine. Break up tomatoes with a wooden spoon. Add parsley, bay leaf, oregano, thyme, cayenne pepper, salt, and pepper. Bring to a boil. Then cover the pot, reduce heat to low, and simmer for 15 minutes.

While soup is cooking, scrub clams and mussels, and put in a large saucepan. Pour in clam juice. Bring to a boil over high heat. Then cover the pot, turn the heat to moderate, and cook for 4–5 minutes or until shells have opened. Discard any clams and mussels that do not open. Remove to a bowl.

Strain cooking fluid and add to simmering soup. After soup has cooked for 15 minutes, add fish, shrimp, and scallops. Cover the pan and cook for about 4–5 minutes, or until fish is just cooked through. Place equal amounts of crab, clams, and mussels in large soup bowls. Ladle Cioppino into bowls and serve.

Baked Mahi-Mahi with Macadamia Crust

This dish is suitable for everyday or company dinners. If you can't get mahi-mahi, substitute pompano, grouper, striped bass, or Spanish mackerel. Mahi-mahi is also called dolphinfish, but it is not related to dolphins.

Prep time: less than 15 minutes • Makes 4 servings

Special equipment: food processor or blender

4 filets of mahi-mahi	2 TB. fresh parsley, freshly chopped
1/2 cup lime juice	2 tsp. fresh rosemary, freshly chopped
2/3 cup plain dry breadcrumbs	1/4 tsp. salt, or to taste
1/2 cup macadamia nuts, chopped	1/3 cup olive oil

Place fish in a glass, ceramic, or other nonreactive dish. Pour all but 1 tablespoon lime juice over fish. Let fish rest about 1 hour.

Preheat the oven to 350°.

Place breadcrumbs and nuts in a food processor or blender. Pulse quickly to combine ingredients as fine crumbs. Place crumbs in a bowl and mix in parsley, rosemary, salt, olive oil, and remaining lime juice.

Place fish in a baking dish. Press crumb mixture onto tops of filets. Bake 20–25 minutes or until filets are cooked through.

Western Omelet

My Dad, William Vail, specializes in this wonderful breakfast treat. You can make a western sandwich by stuffing the omelet between slices of buttered white bread or sourdough toast.

Prep time: less than 15 minutes   •   Makes 2 servings

4 eggs

3 TB. milk

2 scallions, finely chopped

$^1/_4$ cup red bell pepper, finely chopped

$^1/_2$ cup boiled ham, finely chopped

Salt and freshly ground black pepper, to taste

$1^1/_2$ TB. butter

Beat eggs in a bowl. Stir in milk, scallions, red pepper, ham, salt to taste, and a few grindings of black pepper. Melt butter in an omelet pan over low to moderate heat. When butter has melted and looks foamy, add egg mixture.

Cook for a minute or so. When eggs begin to set at edges, stir mixture gently with a fork. Bring hardened edges toward center to allow uncooked egg portions to reach the heat at the bottom of the pan. Continue cooking and stirring this way occasionally for 1–2 minutes. Then cook undisturbed for a minute or so more, until eggs are set but still looking moist. Fold omelet in half to serve.

Chicken Basque Style

This colorful dish goes well with cooked white rice or polenta and a green vegetable.

Prep time: less than 30 minutes • Makes 4 servings

4 oz. ham, diced

1 broiler-fryer chicken, cut into 8 pieces

2 TB. olive oil

1 onion, sliced

2 cloves garlic, minced

1 red bell pepper, seeded and sliced

1 green bell pepper, seeded and sliced

Salt and pepper, to taste

2 TB. freshly chopped parsley

$\frac{1}{2}$ cup dry white wine

1 cup frozen peas, thawed

Cook ham in a large skillet over moderate heat for 3–4 minutes or until dice begin to crisp. Remove ham and set it aside.

Wash and dry chicken pieces. Add olive oil to the pan. Brown chicken a few pieces at a time on all sides (this will take 12–15 minutes). Remove chicken and set aside.

Discard all but 2 tablespoons pan fat. Add onion and garlic, and cook over moderate heat for a minute or so. Add red and green peppers and cook for 2–3 minutes. Return chicken to the pan, including any juices accumulated. Scatter vegetables on top of chicken and sprinkle with salt, pepper, and parsley. Pour in wine.

Cover the pan, turn the heat to low moderate, and cook for 25 minutes, or until chicken has cooked through, basting occasionally. Add peas and ham. Cover the pan and cook 2–3 minutes. Serve chicken topped with vegetables and meat.

Chicken Fried Steak

A favorite from the Wild West days! This is easier to make today than in days of old, thanks to more tender cuts of meat.

Prep time: less than 15 minutes   •   Makes 4 servings

Special equipment: cake rack

4 sirloin tip steaks, cube steaks, or top round steaks, $^1/_4$" thick (about 1$^1/_2$ lbs.)

2 eggs

2 TB. milk

$^1/_2$ cup all-purpose flour

$^1/_2$ cup dry breadcrumbs

1 tsp. salt

$^1/_2$ tsp. black pepper

$^1/_2$ tsp. garlic powder

$^1/_2$ tsp. paprika

Vegetable shortening or oil

1 cup light cream

$^1/_2$ cup beef stock or milk

Salt and pepper, to taste

Preheat the oven to 140° (warm).

Cut meat into 4 equal pieces. Combine eggs and milk in a bowl and beat to blend thoroughly.

In another bowl, blend flour, breadcrumbs, salt, pepper, garlic powder, and paprika. Dredge steaks in flour mixture, and then in egg mixture. Dredge again in flour mixture. Let steaks air dry on a cake rack for 10 minutes. Dredge again in flour mixture. Reserve 2 tablespoons of flour mixture.

In a large skillet, heat enough vegetable shortening or oil to come up $^1/_4$" on the sides of the pan. When the fat is hot enough to make a bread crumb sizzle quickly (about 365°), add 2 steaks. Cook steaks about 3 minutes per side, or until golden brown. Drain on paper towels. Transfer to a serving platter and keep warm in the oven. Repeat with remaining 2 steaks.

Remove all but 2 tablespoons fat from the pan. Add reserved flour and stir, scraping up any browned bits at the bottom of the pan. Cook over low heat about 1 minute. Gradually add cream and stock. Stir, preferably with a whisk, until mixture has thickened. Season to taste with salt and pepper, and then pour gravy over steaks and serve.

Hot Tip

Fried foods need room in the pan or they will steam and get soggy. That's why you cook these steaks two at a time. Use two pans if you want the steaks to be ready at the same time.

Grilled Lamb Kebabs in Mustard-Herb Dressing

These kebabs are all-purpose: Substitute beef or chicken! Serve with potato salad, and the meal is complete.

Prep time: less than 30 minutes • Makes 4 servings

1½ lbs. boneless lamb, cut into chunks

½ cup olive oil

¼ cup lemon juice

1½ TB. Dijon-style mustard

2 TB. minced fresh chives

1 TB. minced fresh oregano (or 1 tsp. dried oregano)

1 large clove garlic, minced

¾ tsp. salt or to taste

½ tsp. grated lemon peel

⅛ tsp. cayenne pepper

2 bay leaves

1 large sweet red pepper, seeded

12 scallions

1 small zucchini

12 white mushroom caps

Put meat in a glass, ceramic, stainless-steel, or other nonreactive bowl. Mix together olive oil, lemon juice, mustard, chives, oregano, garlic, salt, lemon peel, and cayenne pepper, and pour mixture over meat. Press bay leaves into liquid. Let meat marinate 2–3 hours, tossing 2 or 3 times while marinating.

While meat marinates, cut red pepper into 1½" chunks, scallions into 1½" lengths, and zucchini into 1"-thick slices. When meat has finished marinating, skewer meat and vegetables alternately, including mushrooms, onto long skewers. Brush vegetables with marinade.

Preheat the broiler or grill. Broil or grill kebabs 8–15 minutes, turning to brown all sides, depending on whether you like them rare, medium, or well done. Brush meat and vegetables occasionally with marinade during broiling process.

Hangtown Fry

The rich folks' dish! You don't need to strike gold to feast on this, though. It's a good choice for Sunday brunch, but makes a filling dinner, too.

Prep time: less than 15 minutes • Makes 4 servings

12 shucked oysters	Pinch of paprika
3 TB. all-purpose flour	2 TB. vegetable oil
1 egg, beaten	1 TB. butter
1/4 cup cracker crumbs	6 to 8 eggs, beaten
1/2 tsp. salt, or to taste	2 TB. chives, chopped
1/4 tsp. freshly ground black pepper, or to taste	2–3 pieces cooked bacon per person

Dredge oysters in flour and shake off excess. Coat with beaten egg. Mix cracker crumbs, salt, pepper, and paprika in a small bowl and cover egg-coated oysters with this mixture. Heat vegetable oil in a small skillet and fry oysters over moderate heat for 2–4 minutes or until crispy on both sides. Drain oysters on paper towels.

Heat butter in a cast-iron or other heavy skillet over moderate heat. When butter has melted and looks foamy, add eggs. As eggs begin to set at edges after about a minute, stir mixture gently with a fork, bringing hardened edges toward center to allow uncooked egg portions to reach the heat at the bottom of the pan.

When eggs are partially set, add oysters, pressing in gently. Sprinkle chives over ingredients and continue to cook until eggs have set completely. Spoon onto a serving platter and surround with cooked bacon.

Shepherd's Pie

This dish may have originated in England, but gained popularity when sheepherding became big business in the west.

Prep time: less than 30 minutes • Makes 4 to 6 servings

2 carrots, chopped

6 medium all-purpose or Yukon Gold potatoes

6 TB. butter

½ cup milk

Salt and pepper, to taste

5 TB. all-purpose flour

2½ cups beef or lamb stock

2 TB. olive oil

1 onion, chopped

5–6 cups cooked lamb, chopped

1 (10-oz.) pkg. frozen peas

2 TB. fresh parsley, chopped

Preheat the oven to 350°.

Cook carrots in lightly salted water for 3–4 minutes or until softened slightly. Drain carrots and set aside.

Peel potatoes, cut into chunks. Cook in lightly salted water for 10–15 minutes, or until tender. Drain potatoes, add 2 tablespoons butter, milk, and salt and pepper to taste. Mash potatoes and set aside.

Heat remaining butter in a saucepan over moderate heat. When butter has melted and looks foamy, turn heat to low and add flour. Cook for 2 minutes. Gradually add stock, stirring constantly for about 2–3 minutes, until thick and smooth. Set aside.

Heat olive oil in a skillet set over moderate heat. Add onion and cook for 2–3 minutes, or until softened. Add lamb, carrots, peas, and parsley. Sprinkle in salt and pepper. Remove the pan from heat.

Stir in sauce. Spoon mixture into a baking dish. Top lamb with mashed potatoes. Bake for 35–40 minutes or until browned and crispy.

Stuffed Artichokes

Fabulous first course; it takes a little practice and some hard work, but the taste is worth it.

Prep time: less than 1 hour   •   Makes 4 servings

4 large artichokes	$^1/_2$ lb. beef or turkey, chopped
1 lemon, cut into quarters	1 cup plain fresh breadcrumbs
6 TB. olive oil	1 egg
1 medium onion, chopped	$^1/_2$ tsp. dried oregano
1 large clove garlic, chopped	$^1/_2$ tsp. salt, or to taste
$^1/_2$ cup mushrooms, chopped	Black pepper, to taste
$^1/_4$ cup Italian parsley, chopped	2 TB. lemon juice

Cut stems of artichokes to produce a flat, stable bottom. Rub surface with the cut side of lemon. Discard any small leaves at the base and any discolored leaves. Cut off about 1" from the top of artichoke, and rub the cut surface with lemon. With a scissors, snip each thorny leaf tip. Rub with more lemon. Separate center leaves with your hands, and scoop out hairy choke with a spoon or a melon-baller. Turn artichokes upside down. Press firmly to flatten slightly and to separate leaves.

Preheat the oven to 375°.

Lightly grease a baking dish. Heat 4 tablespoons olive oil in a skillet over moderate heat. Add onion, garlic, mushrooms, and parsley, and cook for 2 minutes. Add meat and cook for another 2–3 minutes, or until meat has turned color. Remove pan from heat. Add breadcrumbs to the pan and stir ingredients to combine. Stir in egg, oregano, salt, pepper, and lemon juice. Spoon some of the filling into centers of artichokes, and stuff the rest between leaves.

Put the artichokes inside the baking dish. Pour enough hot water inside the baking dish to be 1" deep. Sprinkle artichokes with remaining olive oil. Cover the dish with aluminum foil. Bake for 30 minutes. Remove cover and bake for another 25–30 minutes or until artichoke base is tender.

Hot Tip

For a different flavor, spoon some tomato sauce on top of the artichokes for the last 25–30 minutes of baking time.

Caramel Corn Balls with Dried Fruit

You can use any kind of dried fruit for these crunchy treats; if you like, make them with packaged, chopped dried fruit bits.

Prep time: less than 15 minutes • Makes 12 balls

Special equipment: candy thermometer

2 TB. vegetable oil	$^1/_4$ cup light corn syrup
$^1/_2$ cup popcorn kernels	$^3/_4$ tsp. white vinegar
1 cup dark brown sugar	$^1/_2$ cup golden raisins
$^1/_4$ tsp. salt	$^1/_2$ cup dried fruit, chopped
$^3/_4$ cup water	

Heat vegetable oil in a large pot or popcorn popper. Add popcorn kernels and cook over moderately high heat until all kernels have popped. Place popped corn in a large bowl. Combine brown sugar, salt, water, corn syrup, and vinegar in a saucepan and bring to a boil over moderate heat. Stir until mixture starts to boil.

Raise heat to high, and cook until mixture reaches 250° on a candy thermometer. Quickly pour over popped corn. Stir in raisins and fruit. Let cool slightly so that the sugar won't burn your hands. Butter your hands lightly, and shape mixture into balls.

Hot Tip

If you don't have a candy thermometer, you can test the temperature by dropping a small amount of the mixture into a dish of cold water. A hard ball should form.

Macerated Pineapple with Chips

Really easy to make and powerfully flavorful! Hawaiian pineapples are the best to use; they are sweet and juicy.

Prep time: less than 15 minutes   •   Makes 4 servings

1 large fresh pineapple, preferably Hawaiian	1 cup heavy whipping cream
6 TB. confectioner's sugar	1 tsp. sugar
3 TB. orange-flavored liqueur	$^1/_2$ cup packaged toffee chips
3 TB. rum, brandy, or kirschwasser	

Cut pineapple in half, keeping leaves intact. Cut flesh out of pineapple shell with a small knife. Use a spoon to scoop portions the knife doesn't reach. Reserve pineapple shells. Cut away and discard hard core in center of flesh. Cut pineapple flesh into bite-size pieces.

Place pineapple pieces in a bowl and add confectioner's sugar, orange-flavored liqueur, and rum or brandy. Toss fruit to dissolve sugar. Macerate fruit at least 1 hour in the refrigerator.

Before serving, put fruit and accumulated juices back into reserved pineapple shells. Whip cream and sugar together until mixture is thick enough to stand in peaks. Put equal amounts of whipped cream on top of two pineapple halves. Garnish with toffee chips.

Hot Tip

Macerate is similar to marinate, but is the term used for fruits and vegetables rather than for meat.

Angel-Food Cake

This classic tall cake is wonderful plain, but gets some glamour when served with ice cream or crushed, sweetened berries. Make sure you let the cake cool completely in the pan, or it might collapse. For best results, always use a serrated knife to cut angel-food cake.

Prep time: less than 30 minutes   •   Makes 1 (10") cake

Special equipment: angel-food cake pan, cake rack

1 cup cake flour	1$\frac{1}{2}$ tsp. cream of tartar
1$\frac{1}{2}$ cups superfine sugar	1 tsp. vanilla extract
$\frac{1}{4}$ tsp. salt	$\frac{1}{2}$ tsp. almond extract
1$\frac{1}{2}$ cups egg whites, at room temperature	

Preheat the oven to 350°.

Sift cake flour, half the sugar, and salt together three times. In an electric mixer bowl (or using a hand mixer) set at medium speed, beat egg whites until foamy. Add cream of tartar and beat whites until they stand in soft peaks. Gradually add remaining sugar and beat until whites stand in stiff peaks. Stir in vanilla and almond extracts. Fold in flour mixture in thirds, making sure each addition is thoroughly incorporated.

Pour batter into an ungreased angel-food pan or 10" tube pan. Bake for 40 minutes or until puffy and golden brown, and a cake tester inserted into the center comes out clean. Remove cake from the oven and set cake upside down on a cake rack to cool completely. If using a tube pan, invert cake onto a glass bottle. When cool, loosen cake edges with the tip of a sharp knife and unmold. Invert right side up.

Hot Tip _____

Try these variations:

- ◆ Substitute $\frac{1}{4}$ cup unsweetened cocoa for $\frac{1}{4}$ cup of the flour.
- ◆ Add $\frac{1}{2}$ cup finely ground hazelnuts to the sifted flour mixture.
- ◆ Add 1 teaspoon orange extract and 2 tablespoons freshly grated orange peel to the batter with the vanilla and almond extracts.

Macadamia-Date Tart

A sweet confection, similar to Pecan Pie. You can freeze this tart for months.

Prep time: less than 30 minutes   •   Makes 1 (10") tart

Special equipment: tart pan with removable bottom

For the crust:

1½ cups all-purpose flour

½ tsp. salt

½ tsp. sugar

6 TB. butter, cut into small chunks

2 TB. chilled shortening, cut into small chunks

3–4 TB. milk (approximately)

Preheat the oven to 400°.

Mix flour, salt, and sugar in a bowl. Add butter and shortening. Work pieces into flour mixture with your fingers or with a pastry blender until mixture resembles coarse meal. Add 2 or 3 tablespoons milk and stir, using more milk if necessary, but just enough to form soft ball of dough.

Let dough rest for 30 minutes, and then roll out to fit a 10" tart pan with a removable bottom. Prick dough with tines of a fork. Cover dough with aluminum foil and add baking weights. Bake for 10 minutes. Remove weights and foil, and bake for another 4 minutes.

For the filling:

¾ cup light corn syrup

½ cup light brown sugar

3 eggs

2 TB. melted butter

1 TB. all-purpose flour

½ tsp. salt

1 tsp. cinnamon

¼ tsp. ground nutmeg

2 tsp. white vinegar

1 tsp. vanilla extract

1½ cups macadamia nuts, coarsely chopped

¾ cup dates, chopped

Combine corn syrup, brown sugar, eggs, and melted butter in a bowl. Whisk ingredients until well blended. Add flour, salt, cinnamon, nutmeg, vinegar, and vanilla extract, and whisk ingredients until well blended.

Stir in nuts and dates. Pour filling into partially baked shell. Bake for about 45 minutes or until golden brown.

Chapter 8

The Northwest

In This Chapter

- ◆ Salmon: the king of fish
- ◆ Oysters and their cousins
- ◆ Mushroom madness
- ◆ Bountiful apples, pears, and cherries
- ◆ From sweet onions to a good cup of coffee
- ◆ Alaska's giants

Fresh *everything* is a hallmark of northwest cooking. This is a region rich in natural abundance. Fish, particularly salmon, is bountiful, as are oysters, clams, crabs, and mussels. These are the foods that kept the pioneers from starving after their long trek here, and to this day, seafood is at the core of the cuisine. All sorts of berries flourish here: blackberries, strawberries, raspberries, and boysenberries, to name a few. And mushroom varieties known by Native Americans thrive here, too, to be savored in dishes as diverse as Mushroom Crostini and Pan-Fried Trout, or used in stuffings for wild game birds or roasted with chicken.

The pioneers who came here brought seedlings from other places. These became the orchards that now supply a nation: apples for pie, pears for poaching, hazelnuts for cake. There's a growing wine industry, and a few cheesemakers, too. Seattle is big on coffee—it's where Starbucks got its start. Alaska, our biggest state, grows giant produce—rhubarb for cobbler, and huge cabbages and turnips. The King Crabs are enormous, too, just right for a feast.

Like other American regions, the Northwest blends ethnic variety in its cuisine. Scandinavians, Russians, Basques, Italians, and Chinese have made their homes here, as well as Japanese, who have had a particularly profound influence on the regional menu. Thanks to them, we know about Asian pears, Sushi, and Chicken Teriyaki.

The Last Frontier

When Lewis and Clark explored the Northwest, they were awestruck by the region's beautiful mountains, the crystal-clear Columbia River, the abundance of fish and wild game, and the extraordinary possibilities for America. Still, settlers didn't come for nearly a quarter-century, beginning in the 1840s. Traversing the Oregon Trail was a daunting task: There was a vast wilderness to get through, and nearly impassable mountains. There were also hostile Native Americans to consider, as well as the prospects of severe weather.

Salmon and Other Fish

Most settlers made the long trip westward in wagon convoys, and they needed to bring almost a half-year's supply of food with them. Like other pioneers, they subsisted on meager supplies of beans, cornmeal, bacon, flour, and other staples, and relied on wild game to supplement their diet. By the time the trailblazers reached the coast, many were out of food. Thanks to the abundance of fish, they averted starvation.

Salmon were so bountiful that they were a staple food among native northwest Native American tribes. Today, supplies are more limited, and much of the harvest is farmed. Some fish markets sell Alaskan wild salmon, a worthwhile purchase because of its intense flavor. Salmon's big flavor means you don't have to fuss with it; it's a wonderful meal when grilled, roasted, or poached, with a few simple seasonings. Salmon tastes best when cooked until it's still somewhat translucent in the center—medium rare. There are several varieties on the market, including Atlantic salmon, which is rich and bountifully flavored. Pacific Northwest varieties include the following:

   ◆ **Chinook (King)**   The largest salmon, with the most fat and flavor; excellent when grilled. A few markets may offer albino salmon, a Chinook with white flesh.
   ◆ **Coho (Silver)**   Red-fleshed and somewhat smaller than the Chinook, and with less fat and less flavor. Some of the catch is canned.

◆ **Pink (Humpback)**   The smallest variety; it has a pale flesh and mild taste. Much of it is canned.

◆ **Chum (Dog)**   Moderately fat with a mild taste and pale orange flesh.

◆ **Sockeye (Red, Blueback)**   Dark-orange and fabulously oily and rich tasting. At one time, almost all sockeye salmon was canned; today you can buy it fresh.

Although salmon is the Northwest's most well-known fish, the region rightfully boasts several other varieties. Halibut is an abundant and important catch. There are also significant supplies of trout, smelt, sturgeon, black cod (sablefish), walleye perch, and rockfish. Sturgeon eggs are served as caviar.

 **Fein on Food**

A once-common festival among the northwest Native American tribes was the potlatch, during which the host would give away possessions that he had received at someone else's potlatch. The ritual was accompanied by a feast that always included salmon. Invited families brought other seasonal foods to be shared. The custom of potlatch, which means "gift," lives on in our potluck dinners.

The World's Your Oyster

The Pacific Ocean and Alaskan waterways are home to a variety of shellfish. For Native Americans, oysters, clams, and other seafood were mainstays. Today the cuisine of the Northwest continues to reflect the bounty, with seafood a regular item on restaurant menus and at home. Thanks to quick transport, some of the harvest is shipped to other areas of the United States. People in New York, Illinois, or Oklahoma can enjoy fresh Pacific oysters anytime. Shellfish varieties from the Northwest include these:

◆ **Oysters**   Four species including the indigenous Olympias, which are small and have a delicate flavor. Also the mild-tasting Pacific and Kumamoto (both introduced to the waters by Japanese settlers) and the European flat oysters, which have a more pronounced briny flavor. Names such as Westcott Bay refer to harvesting grounds of these species.

◆ **Clams**   Dozens of varieties including large "razor" clams, (so-called because the elongated, slightly curved shape resembles a barber's razor), which are steamed or used for sushi; tiny Manila clams, which are steamed or put into chowder; and Geoducks. Geoducks have an elongated neck-like protrusion that is chopped (for chowder or fritters) and an enormous body that may be pan-fried, made into "burgers," or used for sashimi or sushi.

♦ **Crab**   Three major types, all have rich, sweet meat. Dungeness Crab is cooked and served hot or cold, and is one of the most popular ingredients for Cioppino, a fish stew. Alaskan King Crab, the largest and most well-known species, has large, long legs that are steamed and served hot or cold with drawn butter or cocktail sauce. Snow Crab is typically cooked, flaked into tins, and sold fresh or frozen, to be used in crabcakes, salad, and other dishes.

♦ **Mussels**   Small blue mussels and larger Mediterranean mussels; they are usually steamed with wine and flavoring ingredients, such as tomato, garlic, and onion.

Kitchen Clue

At one time, no one ate oysters in months that didn't end in "r." It was thought that oysters were poisonous at these times. Most likely this myth took hold because, in the old days, lack of refrigeration caused many oysters to go bad in the hot weather. In fact, most oysters spawn during the summer and can be flaccid and tasteless. However, with modern methods of controlling the temperature of oyster beds, and the easy means of transporting shellfood from colder climates, plump, deliciously briny oysters are available 12 months a year.

From the Forest Floor

A generation ago, only a mycologist would have been interested in wild mushrooms. Today, these fungi are everyday fare, as they were when Native Americans populated the area. You will find several varieties in the market:

♦ **Morel** mushroom season in the Northwest begins in April. (For more information on this variety, see Chapter 4.)

♦ **Chanterelle** mushrooms look like inside-out umbrellas. Their colors range from ecru to bright red. They pair well with poultry and game dishes that include nuts, but also are lovely as a simple sauté: Cook them in butter to serve alone as a side dish.

♦ **Chicken-of-the-woods** (sometimes called Hen-of-the-woods) is an enormous mushroom, usually sold in sections, each resembling hen feathers sticking out of a clump. The wispy "feathers," which are gray or brown, are soft and tender; the clump is firm and chewy. This mushroom has a deep, earthy flavor (some say it tastes like chicken) that stands up well to poaching in stock, baking in parchment paper (sprinkle with olive oil, salt, and pepper), braising with wine and herbs, or sautéing in olive oil and butter.

♦ **Lobster** mushrooms have a deep, orange-red surface and bright white flesh. Its coloration and briny taste are reminiscent of lobster, hence the name. The cap is brittle with an irregular but flat shape. Use these for sautés, stir-fries, or in braised dishes and casseroles.

- **Oyster** mushrooms are bland, and aren't at all sea-flavored like oysters. The name refers to their shape: the tops do not cap the stem but are more like lobes that resemble oyster shells. Sauté, grill, or deep-fry these.

- **Boletus** mushrooms (Cepes) have a thick stem and lovely, rounded hat. They are the most treasured of mushrooms for their full-bodied, earthy flavor. When dried, they are known as Porcini, which are amazingly flavorful. Grill, braise, or sauté them, or put them into risotto.

- **Portobello** mushrooms are giant, large-capped, overgrown crimini, or common brown mushrooms. Unknown just a few years ago, today they are the most popular variety. Some people use them as a meat substitute: Brush the surface with olive oil and grill until softened. They're used in all sorts of recipes, from stir-fries to pasta dishes.

Did You Know ...

You can use dried mushrooms if fresh are unavailable, and there's a bonus: The water used to reconstitute and soften dried mushrooms can be used to flavor soups, casseroles, gravies, vinaigrette dressings, or sauces. Soak the mushrooms in hot water for 15 to 30 minutes, and then strain the liquid through cheesecloth.

- **Shiitake** mushrooms are rich, substantial and smokey-flavored, standing up well to hearty ingredients such as garlic and sausage. The flat cap has a chewy texture, while the fibrous stem is inedible. They are wonderful when added to stir-fries or pasta dishes, steamed with vegetables, or put into soups or risotto.

- **Matsutake** mushrooms were ignored in the northwest until Japanese settlers made their home in the region. They were familiar with this variety, which also grows in Japan. Matsutakes have an earthy flavor and an almost spicy aroma. The entire mushroom can be eaten. Use them in stir-fries, pasta, risotto, or soup.

Under the Influence

Pioneers headed to the Northwest for many reasons. Settlers from other states arrived in search of land. Prospectors came seeking gold. Scandinavians sought out the area because the terrain and weather reminded them of home. Basques tended sheep in the mountains of eastern Oregon. Chinese, Japanese, and Italians found jobs building the railroads or working in the lumber or seafood-canning industries. As in all other regions, the heterogeneous makeup of the settlers had an impact on the cuisine.

In the Northwest, though, an Asian, particularly Japanese, influence is profound, first in the use of ginger, which has been popular as an all-purpose seasoning for decades, and, more recently, for daikon, cilantro, and Asian pears. Some unique Japanese specialties are now everyday fare: Teriyaki Chicken, a familiar barbecue choice, and fresh sushi, which you can find in gourmet stores and even some supermarkets.

Fein on Food

James Beard, considered by experts to be the Dean of American Cooking, was the son of pioneers. His father's family came from Iowa in a covered wagon. Beard made a number of enduring contributions to American cookery, including his many cookbooks, his enthusiasm for American food, his encouragement of others to cook, and his insistence on using fresh, local, seasonal ingredients.

How Does Your Garden Grow?

Whatever their reasons for making the long, arduous journey to the Northwest, what the settlers found was a wealth of fine, fertile land. Despite frequent drizzle and a serious lack of sunshine, they turned the area into a vast garden yielding some of America's most important produce. Wild strawberries, blackberries, and cranberries always grew lavishly in the area. Today, Washington and Oregon furnish a huge amount of the nation's raspberries and other berry types. Cultivated crops such as rhubarb, cabbage, and peas actually prosper without a lot of sunlight. Seattle's famous Pike Place Market, founded in 1907, is an impressive showcase of abundant fresh produce (also fish, cheese, and other foods) of the area.

Don't Sit Under the Apple Tree

The apple culture begun in the Midwest by Johnny Appleseed became one of the Northwest's most important businesses, with Washington being the biggest apple-growing area in the country. Commercial orchards got their start in the 1840s with seedlings transplanted from Iowa. One of them was the forerunner of the Red Delicious, America's favorite apple (it constitutes more than half the output in Washington), but other varieties grow here as well, including these:

◆ **Fuji (Mutsu)**   A yellow-green apple with red markings; its mild taste and snappy-crisp texture make it a good eating apple.

◆ **Gala**   A yellow apple with pink-red blush, it is crisp and juicy, best for munching.

◆ **Golden Delicious**   A yellow-skinned, delicately sweet, all-purpose variety that is also fine for pie and applesauce.

◆ **Granny Smith**   A tart, crisp green apple used for pie and for recipes using savory ingredients.

◆ **Jonathan**   A firm, crisp, medium-red variety, sometimes with yellow markings; for salad, applesauce, and eating out of hand.

◆ **Rome Beauty**   A large, dark-red apple with sweet, dry, firm flesh; best for baking whole.

◆ **Winesap**   A crisp, juicy red apple excellent for pie, applesauce, salads, and eating out of hand.

Mini-Recipe

Rich Applesauce (6 servings)   Peel and remove the seeds and cores of 8 apples. Slice them into a saucepan. Add $1/2$ cup sugar, 1 tablespoon lemon juice, $1/2$ teaspoon ground cinnamon, 2 tablespoons butter, and $1/4$ cup orange marmalade or apricot preserves. Cover the pan, cook the apples on low heat, stirring occasionally, for 20–25 minutes, or until very tender.

Have a Pear

Pears are another transplant from Iowa. The trees flourished profusely in Oregon and Washington. You may find several pear varieties in the market, including the following:

◆ **Bartlett,** either green or red   This is the first variety to ripen, opening the pear season in late summer. It is medium sized, with thin skin and sweet, juicy flesh. Good for eating and cooking.

◆ **Anjou**   Ready in October, is green and bulbous, with smooth skin and sweet, juicy flesh. Fine for eating and cooking.

◆ **Comice**   A winter pear, is a rotund, squat pear with thick green skin and sweet, creamy, flavorful flesh. Best for eating out of hand.

◆ **Bosc**   A winter pear with a long body, tapering neck, and granular-looking brownish skin. The cream-colored flesh is rich-tasting. Fine for eating or cooking.

◆ **Forelle**   A small winter pear with yellow skin and red blush. The delicate flesh makes this variety good for nibbling.

Kitchen Clue

Pears are rock hard in the stores because they are picked before they mature. Unlike most fruit, pears become gritty and mealy if left to ripen on the tree. Think ahead when buying pears. Leave them at room temperature and they will be ready in two or three days. Handle them carefully; pears are fragile and will show bruising as they ripen.

◆ **Seckel**   A small, round winter pear with thick, drab skin and firm flesh. Use this variety for cooking or preserves.

◆ **Asian Pears**   Sometimes called apple pears or salad pears, are crisp and juicy and have a distinctive texture reminiscent of sweet onions. There are three main types, but all are fine for eating out of hand. Unlike other varieties, Asian pears do not change texture after they are harvested.

Cheery Cherries

America's favorite cherry is the Bing, a dark-red, sweet variety from the northwest. Lambert cherries are another red variety, very dark, large, and sweet. Rainier and Royal Anns, both sweet varieties, are pale with a red blush. Sweet cherries are always sold ripe; look for plump, firm, glossy fruit. They are perfect for eating out of hand, but you can also cut them into homemade vanilla ice cream or pancake batter, use them between chocolate cake layers, dip them into chocolate fondue, or macerate them in sugar and kirsch (cherry brandy). Pale Rainiers and Royal Anns are wonderful when poached (see the Poached Fruit recipe in Appendix C). Sour red cherries are used for pie and cobbler; these are bright red (for a cobbler recipe, see Chapter 4).

Nuts to You

Hazelnuts were once called filberts to honor St. Philbert, whose name day is August 22, which coincides with Europe's hazelnut harvest. Today we only know them as hazelnuts, so called because they look somewhat like helmets, and the old Anglo-Saxon word *haesel* meant helmet. Hazelnuts grew wild in the northwest and were important in the early settlers' diets. But a French immigrant planted an orchard of nut trees in Oregon's Willamette Valley, and out of it came a major industry, providing almost all of the nation's hazelnut supply. Hazelnuts are hard, dense, and faintly sweet. They contain less oil than other varieties of nuts, which means you can grind them easily, and the texture will be light, dry, and fluffy, making them useful for cake, pie crust, and cookies.

Kitchen Clue

Many recipes call for blanched hazelnuts. Here's an easy method of removing the nut's thick skin: Toast the nuts on a cookie sheet in a preheated 375° oven for about 8 minutes, and rub off the skins with a kitchen towel. If that fails, cover the toasted nuts with boiling water, let stand for 2 minutes, and rub with a kitchen towel. On the other hand, you really don't have to blanch the nuts. Blanching does not affect taste, only color, and you can adapt recipes using unblanched nuts.

These Won't Make You Cry

One of Washington's more interesting crops is the Walla-Walla onion, a sweet variety. Like Georgia's Vidalias and Hawaii's Maui onions, Walla-Wallas are delicate, and some people like to eat them as a sandwich filling between buttered crusty French bread. They have a bit of a bite, though, so you can use them as you would any other onion, but they are particularly fine in salad, paired with tomatoes and blue cheese.

Great Pastures Mean Great Cheese

Oregon's fertile farmland was an inspiration for dairy farmers, who founded a major cheese industry in Tillamook, Oregon, toward the end of the nineteenth century. The first variety for commercial production was cheddar, made by a dairyman from Ontario, Canada. Today, Tillamook cheddar is well known throughout the States. Other cheesemakers in the northwest provide Blue, Jack, Colby, and goat's-milk and sheep's-milk cheeses. At Washington State University, the campus creamery produces Cougar Gold, a sharp, nutty-tasting, white cheddar type sold in tins.

A Little Vino with that Cheese

The fabulous soil and mild, damp climate of the northwest makes it a prime place for grape-growing and wine production. There are reds, including Merlots and Cabernets, white Chardonnays, and a variety of sweet whites, such as Reisling and Gewurztraminer.

Latte Land

In 1971, the city of Seattle almost demolished the famed Pike Place Market, but it was saved by community activists. That same year, Starbucks opened its first store in the market. Well before Starbucks took America by storm, Seattle was a coffee-lover's paradise, with several coffee roasters providing beans for the morning brew, and numerous outdoor carts selling a variety of espresso beverages. Starbucks was one among many bean wholesalers, but a New York entrepreneur bought the business and began a

What Is It?

In case there is any confusion about espresso beverages, here are some basics. **Cappuccino** is espresso coffee sometimes mixed with steamed milk and always capped with a thick layer of frothed milk. **Latte** is espresso mixed with steamed milk. **Macchiato** is espresso with a dollop of steamed milk on top.

coffee-house empire. Today, coffee and espresso-based beverages such as *cappuccino*, *latte*, and *macchiato* are more popular than ever, throughout the United States.

North to Alaska

At one time it was Seward's Folly, so called after Secretary of State William Seward negotiated the purchase of Alaska in 1867 for $7.2 million from Russian Czar Alexander II. It was a big, barren place and good for nothing. Or so it seemed until gold was discovered in the Klondike, and later, vast stores of oil. Native Americans, Inuits, and Aleuts had prospered there, despite the cold, living on fish, seabirds, and caribou; the only whites were Russians, who had come as fur trappers. The Russian culinary influence still informs the local cuisine, with families preparing traditional salmon piroghis (pies) and buckwheat groats (kasha). But it would probably surprise even Seward to understand the value Alaska's culinary contributions. In addition to the well-known, well-loved King Crab, there's Alaska's produce. The state has unique growing conditions—a short season but with extremely long daylight hours and cool weather. As a result, produce can be gigantic. Fifty-pound cabbages have been reported, as well as four-foot high rhubarb. In Alaska, crops are no folly: Beets, carrots, onions, potatoes, rhubarb, cabbage, berries, radishes, sunflowers, broccoli, and turnips all thrive.

The Least You Need to Know

- The cuisine of the Northwest bespeaks an abundance of fresh fish, shellfish, and produce; it also culls influences from the varied ethnic groups that have made their home in the region.

- Salmon is so flavorful that it's best when prepared simply. It also tastes best when cooked still rare in the center.

- Oysters, clams, and other seafood are bountiful in the Northwest, and are mainstays on restaurant menus and at home.

- Several varieties of fresh or dried mushrooms, such as morel and chanterelle, are used in all sorts of recipes, from stir-fries to pasta dishes.

- The Northwest furnishes a huge amount of the nation's berries, apples, pears, and cherries.

- Despite the short but thriving growing season, Alaska produces a bountiful crop of cabbage, rhubarb, beets, carrots, onions, potatoes, berries, radishes, sunflowers, broccoli, and turnips.

Wild Mushroom Crostini

These rich-tasting toasts are perfect for parties.

Prep time: less than 30 minutes   •   Makes about 3 dozen

Special equipment: food processor

$^1/_2$ oz. dried mushrooms

$^1/_2$ cup hot water

2 TB. olive oil

1 large shallot, chopped

1 clove garlic, chopped

12 oz. fresh wild mushrooms, such as oyster, lobster, chanterelle, or Shiitake, finely chopped

Salt and pepper, to taste

$^1/_2$ cup cream

10 TB. Parmesan cheese, freshly grated

A baguette bread

Soak dried mushrooms in hot water for several minutes until softened. Drain and squeeze mushrooms dry, and chop in a food processor. Strain soaking water and set aside.

Heat olive oil in a skillet over moderate heat. Add shallot and cook for 2 minutes, or until softened. Add garlic and cook for 1 minute. Add fresh and dried mushrooms, and cook for 5–6 minutes, stirring occasionally, or until juices have evaporated. Add soaking water and cook for another 3–4 minutes or until juices have evaporated. Sprinkle mushrooms with salt and pepper to taste. Stir in cream, and cook for 4–5 minutes or until mixture is thick and liquid has evaporated. Stir in 6 tablespoons cheese, and then remove from heat and let cool.

Cut bread into $^1/_4$" slices. Spread mushroom mixture on top of slices. Sprinkle with remaining Parmesan cheese. When ready to serve, preheat an oven broiler. Place crostini on a baking sheet. Broil about 6" away from the heat for 2–3 minutes, or until hot and bubbly.

Hot Tip

To keep these hors d'oeuvres from becoming soggy, don't spread the mushroom mixture onto the bread until just before you are ready to serve.

Sweet Onion and Tomato Salad

This is a beautiful salad that takes just a few minutes to make. It goes well with just about any grilled meat, fish, or poultry as a side dish—or serve it as a light first course.

Prep time: less than 15 minutes • Makes 4 servings

$\frac{1}{4}$ cup olive oil

3 TB. red-wine vinegar

1 tsp. Worcestershire sauce

$\frac{1}{2}$ tsp. Dijon mustard

Salt and pepper, to taste

8 romaine lettuce leaves, washed and dried

2 large, ripe tomatoes

1 large sweet onion such as Walla-Walla or Vidalia

$\frac{1}{2}$ cup Gorgonzola cheese, crumbled

2 TB. fresh parsley, chopped

Combine olive oil, red-wine vinegar, Worcestershire sauce, Dijon mustard, and some salt and pepper to taste. Set aside in a bowl.

Place 2 lettuce leaves on each of 4 plates. Slice tomatoes and arrange over lettuce. Peel and thinly slice onion, and arrange slices over tomatoes. Sprinkle with crumbled Gorgonzola cheese. Mix dressing ingredients and pour over salads. Sprinkle with parsley and serve.

Oyster Stew

You can serve this rich, creamy soup in any season. It warms you up in winter and refreshes in summer. The cayenne pepper gives it just a bit of a bite. If you make it the alternative way, with sherry, you'll find the dish transformed into soup that's magically sweet.

Prep time: less than 15 minutes • Makes 4 servings

2 TB. olive oil

1 TB. butter

1 medium onion, chopped

2 stalks celery, chopped

2 cups whipping cream

$1^{3}/_{4}$ cups whole milk

1 pint shucked oysters

The oyster liquor (1 pint of shucked oysters will yield about $^{3}/_{4}$ cup of liquid)

$^{1}/_{4}$ tsp. cayenne pepper

1 TB. Worcestershire sauce

Salt, to taste

2 TB. freshly minced parsley

2 tsp. sweet cream sherry

Heat olive oil and butter in a large saucepan over moderate heat. Add onion and celery, and cook for 7–8 minutes, stirring occasionally, or until vegetables have softened completely. Add cream and milk, and bring to a simmer.

Add oysters and their liquid, cayenne pepper, and Worcestershire sauce. Bring to a simmer again, and cook 1–2 minutes. Taste for seasoning, and add salt to taste. Sprinkle with parsley, stir in the sherry, and serve.

Steamed Mussels

This dish is delightfully sea-flavored. You can use it as a first course, or serve it for dinner. The garlic toasts are great for dunking into the sauce.

Prep time: less than 15 minutes • Makes 4 to 6 servings

4 lbs. mussels

2 TB. olive oil

1 medium onion, chopped

4 large cloves garlic, chopped

1 large tomato, chopped

$\frac{1}{2}$ cup dry white wine

$\frac{1}{2}$ cup tomato sauce

1 TB. lemon juice

Toasted garlic bread or packaged garlic toasts, optional

Scrub mussels and set aside. Heat olive oil in a large saucepan over moderate heat. Add onion and cook for 1 minute. Add garlic and tomato, and cook for another minute. Add wine, tomato sauce, and lemon juice, and stir to blend ingredients.

Put mussels in pan. Cover pan and turn heat to high. Steam mussels for 8–10 minutes, or until shells open, shaking the pot occasionally. Place mussels into 1 large or 4 individual serving dishes, and pour liquid over them. Serve plain or with toasted garlic bread or toasts.

 Hot Tip

Before preparing this dish, be sure to discard any mussels with shells that are cracked or open, or that do not close immediately if you tap them.

Roasted Chicken with Apples, Cider, and Wild Mushrooms

What a festive dish this is! Serve it with a green vegetable, such as sautéed spinach or steamed green beans, and some white rice or egg noodles.

Prep time: less than 30 minutes • Makes 6 servings

1 roasting chicken, about 5 lbs.

2 TB. softened butter

Salt and pepper

8 shallots, peeled

8 cloves garlic, peeled

1 cup apple cider

10 ounces fresh wild mushrooms, such as shiitake, chanterelles, morels, or portobellos

3 tart apples, peeled and cut into large chunks

$1/3$ cup bourbon

$1/4$ cup whipping cream

Preheat the oven to 400°.

Wash and dry chicken. Rub skin with softened butter, and sprinkle with salt and pepper. Place chicken, breast-side down, on a rack in a roasting pan. Add shallots and garlic to the pan. Reduce oven heat to 350°, and roast chicken 1 hour, basting occasionally with apple cider.

Turn chicken breast-side up. Add mushrooms and apple chunks to the pan. Continue to roast until a meat thermometer inserted into thickest part of thigh registers 165 to 180°. Baste occasionally with pan juices until 15 minutes before you expect the chicken to be done.

Remove chicken to a carving board, and let rest for 15 minutes before carving. Reduce oven heat to 140°. Remove vegetables and apples with a slotted spoon, and keep warm in the oven. Add bourbon to the roasting pan, stir, and bring liquid to a boil. Cook over high heat for about 2 minutes or until sauce has reduced to the consistency of heavy cream.

Add cream, stir, and keep warm over low heat. Taste for seasoning, and add salt and pepper to taste. Carve chicken, and place pieces on a serving dish surrounded by vegetables and apples. Pour sauce over vegetables and serve.

Hot Tip

The USDA recommends cooking chicken to 180° as measured in the thickest part of the thigh, but the meat is juicier when cooked to 165°, and many cooks follow this practice. You must decide whether or not to use the more conservative USDA guidelines; I have suggested alternative temperatures. Use a meat thermometer or instant read thermometer to check temperature. In any case, be sure to follow safe food-handling basics: Wash hands and defrost, wrap, and refrigerate the meat properly to keep pathogens away.

Roast Stuffed Quail

Early settlers depended on wild game to supplement their diets. It is still popular in the northwest. Quail, which is farmed now, is available in most markets, and most people find its meat mild but flavorful. These little birds also make a pretty presentation.

Prep time: less than 30 minutes • Makes 6 servings

$^1/_4$ cup dried wild mushrooms

$^1/_2$ lb. sweet Italian sausage

2 TB. olive oil

3 TB. hazelnuts, chopped

2 large shallots, chopped

1 clove garlic, chopped

2 TB. fresh parsley, chopped

$1^1/_2$ TB. fresh rosemary, chopped or $1^1/_2$ tsp. dried rosemary, crushed

4 slices homestyle white bread

Salt and pepper, to taste

12 quail

2 TB. softened butter

Preheat the oven to 425°.

Place mushrooms in a small bowl, cover with hot water, and let soak for 15 minutes, or until softened. Drain mushrooms, chop, and set aside.

Cook sausage in a skillet set over moderate heat, breaking up pieces, for 4–5 minutes or until browned. Use a slotted spoon to remove sausage from the pan, and add to mushrooms. Discard pan fat.

Heat olive oil in the pan. Add hazelnuts and cook for 2 minutes, or until brown. Add shallots and cook for another minute. Then add garlic, and cook briefly, or until shallots have softened. Add parsley and rosemary, stir, and remove pan from heat.

Trim and discard the crusts from the bread and crumble the bread into the pan. Add the sausage and mushrooms and toss the ingredients to distribute them evenly. Season with some salt and pepper.

Wash and dry quail, and then stuff with the bread mixture. Rub quail with softened butter, and sprinkle with salt and pepper. Place quail breast-side up on a rack in a roasting pan. Roast for 20–25 minutes, turning birds every 5 minutes, or until browned.

Pan-Fried Trout with Wild Mushrooms and Hazelnuts

The delicate flavor of the trout pairs nicely with the bolder wild mushrooms and hazelnuts. This dish works well with steamed or mashed potatoes and fresh cooked green peas.

Prep time: less than 30 minutes • Makes 4 servings

4 large trout filets	2 TB. olive oil
$\frac{1}{2}$ cup milk	Salt, to taste
$\frac{1}{2}$ cup all-purpose flour	$\frac{1}{3}$ cup chopped hazelnuts
$\frac{1}{2}$ tsp. salt, or to taste	$\frac{3}{4}$ cup chopped fresh wild mushrooms, such as portobello, boletus, shiitake, or oyster
$\frac{1}{4}$ tsp. paprika	2 TB. chopped fresh parsley
Black pepper, to taste	6 TB. fresh lemon juice
4 TB. butter	

Preheat the oven to 140° (warm).

Place trout filets in a dish, and pour milk over them, making sure fish is coated on all sides with milk. Combine flour, salt, paprika, and black pepper on a plate. Dredge milk-coated fish in flour mixture and set aside.

Heat 2 tablespoons butter with olive oil in a large skillet, over moderate heat. When butter has melted and looks foamy, add fish. Sprinkle with salt to taste. Cook fish for 3–4 minutes per side, or until lightly crispy. Place on a serving platter and keep warm in the oven.

Melt remaining butter in the skillet. Add nuts, and cook for 2 minutes. Add mushrooms and parsley, and cook for another 2 minutes, or until nuts are lightly browned. Add lemon juice, stir, and remove from heat. Spoon sauce over fish, and serve.

Hot Tip

Be sure the trout filets are each large enough to serve one person (6–8 ounces). Instead, you may use small whole, filleted, and butterflied trout, 1 fish per person.

Oysters with Spinach and Crème Fraîche

This is a rich, extravagant dish, perfect as a first course at dinner when you are expecting company.

Prep time: less than 30 minutes • Makes 6 servings

2 dozen oysters

10 oz. fresh spinach

2 TB. butter

1 large shallot, chopped

¼ cup plain dry breadcrumbs

½ cup apple cider or applejack

5 TB. Crème Fraîche or dairy sour cream

Preheat the oven to 450°.

Have oysters shucked, but ask the fishmonger to save half the shells (24) and the oyster liquor (the liquid from the oysters). Bring a large pot half-filled with water to a boil. Wash spinach and put into boiling water for 30 seconds. Drain spinach under cold water. Squeeze to remove as much water as possible. Chop spinach and set aside.

Heat butter in a skillet over moderate heat. When butter has melted and looks foamy, add shallot, and cook for 2 minutes, or until softened. Add spinach, and cook for a minute or so to evaporate any remaining liquid. Add breadcrumbs, mix in thoroughly, and cook for another minute. Remove from heat and set aside.

Combine oyster liquor and apple cider in a saucepan, and bring to a boil over high heat. Cook until liquid has reduced to ¼ cup. Add this and the Crème Fraîche to the spinach mixture. Place each oyster on a half shell. Top with spinach. Bake for 5 minutes, or until hot.

Hot Tip

Crème Fraîche is available in the dairy cases of many supermarkets and gourmet specialty shops. Or you can make your own Crème Fraîche: Combine 1 cup whipping cream (not ultra-pasteurized) and 3 tablespoons stirred plain yogurt or buttermilk. Whisk ingredients until well blended, pour mixture into a saucepan, and cook over moderate heat for 2 minutes or until mixture is lukewarm. Pour ingredients into a jar. Cover the jar and let mixture stand at room temperature for 12–15 hours or until it has thickened to the consistency of stirred yogurt. Refrigerate the sauce at least 24 hours to allow the flavors to mellow.

Oven-Roasted Salmon with Horseradish Crust

This dish is incredibly easy to make. You can prepare it a few hours ahead of serving time, and pop it into the oven just before dinner.

Prep time: less than 15 minutes • Makes 4 servings

$1\frac{1}{2}$ to 2 lbs. filet of salmon, preferably wild salmon

3 TB. Dijon mustard

3 TB. prepared white horseradish

Juice of half a large lemon

Salt and pepper

Preheat the oven to 475°.

Place salmon in a baking dish. Mix mustard and horse-radish together, and spread over the surface of fish. Sprinkle with lemon juice, salt, and pepper. Roast fish for 12–20 minutes, depending on thickness and degree of doneness desired.

Hot Tip
Salmon tastes best when it is almost cooked through, but still rare at the center.

Grilled or Broiled Salmon

This simple dish is easy to prepare; perfect when you need an easy but tasty dinner.

Prep time: less than 15 minutes • Makes 4 servings

6 TB. olive oil

3 TB. lemon juice

2 tsp. Dijon mustard

1 TB. fresh parsley, chopped

1 TB. fresh oregano (or 1 tsp. dried), chopped

1 TB. fresh chives, chopped

Salt and pepper

4 salmon steaks, $1\frac{1}{4}$"–$1\frac{1}{2}$" thick

Mix olive oil, lemon juice, mustard, parsley, oregano, chives, and some salt and pepper in a small bowl. Place salmon in a stainless-steel, ceramic, or other nonreactive dish. Pour marinade over the fish, and coat all sides. Let fish marinate, refrigerated, for 15–60 minutes.

Preheat an outdoor grill or oven broiler. Cook steaks, turning once, for 5–6 minutes per side, or until cooked to desired doneness.

Grilled Teriyaki Chicken

The sweet, soy-based marinade keeps the white meat moist and gives it lots of flavor. The honey gives the breasts a gorgeous brown color.

Prep time: less than 15 minutes • Makes 4 servings

4 large skinless, boneless chicken-breast halves

1 clove garlic, finely chopped

2 scallions, finely chopped

1 TB. fresh ginger, chopped

$^{1}/_{2}$ tsp. powdered mustard

3 TB. soy sauce

2 TB. rice wine or sherry

1 tsp. sesame oil

$^{1}/_{2}$ cup honey or corn syrup

Remove any fat and cartilage from breasts and set aside in refrigerator.

Place garlic, scallions, ginger, mustard, soy sauce, rice wine, sesame oil, and honey into a small saucepan. Bring to a simmer, and cook 10 minutes over low-moderate heat. Let mixture cool. Pour cooled mixture over chicken, and marinate for 30 minutes.

Preheat an outdoor grill or oven broiler. Remove chicken from liquid, and grill or broil at moderate temperature. Turn pieces occasionally, brushing with more sauce, for 12–15 minutes, depending on thickness of breasts, or until cooked through.

Hot Tip

For a good party hors d'oeuvre, make this dish with chicken wings. Use 18 chicken wings, cut the wings at the joints into 3 separate pieces, discard the wing tips, and grill for about 15 minutes, turning occasionally.

Spiced Iced Coffee

This is a refreshing drink on a summer's day. To jazz it up, you could add half a scoop of ice cream.

Prep time: less than 15 minutes   •   Makes 4 servings

4 cups strong coffee

3 TB. brown sugar

1 (4-inch) cinnamon stick, broken

8 whole cloves

8 whole dried allspice berries

1/3 cup brandy

Ice cubes

Cream, if desired

Pour coffee into a bowl. Add brown sugar, cinnamon stick, cloves, allspice berries, and brandy. Let coffee cool in refrigerator. Strain coffee into tall glasses filled with ice cubes. Stir in cream to taste, if desired.

Blackberry Fool

This simple, fluffy dessert is easy to make, and you can do it well ahead of serving time.

Prep time: less than 15 minutes   •   Makes 8 servings

3 cups fresh blackberries

1/4 cup sugar

1 tsp. freshly grated orange peel

2 cups whipping cream

2 TB. dark rum or brandy, or 2 tsp. vanilla extract

Crush berries using the back of a fork, or pulse in a food processor, but do not purée completely. Berries should be in small pieces. Add sugar and orange peel, and toss gently.

Let mixture macerate for 30 minutes. Whip the cream until it stands in stiff peaks. Stir in rum. Fold whipped cream and berries together. Spoon into individual serving dishes, and refrigerate for at least 30 minutes.

Hot Tip

Try these variations:

- ◆ Use strawberries, raspberries, blueberries, or a mixture of berries, instead of the blackberries.
- ◆ Omit the orange peel, and substitute 1 teaspoon ground cinnamon, nutmeg, or ginger.

Baked Apples with Dried Figs, Hazelnuts, and Cider

It may be worth preparing these just for their fragrance as they bake in the oven. Baked apples are great for dessert, but they also make a splendid breakfast. The best apple varieties for baking are York Imperial, Rome Beauty, and Cortland.

Prep time: less than 15 minutes • Makes 4 servings

Special equipment: apple corer

4 large baking apples	1 cup apple cider
½ cup chopped dried figs	Ground cinnamon
2 TB. lightly toasted hazelnuts	1 TB. butter
2 TB. honey	

Preheat the oven to 375°.

Wash and core apples. Leave small portion of core at the bottom. Peel apples halfway down from the top, and put in a baking dish. Mix together chopped dried figs, hazelnuts, honey, and 3 tablespoons cider. Place mixture inside hollowed apple cores. Pour remaining cider over apples.

Sprinkle apples lightly with cinnamon. Cut butter into four equal portions, and place on top of apples. Bake apples for 50–60 minutes or until tender, basting occasionally with juices.

Hot Tip

Try these variations:

- ◆ Use raisins instead of dried figs.
- ◆ Use almonds instead of hazelnuts.
- ◆ Use maple syrup instead of honey.
- ◆ Use orange juice instead of apple cider.

Strawberry Rhubarb Pie

This pie is tangy and sweet all at the same time. Serve it still-warm with a scoop of vanilla ice cream so that it can melt into the fruit.

Prep time: less than 30 minutes   •   Makes 1 (9") pie

Dough for two-crust pie (see Basic Pie Dough, Appendix C)

1–1¼ lbs. rhubarb, cut into 1" slices

1 pint strawberries, cut in half

⅔ cup sugar

¼ tsp. salt

5 TB. all-purpose flour

1 tsp. grated lemon or orange peel

¼ tsp. grated nutmeg

1 TB. butter

Milk

On a floured surface, roll out half the dough and fit into a 9" pie pan. Preheat the oven to 400°.

Combine rhubarb, strawberries, sugar, salt, flour, lemon or orange peel, and nutmeg in a bowl. Spoon filling into pie pan. Cut butter into small chunks and place on top of filling.

Roll remaining dough, and place on top of fruit. Crimp edges to seal pie. Brush the crust with a small amount of milk. Bake for 45 minutes or until crust is crisp and golden brown.

Pear and Ginger Crisp

The fresh ginger gives warmth and energy to this tender-filled, crispy-topped dessert.

Prep time: less than 30 minutes • Makes 6 servings

For the filling:

6 ripe pears, preferably Comice, Anjou, or Bartlett

Juice of a half lemon

1 tsp. fresh ginger, grated

$^1/_2$ tsp. cinnamon

6 TB. brown sugar

2 TB. all-purpose flour

Pinch of salt

Preheat the oven to 400°.

Peel, core, and slice pears. Toss with juice of half a lemon. Add ginger, cinnamon, brown sugar, flour, and salt. Mix ingredients and put in a baking dish. Set aside.

For the topping:

$^3/_4$ cup all-purpose flour

$^1/_2$ cup light brown sugar

$^1/_4$ tsp. salt

6 TB. butter

To make topping, combine flour, brown sugar, and salt. Add butter in chunks, and work into dry ingredients with your hands or with a pastry blender until mixture resembles coarse meal. Scatter over pear mixture.

Bake for 35 minutes or until golden brown. Let cool slightly before serving. Best if served warm.

Hazelnut Cake

This is a beautiful cake and a fabulously moist, rich, and delicious dessert. It freezes well, too.

Prep time: less than 30 minutes • Makes 1 (10") cake

Special equipment: 10" springform pan

8 eggs, separated	¹/₄ tsp. salt
³/₄ cup sugar	2 cups whipping cream
1¹/₂ cups hazelnuts, ground	1 TB. sugar
¹/₄ cup dry plain breadcrumbs	3 TB. hazelnuts, toasted, chopped
2 tsp. freshly grated lemon peel	

Butter and lightly flour a 10" springform pan. Preheat the oven to 300°.

Beat egg yolks and ¹/₂ cup sugar in an electric mixer set at medium speed for 4–5 minutes, or until thick and pale. Stir in ground hazelnuts, breadcrumbs, and lemon peel.

In a separate bowl, beat egg whites and salt in an electric mixer set at high speed until soft peaks form. Gradually add remaining ¹/₄ cup sugar. Beat whites until they stand in stiff peaks. Fold half the whites into egg yolks, and then fold remaining whites in. Pour batter into the prepared pan.

Bake cake 45 minutes or until golden on top and a cake tester inserted into center comes out clean. Remove cake from the oven and let cool in the pan. Remove the sides of the pan. Slit cake horizontally into 3 layers.

Whip cream with the 1 tablespoon sugar until thick. Spread whipped cream between cake layers and on top of cake. Garnish top with chopped toasted hazelnuts. Refrigerate cake until serving time.

Part 2

An Emerging National Cuisine

During the last several decades of the nineteenth century, America was defining itself politically, culturally, and economically on the world scene. A less localized, more nationally focused cuisine emerged as our country grew, prospered, and changed.

The next two chapters will explain how immigration, political issues, transportation, communication, our curiosity about the foods we eat, and the enormous technological advances that we made all impacted our food traditions and paved the way for mainstream American cookery.

Chapter 9

The Melting Pot

In This Chapter

- America's great culinary melting pot
- Survival by potato: our Irish-American heritage
- How Italian-American cuisine came to be
- Is it kosher? Jewish-American cuisine
- Chop suey comes of age: Chinese cooking in America
- At the bodega: Latino food

America is a land of immigrants. As you've seen in earlier chapters, American cuisine has always reflected elements of other cultures. New England's foods were predominantly English, the Dutch influenced cooking in the mid-Atlantic, and settlers from Europe and Asia brought their food traditions with them as they cleared the plains and prairies to build the west.

The mass migrations of the nineteenth and early twentieth century changed the country's culinary focus quickly, powerfully, and permanently. Millions of people, including Irish, Italians, Chinese, and Eastern European Jews arrived here, leaving their homelands forever. They came to flee religious persecution or to find gold, to escape the aftermath of crop failures, and to take advantage of job opportunities. Most were poor.

These people also brought their food cultures with them, often reinventing dishes by adding new ingredients and adapting new techniques, the way others had done here before them. Their presence changed the way our nation eats. Americans of all backgrounds began to enjoy the specific cuisines of the new groups and learned to eat a variety of ethnic foods—American style.

Subsequent waves of immigration have brought people from Latin America, Asia, Europe, and the Middle East, all of whom have made a contribution to our culinary culture. We are the richer for their input.

America, Land of the Free, the Brave, and the Immigrant

The Pilgrims were foreigners to America, and so were the Dutch tradesmen who developed New Amsterdam. In fact, all Americans, except for those who belong to Native American tribes, are descended from immigrants. American cuisine more or less absorbed the food traditions of the groups that settled here for the first two and a half centuries. Who could deny such American classics as English pie, German frankfurters, French fries, Neapolitan pizza, or Mexican tortillas? But in the middle of the nineteenth century, something changed. Millions of people came to live here from numerous countries, and Americans learned to eat ethnic.

The Pride of Erin

The Irish were the first group who arrived in the massive migrations that began in 1850 and ended in 1920. They comprised the largest number of newcomers from any one country. They fled their homes after a potato blight, which began in 1846, left millions dead or starving. They were dreadfully poor and had been dependent on the potato as the sole source of nourishment.

Kitchen Clue

When mashing potatoes, always use a fork, a potato masher, an implement called a ricer, or a hand mixer set on low speed. These tools will keep potatoes fluffy. Avoid using a food processor to mash potatoes: It turns potatoes into something resembling wallpaper paste.

In Praise of the Potato

Because the potato kept the Irish alive, their cooks became world masters of potato cookery. On holidays, many Irish cooks still prepare some of the traditional dishes. The spud is used in everything from scones and soups to salads and casseroles. Colcannon is a luscious melange of buttery mashed potatoes laden with morsels of fresh cooked cabbage or kale, plus leeks and milk. Boxty is the Irish potato pancake, fluffy inside with a crispy crust, and Champ is a mountain of mashed potatoes with leeks or scallions.

Oat Cuisine

Samuel Johnson, the English lexicographer who wrote the first *Dictionary of the English Language* (1755), called oats "a grain which in England is generally given to horses but in Scotland supports the people." Poor folk in Scotland and in Ireland, where oats flourish in the moist, cool climate, made do with oats, which at the time seemed like lesser stuff than the English gentry's refined white flour. Today, when oats are hailed as healthy and everyone has discovered how delicious they are, Johnson would rethink his definition. Fortunately, Irish and Scottish cooks brought their oat cuisine with them to America and have given us such appetizing fare as oat scones, cooked oatmeal, biscuits, muffins, and quickbreads, all fine for breakfast and coffee breaks, and as accompaniments for soup.

> **Did You Know ...**
>
> Regular and quick-cooking oats can be used interchangeably in recipes, unless otherwise specified. In both cases, the grain is hulled to remove the inedible outer coating, and then cleaned, steamed, toasted, resteamed, and flattened into flakes by steel rollers. The difference is that quick oats are cut into several pieces before being rolled, in order to shorten cooking time. Regular oats are left whole. Instant oatmeal grains are steamed longer, cut into tinier pieces, and rolled thinner. They do not usually work well in recipes calling for regular or quick oats.

Beyond Corned Beef and Cabbage

On St. Patrick's Day, everyone in the United States becomes Irish for a day, and many make corned beef and cabbage, which is famous in America but not well known in the Emerald Isle. Corned beef and cabbage may be popular, but contemporary Irish-American cooks are trying, successfully, to build a proud cuisine that goes well beyond this dish. There's savory Roasted Leg of Lamb or Lamb Stew; Cockle and Mussel Chowder, rich with cream and dotted with crispy bacon; Roasted Chicken basted with Irish whiskey and cider; Trout fried with a crispy oatmeal crust; and moist Irish Soda bread, to name a few.

Mangiare con Gusto!

Over four million Italians came to America after 1880, because economic privation made it difficult to feed their families in Europe. Italian food, above all others, became the most beloved ethnic cuisine in America.

Pan-Italian

As recently as a generation ago, many thought of Italian food as a monolith of red sauce and pasta, antipasto, and minestrone soup. But in Italy, cooking differs from region to region. The first Italians who came to America were from small towns and had little interaction with one another. Tuscan villagers, who ate polenta, were not familiar with Genoa's pesto or with a Neapolitan dish called pizza. But when they lived as neighbors in America, they borrowed freely from each others' regional culinary coffers to create Italian-American cuisine. Ingredients such as pasta, tomato sauce, *olive oil*, and cheese were universally accepted by all Italian-Americans. They supported their culture in every way possible, importing Italian goods such as canned tomatoes and olive oil from Europe, building food industries such as pasta factories, and employing Italian workers in their businesses. Feast days featured pan-Italian items such as grilled sausage and Italian bread, which continue to be staples in the Italian-American kitchen, although back in the old country each town had its own kind of sausage, bread, and other particular foods.

> **What Is It?**
>
> There are three grades of **olive oil**. *Extra virgin*, the highest grade, is the least acidic, and has the finest flavor and the most appealing aroma. It is the best choice for salads and subtle dishes. *Virgin* is the next-best grade, and then *pure*. All are made from the first pressing of olives, but pure may also blend second and third pressings.

The Icon

Most people would pick pasta as the icon of Italian cuisine. But at the time of the migrations to America, it was eaten regularly only among people who had some extra money for their table. The poor ate it only on Sunday and holidays. Small wonder, then, that pasta became the food of choice when the immigrants came to this country. The ingredients were cheaper here, jobs more plentiful, and the people could afford to eat better. By the dawn of the twentieth century, pasta was a favorite not only in Italian-American homes but also Italian restaurants frequented by other Americans. Other than spaghetti or linguine cooked with the ubiquitous tomato sauce, though, most Americans knew little about macaroni products. Pasta came of age in the United States in the 1980s. All of a sudden, people were feasting on Pasta Pesto (fresh basil, Parmesan cheese, and pignoli nuts) and other "new" recipes such as Pasta Puttanesca (tomatoes, olives, capers, and garlic). Today, pasta is thoroughly integrated into American cuisine, and many recipes using macaroni products have no Italian origins. Different pasta shapes take different sauces:

- Strands (spaghetti, fusilli, angel hair) are best with olive oil, butter, thin tomato sauces, and cream sauces.

- Flat ribbons (linguine, fettuccine, papardelle, tagliatelle) pair well with thick cream and cheese sauces, smooth meat sauces, and thick tomato sauces.

- Tubular pastas (macaroni, penne, bucatini, rigatoni, ziti) fare best with hearty, chunky vegetable or meat sauces that coat the surface and cling to the pasta's hollows and grooves. They are also fine for casserole dishes such as macaroni and cheese.

- Odd-shaped pastas (farfelle, orecchietto, rotelle) are fine with cheese sauces and with chunky vegetable and meat sauces.

- Stuffed pastas (manicotti, shells, ravioli, tortellini) have meat, vegetable, or cheese fillings, and may be cloaked with butter, olive oil, or tomato or cream sauce.

- Tiny pastas (ditalini, orzo, pastina) are used in soups and salads.

Be sure to buy pasta made with durum semolina flour, which is made from hard wheat that holds up well during cooking. Use plenty of lightly salted water, and cook the pasta until it is al dente (literally, "to the tooth"), or slightly chewy and resilient. Add sauce as soon as the pasta is drained, to prevent the pieces from sticking together.

It's in the Sauce

Some Italian-Americans make tomato sauce quickly, using fresh Roma (plum) tomatoes and basil, while others prefer long, slow-cooked versions made with canned tomatoes; thick, tangy tomato paste; and enrichments of red wine, pork, sausage, or meatballs. There are many variations on basic tomato sauce (see the Basic Tomato Sauce recipe in Appendix C).

Kitchen Clue

Use plum tomatoes when making sauce; they are less watery than regular tomatoes. If you use canned tomatoes, buy "Italian-style" plum tomatoes, preferably the San Marzano variety. This variety of plum tomato comes from an area near Naples and is considered the best quality for tomato sauce. A 28-ounce can contains about a dozen tomatoes, about $1^1/_4$ pounds, plus a cup of liquid.

A Show of Opulence

When Italians first came to this country, they served pasta and sauce plain, without meat. Other than a few well-known ragus such as Bolognese sauce, authentic Italian sauce contains no meat. Recipes with large amounts of meat—spaghetti and meatballs, for example—were invented by Italian-American cooks as a sign of opulence. One such meat-with-sauce favorite is Veal Parmigiana, made of breaded, fried cutlets topped with tomato sauce and cheese.

From the Pushcarts

It Italy, families depended on vegetables for nourishment, and it was natural, when they came to America, to grow familiar varieties. In the cities, Italian-American vendors sold the vegetables from pushcarts and, later, from produce markets; they were instrumental in introducing other Americans to plum tomatoes, broccoli, zucchini, fava beans, eggplant, and fennel, and to herbs such as basil, oregano, and rosemary. On Sundays and holidays in the old country, the poor ate vegetables with rice or pasta in the form of soup; it became Minestrone Soup in the United States.

Time for Pie

The first pizzeria opened in New York in 1905, serving thin-crusted Neapolitan-style pizza topped with tomato sauce and cheese. Most New Yorkers didn't know about it. In fact, pizza didn't catch on until after World War II. Soldiers who had been in Italy during the war had tasted the stuff and wanted more. Before long, there were pizzerias throughout the country. Some people prefer Chicago-style, deep-dish, thick-crusted pizzas, while others swear by Neapolitan thin, crispy versions. Tomato sauce and cheese toppings are still the favorites. But pizzas, like pasta, have come a long way. Today we can dine on "white" ricotta-cheese pizzas with clams, but no red sauce. Or have our tomato-sauce pizzas topped with a variety of ingredients such as peppers, anchovies, mushrooms, sausage, pepperoni, olives, and so on. And, of course, there are pizzas that have no connection whatsoever with the original Italian versions—fruit pizzas and goat-cheese pizzas, for example.

Cheese, Please

In recent years, Americans have discovered the vastness of Italy's food styles, and have embraced it wholeheartedly. We now enjoy Italian regional dishes such as polenta, risotto, Osso Buco, and frittatas, among others. Two traditional Italian cheeses, mozzarella and Parmesan, have always been American favorites, and today they are more widely available. We also know much more about how to use them to advantage:

- Fresh cow's-milk mozzarella cheese is delicate and spongy, tasting somewhat like rich, fresh, solidified milk. It is fragile, lasting only a few days in the fridge. Immerse it in cold water, and cover with plastic wrap. Use it for hors d'oeuvres or salad.

- Packaged mozzarella does not have the same fresh, vivid taste as the fresh kind and is rubbery, although it is fine for pizza and casseroles. It lasts up to two weeks in the fridge and six months in the freezer.

- Buffalo mozzarella is made from the milk of water buffalo. It has a rich, sweet, intense flavor and is wonderful when grilled or used as an accompaniment to ripe summer tomatoes. Sprinkle with fresh basil, and drizzle with some extra-virgin olive oil.

- Parmesan cheese is robust, rich, and salty, made from partially skimmed cow's milk. The best Parmesan is Parmigiano-Reggiano, with its fruity aroma. Grana Padano is another Parmesan variety, but it is not aged as long as Parmigiano-Reggiano, nor does it have the same rich, intense flavor. Although most Americans grate Parmesan cheese over pasta or salad, you can also serve it as a sideboard cheese. It pairs deliciously with hearty Italian wines such as Barolo, Barbera, Brunello, Barbaresco, and Chianti Riserva.

Most Americans use Parmesan as their grating cheese of choice for pasta and salad. In southern Italy, cooks prefer Pecorino, a nutty-tasting sheep's-milk cheese. You can combine these cheeses for use over pasta, pizza, casseroles, salads, and so on.

Is It Kosher?

Twenty-three people sailed from the West Indies to New Amsterdam in 1654, to escape the Inquisition. They were Sephardic Jews, with origins in Spain and Portugal. Over the next two centuries, Jews from Germany and other central European countries emigrated here. By 1880, there were about 250,000 Jewish-Americans in the United States. At the time, anti-Semitism was virulent in Europe. Restrictive laws made it almost impossible for

 Fein on Food

Potato pancakes (*latkes*) are served in traditional Jewish-American homes on Hanukkah, the Festival of Lights. Originally, latkes were made with meat. But the poorest families in Eastern Europe couldn't afford meat and so they substituted potatoes. No one seemed to mind!

Jews to own property or to engage in certain professions; violent pogroms destroyed entire Jewish towns. Millions fled to America from Russia, Poland, Rumania, and other countries in the East. They were highly literate, but poor. When people talk about traditional Jewish food, they usually mean the cuisine of these Eastern European Jews. Interestingly, their foods differed greatly, depending upon where they lived. But in America, it blended together as Jewish-American cuisine.

Kashruth, the Tie That Binds

Despite differences in Jewish cooking from country to country, the dietary laws governing which foods are fit to eat (*kosher*) and which are prohibited (*treyf*) are common to all observant Jews. No pork is permitted, and, because fish must have fins and scales, shellfood such as shrimp and lobster is forbidden. Meat may not be eaten at the same time as dairy products—no cheeseburgers. Other rules regulate the butchering and preparation of food. At the time of the great migration to America, many Jews could not find kosher products, and others wanted to assimilate into the American culture. Judaism became more lenient in America, and Jewish-Americans felt that they did not have to follow the dietary laws. Today, most Jewish-Americans are not kosher, although some may keep kosher homes, or eat shrimp but not pork, and so on.

Dairy for Dinner

Because Jews ate meatless meals regularly, they developed delicious foods using dairy products. Some of the dishes were so appealing that Americans of almost all ethnic groups came to love them: smoked salmon on bagels with cream cheese, for example, and other fish specialties such as smoked whitefish and pickled herring. Crispy Potato Pancakes with applesauce are also favorites, as are Blintzes, which are pancakes stuffed with cheese or fruit and topped with tangy sour cream. Among the most treasured recipes from the old country are kugels, or noodle puddings. Depending on where the family came from, a recipe for kugel could include chicken fat and onions or cabbage, or it may be sweet and seasoned with cinnamon. Some kugels are *pareve*, while others are dairy-rich with cheese and sour cream and perhaps some chopped fruit or raisins. As for dairy desserts, Jewish-style cheesecake is one of America's top choices. Cheesecake was made famous at Reuben's Restaurant in New York, and then at Lindy's, where the dessert became an American icon.

> **What Is It?**
>
> The word **pareve** marked on food packages indicates that it is a neutral ingredient that Jews may eat with either meat or dairy. Pareve ingredients include eggs, vegetables, grains, and fish.

Putting Meat on the Table

Jewish families, like others who came to America hungry, wanted more meat in their diets. They adapted meat recipes to conform to the dietary laws. Jewish versions of Rumanian pastrami and German frankfurters were reinvented with beef instead of pork. The "deli" became a place where Jews could dine out on foods that became renowned among the American community at large: overstuffed sandwiches made with such Jewish-American specialties as pastrami, salami, tongue, chopped liver, and corned beef, served with pickles and sauerkraut, coleslaw, and sour tomatoes. At home, meat meals often included pot roasts and other kinds of braised dishes that are cooked slowly, for a long time—perfect for tougher, kosher portions such as brisket.

Let's Eat!

Jewish culture encourages eating well. Before the migrations to America, even the poorest families in Europe celebrated the Sabbath as a special time, when the most elaborate meal was served. Familiar foods such as gefilte fish, chicken soup with dumplings (*knaidlach*), and kugel might be on the menu, and, of course, a tender, fluffy, egg-rich challah bread. Dessert could be an ethereally light spongecake or a dense, sticky-sweet Honeycake. Today, traditional Sabbath celebrations may include some of these foods. Religious holidays also have food associations. The New Year (*Rosh Hashanah*) is linked to sweet ingredients such as honey. *Shavuot* features Blintzes and Cheesecake. Hanukkah has its latkes; Purim, its filled triangle pastries (*Haman-taschen*). Passover, an eight-day festival commemorating the Exodus from Egypt, is the most food-oriented. Certain items such as bread and pasta products may not be eaten; but families feast on special foods such as matzah ball soup and other matzah dishes, as well as specific symbolic foods such as haroset, a fruit and nut relish.

Mini-Recipe

Matzah Brei (2 servings)   Break 3 pieces of matzah into pieces and put them in a colander. Pour 3 cups of boiling water over them. Put the moistened matzah into a bowl. Mix in 2 beaten eggs and some salt and pepper. Let rest for 3–4 minutes. Heat some butter in a skillet over moderate heat. When the butter has melted and looks foamy, add the matzah mixture and flatten it slightly. Cook for 2–3 minutes, or until the bottom is lightly crispy. Turn the pancake over and cook on the second side. Serve with maple syrup, applesauce, or sour cream.

The Modern Jewish Table

The Jewish-American diet has changed over the years. Some of the old favorites remain, but today, because of concerns about fat and cholesterol, modern families eat less meat and dairy. Recipes have been updated. Few home cooks use chicken fat, preferring vegetable oil instead, and heavy, time-consuming dishes are part of the memory bank, rather than the recipe file. There's also an increased awareness of Middle-Eastern and other kinds of Jewish dishes such as Hummus, Baba Ghanoush, and Falafel. Jewish-American food, like other ethnic cuisines, keeps changing.

Chop Suey Comes of Age

The first American immigrants from Asia were the Chinese, mostly men, who came to make their fortunes during the California Gold Rush (1848). Unfortunately, as with most others, things didn't pan out. The men went to work in mining camps and as railroad crew. Some opened restaurants, catering mainly to other Chinese. Eventually, a few adventurous Americans of other ethnicities tried the food, and so began the American love affair with Chinese cuisine. At first, the food was tailored to American tastes: No one ever heard of chop suey (a mixture of meat and vegetables such as bean sprouts, mushrooms, and bell peppers) in the old country. Little by little, Americans learned to enjoy egg rolls, fried rice, barbecued spareribs, chow mein, shrimp in lobster sauce, and a host of other savory, mild-tasting Cantonese specialties. When immigration from China opened up in the late 1960s, we began to favor Chinese dishes from other regions, including Peking Duck and hot, peppery Sichuanese Chicken with Peanuts. Chinese cuisine continues to be popular in America. For more information, see Chapter 10.

At the Bodega

In the period after World War II, Americans began to welcome large numbers of settlers from Latin cultures in the Caribbean, including Puerto Rico, Cuba, and the Dominican Republic. The people are a diverse group with Spanish ancestry in common. Their cuisine is a melting pot of Spanish, Caribbean, and African foods and flavors. Like all other immigrants, Latinos brought their culinary traditions to America and continued to adapt recipes and cooking styles. In recent years, this cuisine has become more popular, especially in the large cities where Nuevo Latino cooks are reinventing the old classics. Bodegas, or small groceries, that offer Latino specialties have cropped up everywhere.

To Every Season

Latino flavors depend on special combinations of herbs, spices, and condiments. Some of the core items are the following:

◆ **Sofrito,** a mixture of sautéed vegetables, used in a variety of dishes. It usually contains bell peppers, onion, and garlic, but may also include chorizo sausage or ham, cilantro, chopped olives, chili peppers or tomatoes, and spices and herbs such as cumin and oregano.

◆ **Adobo** is a blend of garlic, salt, black pepper, oregano, and capers mixed with olive oil and vinegar. It provides a heady aroma and bountiful flavor to grilled beef and pork.

◆ **Achiote** (Annatto seeds), has no flavor but is used to give light foods such as rice a vibrant yellow color. The seeds are heated with lard or vegetable oil, and then strained out; the colored cooking fat remains.

◆ **Mojo** is a citrus-based marinade that gives a vibrant flavor to grilled foods. It can also be used as a sauce for vegetables.

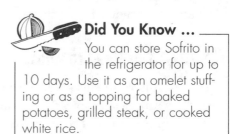

Did You Know ...
You can store Sofrito in the refrigerator for up to 10 days. Use it as an omelet stuffing or as a topping for baked potatoes, grilled steak, or cooked white rice.

An Important Combo

Beans and rice are an integral part of Latino cuisine. Puerto Rican cooks may use red beans, while Cuban cooks almost invariably choose black ones. Traditional recipes combine the two ingredients in one casserole. Classic Beans and Rice, American style, is on the mild side, with a Sofrito base, but some people splash seasonings such as hot pepper sauce or vinegar on top.

Kitchen Clue
Plantains can be difficult to peel. Here's how to do it: Cut off both ends with a sharp knife. Make three or four lengthwise slits on the surface, taking care not to cut into the flesh of the plantain. Place the plantain in a sink full of hot water and let it soak for 10 minutes. Pull the skin off with your fingers.

A Different Kind of Banana

Latino-American cooking often features plantains, which are related to bananas. These banana cousins are used in all states of ripeness from dark green to black-ripe, and may appear at any point of a meal, from appetizer to dessert. Plantains are almost always cooked before being eaten. Two particularly prized dishes are Tostones, which are twice-fried plantain fritters that are hot and crispy and sprinkled with salt, and Mofongo, which are mashed fried plantains and crispy pork cracklings (or other meat) made into small balls.

America the Melting Pot

America has become home to many ethnic groups: Greeks, Japanese, Koreans, Swiss, Bohemian, Czech, Hungarian, Portuguese, and many others. All brought recipes with them, and many of these recipes continue to bring enjoyment to families throughout the United States. While new immigrant groups learned about America and American food, they all contributed in some way to the melting pot of American cuisine.

The Least You Need to Know

- ◆ American cuisine blends dozens of diverse culinary cultures, including Native American; the earliest immigrants from England, Holland, and Spain; and other European, African, and Asian peoples who have made their home here.

- ◆ Irish-American cooks have given us many delicious potato, seafood, and oat-based dishes.

- ◆ Italian-American food is America's best-loved ethnic cuisine, with such favorites as pasta and tomato sauce, Veal Parmigiana, and Lasagna.

- ◆ Jewish-American cuisine embraces the foods of Eastern European Jews and Jews from other parts of the world; although their foods differ, they all have kosher dietary laws in common.

- ◆ Chinese-American cuisine is a rich mixture of dishes such as Chop Suey, invented especially for Americans, and a sophisticated treasure of dishes with origins in various regions of China.

- ◆ Latino foods are becoming more popular in recent years and feature such dishes as Black Beans and Rice and Mofongo, made with plantains.

Mofongo

This recipe was given to me by my friend Jorge Ramos, whose father was a restaurateur in Puerto Rico. He acknowledges that the dish is usually made with pork, but says the lobster makes it all the better! Serve as an appetizer or side dish.

Prep time: less than 30 minutes   •   Makes 12 or more balls

5 green plantains	1 small onion, chopped
Vegetable oil for deep-fat frying	3 large cloves garlic, chopped
2 TB. butter	$\frac{1}{2}$ lb. cooked lobster meat, chopped

Peel plantains and cut into 1" slices. Heat vegetable oil in a deep fryer. Using a few pieces at a time, deep fry plantain slices until golden. Remove pieces with a slotted spoon or skimmer, and place in a bowl.

Heat butter in a skillet over moderate heat. When butter has melted and looks foamy, add onion and cook for 2 minutes, or until begins to soften. Add garlic and lobster meat, and cook for another 2 minutes. Add lobster mixture to plantains. Mash ingredients with a potato masher (or use a mortar and pestle). Shape into 12 or more balls. Serve warm or at room temperature.

Minestrone Soup

This is the traditional Italian-American vegetable soup. A hot, crusty chunk of Italian or garlic bread makes a perfect accompaniment.

Prep time: less than 45 minutes • Makes 8 servings

2 oz. salt pork, cut into pieces

3 TB. olive oil

1 TB. butter

1 medium onion, chopped

2 cloves garlic, chopped

2 large carrots, sliced

2 large all-purpose potatoes, peeled and diced

2 stalks celery, sliced

1 medium zucchini, cut into bite-size pieces

1 1/2 cups frozen peas

1 cup frozen corn kernels

1 (28-oz.) can Italian-style tomatoes, undrained

7 cups vegetable or chicken stock or water

1 bay leaf

1–2 TB. chopped fresh basil, or 1–2 tsp. dried basil

1/2 tsp. dried oregano

Salt and black pepper, to taste

1 cup cooked beans (cannelini or kidney); drained canned beans are fine

1/2 cup elbow macaroni or white rice

Freshly grated Parmesan cheese

Fry salt pork in a soup pot over low-moderate heat for 5–6 minutes or until crispy. Remove pork and set pieces aside.

Drain fat from the pot. Raise the heat to moderate and add olive oil and butter to the pot. When butter has melted and looks foamy, add onion and cook for 2–3 minutes. Add garlic, carrots, potatoes, celery, zucchini, peas, and corn and cook for 2–3 minutes. Add reserved salt pork, tomatoes, stock, bay leaf, basil, oregano, and salt and pepper.

Hot Tip _____
Although salt pork adds a lot of flavor, you can eliminate this step if you prefer.

Cover the pot partially and simmer for 30 minutes. Add beans and rice or macaroni. Cover the pot and cook another 20 minutes or until macaroni or rice is tender. Serve hot, sprinkled with Parmesan cheese.

Irish Cockle and Mussel Chowder

This opulent soup shows the richness of Irish-American cooking. It's fine for any season.

Prep time: less than 45 minutes   •   Makes 8 servings

1¹/₂ lbs. cockles or littleneck clams

1¹/₂ lbs. mussels

2 cups water

¹/₂ cup white wine

1 onion, peeled and quartered

1 stalk celery

2 cloves garlic, cut in half

1 bay leaf

2 sprigs thyme or ¹/₂ tsp. dried

3 sprigs fresh parsley

3 slices bacon

2 leeks

4 medium all-purpose potatoes, peeled and cut into small chunks

Enough water plus stock drained from shellfish to make 6 cups liquid

Salt and freshly cracked black pepper

Freshly grated nutmeg

1 cup cream (light, whipping, or half-and-half)

Scrub cockles and mussels and let soak in cold water for at least one hour. Rinse and place in a large pan with the 2 cups water, white wine, onion, celery, garlic, bay leaf, thyme, and parsley. Cover the pan and bring ingredients to a boil. Lower the heat and simmer, covered, for about 10 minutes, or until all shells have opened. Discard any cockles or mussels whose shells have not opened. Remove meat from shells. Discard shells and reserve meat. Strain broth through 2 layers of moistened cheesecloth. Measure liquid into a bowl and add water to measure 6 cups.

In a soup pan, fry bacon over low heat until pieces are crispy. Remove bacon, crumble into small pieces, and set aside.

Discard dark green part of leeks, remove roots, and clean leeks thoroughly. Chop leeks and add with potatoes to the pan. Cook over moderate heat for 3–4 minutes. Add 6 cups of liquid and sprinkling of salt, black pepper, and nutmeg. Simmer partially covered for about 45 minutes.

Purée ingredients in a food processor or blender. Return soup to the pan. Add reserved shellfish and bacon, and stir in cream. Heat through for 5 minutes.

Chicken Cacciatore

Tender chicken and rich, savory sauce make this dish as special for company as it is heartwarming for family. Serve with pasta or polenta.

Prep time: less than 15 minutes • Makes 4 servings

1 broiler-fryer chicken, cut into 8 pieces	2 TB. tomato paste
$\frac{1}{4}$ cup all-purpose flour	$\frac{1}{2}$ cup red wine
2 TB. olive oil	Salt and pepper, to taste
2 medium onions, sliced	3 TB. fresh parsley, chopped
2 large cloves garlic, chopped	2 TB. fresh basil, chopped
1 (2-lb.–3-oz.) can Italian-style tomatoes, drained	8–10 oz. fresh mushrooms, cut in half

Rinse chicken pieces and pat dry with paper towels. Dredge chicken in flour, shaking off excess. Heat 1 TB. olive oil in a deep skillet over moderate heat and brown chicken a few pieces at a time, adding remaining olive oil as needed to prevent sticking. Browning will take 15–20 minutes.

Remove chicken from the pan. Add onions to the pan. Cook for 3–4 minutes, or until softened. Add garlic and cook for another minute. Add tomatoes, tomato paste, and wine and stir to blend in.

Return chicken to the pan. Sprinkle with salt and pepper, parsley, and basil. Cover the pan and simmer for 15 minutes. Baste ingredients once or twice during this time. Add mushrooms and simmer, covered, another 20 minutes or until chicken is completely cooked through, basting occasionally.

Cheese Lasagna al Forno

This is a traditional version of Italian-American baked lasagna. It is meatless, but you can always add cooked sausage, ground meat, or tiny fried meatballs.

Prep time: less than 45 minutes   •   Makes 6 to 8 servings

3 TB. olive oil	2 TB. fresh parsley, chopped
1 medium onion, chopped	1 TB. dried oregano
3 cloves garlic, chopped	2 tsp. salt, or to taste
1 (2-lb.-3.oz.) can Italian-style tomatoes in thick purée	Freshly ground black pepper, to taste
	2 lbs. ricotta cheese
1 (8-oz.) can tomato sauce	3 cups mozzarella cheese, shredded
1 (6-oz.) can tomato paste	$^{3}/_{4}$ cup Parmesan cheese, grated
$^{3}/_{4}$ cup water	$^{1}/_{4}$ cup fresh parsley, chopped
2 TB. fresh basil, chopped or 2 tsp. dried basil	15 lasagna noodles, about $^{3}/_{4}$ lb.

Heat olive oil in a saucepan over moderate heat. Add onion and cook for 3 minutes. Add garlic and cook for another minute. Add tomatoes with their juice, tomato sauce, tomato paste, water, basil, parsley, oregano, salt, and pepper. Break up tomatoes in the pan with a sturdy wooden spoon. Bring sauce to a simmer and cook for $1^{1}/_{2}$ hours, or until thickened.

Preheat the oven to 350°.

Mix ricotta cheese with one cup of the mozzarella cheese, $^{1}/_{2}$ cup Parmesan cheese, and parsley. Set aside.

Cook noodles until al dente. Let noodles drain. Assemble lasagna as follows: Place about $^{1}/_{2}$ cup sauce in the bottom of a 13" × 9" baking dish. Place 5 noodles on top, overlapping. Cover noodles with half cheese mixture.

Add another layer of 5 noodles. Cover with remaining cheese. Pour half tomato sauce on top and smooth evenly over cheese. Cover with remaining 5 noodles. Top with remaining sauce. Sprinkle remaining 2 cups mozzarella cheese on top. Finally, sprinkle dish with remaining $^{1}/_{4}$ cup Parmesan cheese. Bake for 45 minutes or until hot and bubbly.

Chicken with Peanuts

This is a hot and spicy Sichuanese-American dish, perfect with plain, cooked white rice.

Prep time: less than 30 minutes • Makes 4 servings

2 whole, boneless, skinless chicken breasts

2 tsp. cornstarch

2 TB. soy sauce

1 TB. Chinese rice wine or sherry

1 tsp. sesame oil

$^1/_2$ tsp. white vinegar

1 TB. sugar

$^1/_4$ tsp. salt

3 TB. vegetable oil

5–6 dried whole red chili peppers

4 thick scallions, including half the green portion, chopped into $^1/_4$" pieces

1 tsp. fresh ginger, minced

$^1/_2$ cup shelled roasted peanuts

Cut chicken into bite-size pieces. Discard fat. Discard membrane that connects the 2 halves. Place chicken in a bowl and toss with 1 teaspoon cornstarch. Add some water to be sure cornstarch dissolves into chicken pieces. Set chicken aside.

Mix remaining 1 teaspoon cornstarch with just enough water to make thin paste. Set cornstarch mixture aside.

Mix soy sauce, rice wine, sesame oil, vinegar, sugar, and salt in a bowl. Set the bowl aside.

Heat 2 tablespoons vegetable oil in a wok or stir-fry pan set over high heat. Stir-fry chicken for 2 minutes. Remove chicken from the pan. Add remaining 1 tablespoon vegetable oil to the pan. Add chili peppers and stir-fry briefly, until they begin to turn color.

Add scallion and ginger, stir, and return chicken to the pan. Add soy sauce mixture and stir briefly. Add peanuts and stir briefly. Give cornstarch mixture a stir, and pour into the pan. Stir-fry ingredients for a few seconds or until sauce thickens. Serve immediately.

Pasta Puttanesca

This dish has a rich, tangy sauce that you can use over grilled chicken or steak instead of pasta.

Prep time: less than 15 minutes, plus time to make the Tomato Sauce   •   Makes 4 servings

2 TB. olive oil

1 small onion, minced

2 cloves garlic, chopped

2 cups Basic Tomato Sauce (see Appendix C)

2 TB. capers, drained

12 pitted black olives, preferably imported, cut in half

12 pitted green olives, cut in half

8 anchovy filets, drained and mashed, optional

1 TB. fresh oregano leaves or 1 tsp. dried oregano

$^1/_2$ tsp. dried red pepper flakes

1 lb. pasta, preferably spaghetti or linguine

1 cup freshly grated Parmesan cheese, or to taste

Heat olive oil in a skillet over moderate heat. Add onion and cook over low-moderate heat for 2–3 minutes or until softened. Add garlic and cook for another minute. Add Tomato Sauce, capers, olives, anchovies if used, oregano, and red pepper flakes. Cook for 15–20 minutes or until tangy and slightly thickened.

While sauce is cooking, cook pasta until al dente. Drain pasta. Pour sauce on top and sprinkle with freshly grated Parmesan cheese.

Pot Roast Brisket

This is the quintessential Jewish-American holiday entrée. Every family has its own version; this one is simple and calls for long, slow cooking, which makes the meat very tender.

Prep time: less than 15 minutes • Makes 10 servings

1 beef brisket (about 6 lbs.)

2 TB. vegetable oil

Salt and pepper

2 TB. paprika

2 large onions, sliced

4 large all-purpose potatoes, peeled and cut into large chunks

10 oz. whole medium white button mushrooms

1¹/₂ lbs. carrots, cut into 1¹/₂" chunks

Preheat the oven to 300°.

Dry meat with paper towels. Heat vegetable oil in a Dutch oven over moderate heat. Add meat and brown both flat sides; this should take about 10 minutes. Remove the pan from the heat. Sprinkle meat with salt and pepper and 1 tablespoon paprika. Put onions on top of and around meat. Sprinkle with salt and pepper and the remaining 1 tablespoon paprika. Cover the Dutch oven and put it in the oven. Cook for 3 hours.

Add onions, potatoes, and mushrooms, basting the meat and vegetables with the pan juices. Cover and cook another 1¹/₂–2 hours, or until meat is fork-tender. Remove meat and vegetables and set aside. Degrease cooking juices. If desired, boil cooking juices to make sauce thicker, or purée some vegetables with pan juices. Spoon sauce over meat and vegetables and serve.

Hot Tip

Make this dish a day or two ahead. The flavors mellow and it is easy to degrease the dish after refrigeration. Separate the meat, vegetables, and juices. The fat will rise to the top of the juices and you can scoop it off easily.

Cuban-Style Roast Chicken with Rice Stuffing

This is both festive looking and fabulous tasting; the mild chicken is the perfect foil for the tangy rice dressing stuffed inside.

Prep time: less than 30 minutes • Makes 4 to 6 servings

1 roasting chicken, about 4–5 lbs.	$^1/_2$ cup chorizo sausage, chopped
3 TB. olive oil	$^1/_2$ cup green olives, chopped
Salt, to taste	$^1/_4$ cup pignoli nuts, toasted
Cayenne pepper	2 TB. capers, drained
3 cups cooked white rice	$^1/_2$ cup chicken stock
$^1/_2$ cup dark raisins	$^1/_2$ cup sherry, preferably Amontillado

Preheat the oven to 400°.

Rinse chicken and pat dry with paper towels. Rub surface with one tablespoon olive oil and sprinkle with salt and cayenne pepper. Set aside.

In a bowl, combine rice, raisins, sausage, olives, nuts, capers, and the remaining 2 tablespoons olive oil. Season with salt. Stuff mixture inside cavity of chicken. Secure cavity closed with a toothpick.

Place chicken breast-side down on the rack in a roasting pan. Place any stuffing that does not fit inside chicken inside the roasting pan. Roast chicken for 10 minutes, and then lower the heat to 350° and cook another 10 minutes. Mix stock and sherry together and pour some of mixture over chicken. Roast another 20 minutes and pour remaining liquid over chicken.

Roast another 10 minutes and turn chicken breast-side up. Continue to roast chicken for another 50–75 minutes, or until a meat thermometer inserted into thickest part of thigh registers 160° to 180°. Baste occasionally with pan fluids until 15 minutes before you expect chicken to be done. Remove chicken to a carving board and let rest 15 minutes before carving.

Hot Tip

The USDA recommends cooking chicken to 180° as measured in the thickest part of the thigh, but the meat is juicier when cooked to 165°, and many cooks follow this practice. You must decide whether or not to use the more conservative USDA guidelines; I have suggested alternative temperatures. Use a meat thermometer or instant read thermometer to check temperature. In any case, be sure to follow safe food-handling basics: Wash hands and defrost, wrap, and refrigerate the meat properly to keep pathogens away.

Shrimp in Lobster Sauce

This old-fashioned Chinese entrée is still a favorite; serve it with cooked white rice. This recipe was adapted from one given to me by Florence Lin, who was a well-known cookbook author and a teacher at New York City's China Institute.

Prep time: less than 30 minutes • Makes 4 servings

3 TB. vegetable oil	$^1/_4$ tsp. sugar
1 lb. shrimp, shelled and deveined	1 TB. soy sauce
1 TB. Chinese rice wine or sherry	$^1/_2$ cup water
4 medium scallions, chopped	$^1/_2$ cup chicken stock
2 medium cloves garlic, chopped	$1^1/_2$ TB. cornstarch
4 oz. ground pork	2 eggs, beaten
$^1/_4$ tsp. salt, or to taste	

Heat 2 tablespoons vegetable oil in a wok or stir-fry pan over high heat. Add shrimp and stir-fry for half a minute, until they begin to turn pink. Add rice wine, cover the pan, and cook for 1 minute. Remove shrimp and set aside.

Heat remaining 1 tablespoon vegetable oil in the pan. Add scallions and stir-fry for 1 minute. Add garlic and pork, and cook for 2 minutes, making sure all traces of pink disappear from pork. Add salt, sugar, soy sauce, water, and chicken stock. Bring mixture to a boil. Add shrimp.

Mix cornstarch with enough water to make a paste and add to the boiling liquid in the pan. Stir until sauce has thickened. Slowly add beaten eggs. Mix gently with chopsticks or a wooden spoon and serve immediately.

Stuffed Cabbage

You can use stuffed cabbage as an entrée or as first course. These freeze well: Place them into separate baking dishes and pop them into the oven when you need them.

Prep time: about 1¹/₄ hours   •   Makes 8 to 12 main-course servings, or 18 first-course servings

2 large heads of green cabbage	3 slices white bread, crusts trimmed
2 (1-lb.) cans jellied cranberry sauce	1 lb. ground beef
4 cups canned tomato purée	1 lb. ground veal
2 cups water	2 eggs
¹/₃ cup lemon juice	1 medium onion, grated
¹/₂ cup brown sugar	¹/₄ cup ketchup
1 cup raisins	¹/₄ cup water

Preheat the oven to 350°.

Remove hard core of cabbages, and discard thick outer leaves, if any. Bring a large pot half-filled with water to a boil. Immerse cabbages one at a time and cook, covered, for 8–10 minutes or until you can remove leaves easily from head. Drain cabbages under cold water, carefully remove leaves, and set aside. (Save tiny innermost leaves for other purposes.)

Combine cranberry sauce, tomato purée, water, lemon juice, and brown sugar in a saucepan. Bring to a simmer over moderate heat, stirring with a whisk occasionally to blend ingredients thoroughly. When sauce is smooth, let cook about 10 minutes, and then add raisins and cook another 6–7 minutes. Set sauce aside.

Break white bread into pieces into a bowl and cover slices with water. Let bread soak for about 3–4 minutes, and then squeeze out the excess water. Return bread to the bowl and add beef, veal, eggs, onion, ketchup, and water. Blend ingredients to make uniform mixture. Place some filling on each of the leaves, and wrap filling to completely enclose meat. Place stuffed leaves seam-side down in baking dishes.

Cover stuffed cabbage with half of sauce. Cover the baking dishes with aluminum foil and bake stuffed cabbage 1 hour. Remove the cover and bake another 45 minutes. Add remaining sauce and cook, uncovered, another 45–60 minutes.

Veal Parmigiana

Veal Parmigiana has always been a favorite. Make a large batch of it and save some for the future. This dish goes nicely with spaghetti and plain tomato sauce. If possible, use a good Parmigiano-Reggiano cheese.

Prep time: less than 15 minutes, plus time to make the Tomato Sauce • Makes 4 servings

8 veal cutlets	Salt and pepper, to taste
1/4 cup all-purpose flour	6 TB. olive oil, approximately
2 eggs	2 cups Basic Tomato Sauce (see Appendix C)
1 cup dry plain breadcrumbs	8 oz. mozzarella cheese, shredded
3 TB. Parmesan cheese, grated	1/4 cup Parmesan cheese, grated

Dredge veal in flour; shake off excess. Beat eggs, and dip each floured cutlet into beaten egg, covering entire piece. Mix breadcrumbs, 3 tablespoons Parmesan cheese, and salt and pepper to taste. Coat veal with breadcrumbs. Let meat rest, preferably on a cake rack, for 15 minutes.

Preheat the oven to 350°. Heat 2 tablespoons olive oil in a skillet over moderate heat. Brown breaded veal in oil, a few pieces at a time, until lightly browned, about 4–5 minutes. Add more olive oil to the pan as necessary to prevent sticking.

Place veal in a large baking pan. Spoon 1 1/2–2 cups tomato sauce over meat. Top with mozzarella cheese; sprinkle with 1/4 cup Parmesan cheese. Cover the pan with aluminum foil. Bake 15 minutes. Uncover the pan and bake another 5–10 minutes.

Colcannon

Fluffy potatoes spiked with tender cabbage make this a tasty side dish for roasted or grilled meat or poultry.

Prep time: less than 30 minutes   •   Makes 6 to 8 servings

6 medium all-purpose potatoes (about 2 lbs.)	5 TB. butter
Lightly salted water	1 tsp. salt, or to taste
1 lb. green cabbage (or substitute kale)	Freshly ground black pepper, to taste
1 large leek	Freshly grated nutmeg
³/₄ cup hot milk	

Peel potatoes and cut into chunks. Place in a saucepan and cover with lightly salted water. Bring water to a boil, lower the heat, and simmer potatoes for 15–20 minutes or until fork-tender.

While potatoes are cooking, remove hard core from cabbage, cut leaves into coarse chunks, and cook cabbage in lightly salted water for 12 minutes or until leaves have wilted. Drain cabbage thoroughly and set aside.

Discard dark green part of leek, remove roots, and clean leek thoroughly. Chop leek and place in a saucepan with milk. Bring to a simmer and cook for 6–8 minutes. Set milk mixture aside.

Drain potatoes. Mash with a potato masher, fork, or electric mixer set on low speed. Add butter in chunks and continue to mash until mixture is free of lumps. Add cabbage and leek-and-milk mixture, salt and pepper, and a few grindings of fresh nutmeg. Stir briefly until ingredients are smooth and thoroughly blended.

Black Beans and Rice

This is the classic version of this dish. If you like it spicy, substitute two hot peppers for the mild Cuban peppers, and serve it with some hot pepper sauce.

Prep time: less than 15 minutes • Makes 6 to 8 servings

2 TB. lard or olive oil

1 large onion, chopped

$^1/_2$ large green bell pepper, seeded and chopped

3 or 4 Cuban yellow or Caribe peppers or 2 Anaheim peppers, seeded and chopped

3 large cloves garlic, chopped

$^1/_4$ cup chopped green olives

1 tsp. dried oregano

2 cups long-grain white rice

$3^1/_2$ cups chicken stock

Salt and pepper, to taste

2 (15-oz.) cans black beans, undrained

2 TB. fresh cilantro, choped

Heat lard or olive oil in a skillet over moderate heat. Add onion, green pepper, Cuban pepper, garlic, and olives, and cook for 2–3 minutes. Add oregano and rice, and stir ingredients to spread evenly in the pan. Pour in chicken stock. Sprinkle with salt and pepper. Bring liquid to a boil. Turn heat to low, cover the pan, and simmer for 18–20 minutes.

Add beans and their liquid, and cilantro. Stir to spread ingredients evenly. Cover the pan and cook for another 15 minutes or until rice and beans are soft and liquid has been absorbed. Taste for seasoning and add salt and pepper to taste.

Irish Oat Scones

These tender, crumbly pastries are terrific for breakfast or coffee breaks. Slather them with fresh sweet butter or strawberry preserves.

Prep time: less than 15 minutes   •   Makes 6 to 8 scones

1 cup quick-cooking oats (not instant)	$^1/_2$ tsp. salt
1 cup all-purpose flour	$^1/_2$ cup butter, cut into small chunks
4 tsp. baking powder	$^2/_3$ cup milk

Preheat the oven to 425°.

Lightly grease a cookie sheet. Cook oats in an ungreased skillet over moderate heat for 5–6 minutes, or until lightly browned. Set aside.

Combine flour, baking powder, and salt in a bowl. Add butter and work into flour mixture with your hands or a pastry blender until mixture resembles coarse meal. (You can also use a food processor; pulse quickly about 36 times to obtain mealy texture. Stir in oatmeal.)

Pour in milk and stir to make a soft dough. Knead dough briefly on a floured surface, and then press dough into a $^3/_4$"-thick circle. Cut circle into six or eight wedges. Place wedges on the cookie sheet and bake for 12–15 minutes or until golden brown.

Noodle Kugel with Cornflake Crust

I got this recipe from my friend Susan Blomberg, who got it from her friend Linda Gratt, who got it from her mother, who got it from someone else. It's the best Kugel I've ever tasted.

Prep time: less than 30 minutes   •   Makes 8 servings

1 pound wide, flat egg noodles

8-oz. package cream cheese

$\frac{1}{4}$ lb. butter (1 stick)

1 cup sugar

2 cups sour cream

6 eggs, beaten

1 tsp. cinnamon

1 cup raisins

2 cups crushed cereal such as cornflakes, crispy rice, or frosted cornflakes

4 TB. butter, melted

Preheat the oven to 350°.

Cook noodles in lightly salted water until tender but still slightly firm.

In an electric mixer, beat together cream cheese and butter until well blended and fluffy. Beat in sugar until well blended. Blend in sour cream, eggs, and cinnamon, and stir in raisins. Pour mixture over noodles and toss to coat.

Place mixture in a lightly buttered baking dish. Mix cereal and melted butter, and sprinkle mixture on top of Kugel. Bake for about 40 minutes or until well browned and crispy.

Kourabiedes

These are Greek butter cookies; very tender, and the hint of cloves gives them a warm, winter-holiday feel—but they are fine without it, too. These freeze well.

Prep time: less than 30 minutes   •   Makes about 4 dozen cookies

1 cup butter (2 sticks)	2 cups all-purpose flour
1 egg yolk	$^1/_3$ cup almonds, ground
3 TB. confectioner's sugar	Confectioner's sugar for coating
$^1/_4$ tsp. salt	Ground cloves, optional

Beat butter with an electric mixer set on medium speed for 2–3 minutes, or until light and fluffy. Add egg yolk, confectioner's sugar, and salt, and beat until ingredients are well blended. Thoroughly blend in flour and almonds. Wrap dough in plastic wrap and refrigerate for at least 1 hour.

Preheat the oven to 325°.

Shape dough into balls about 1" in diameter. Place balls on ungreased cookie sheets and bake for about 25 minutes or until lightly tanned. Let cool. Roll cookies in confectioner's sugar to coat entire surface. Place on a serving tray and sprinkle with ground cloves if desired.

Honeycake

This dense, sticky-sweet cake is traditionally eaten during Rosh Hashanah, but you can enjoy it anytime.

Prep time: less than 30 minutes • Makes 2 loaf cakes

Special equipment: cake rack

3½ cups all-purpose flour	1 TB. freshly grated orange peel
2½ tsp. baking powder	2 tsp. freshly grated lemon peel
1 tsp. baking soda	4 eggs
½ tsp. salt	¾ cup sugar
1 tsp. ginger, ground	2 cups honey
1 tsp. cinnamon	1 cup cold double-strength coffee
¼ tsp. nutmeg, ground	3 TB. vegetable oil

Preheat the oven to 300°.

Lightly oil two 9"×5" loaf pans, then line pans with aluminum foil. Sift together flour, baking powder, baking soda, salt, ginger, cinnamon, and nutmeg. Stir in orange and lemon peel.

In bowl of an electric mixer set at medium speed, beat eggs and sugar together for 2–3 minutes or until thick and fluffy. Add honey, coffee, and vegetable oil and mix ingredients thoroughly. Add dry ingredients to bowl. Stir only to blend ingredients; do not over mix. Pour batter into prepared pans.

Bake about 1¼ hours or until cake tester inserted into center of cakes comes out clean. Remove cakes to a cake rack to cool completely.

Invention, Innovation, and Culture

In This Chapter

- ◆ Convenience foods come of age
- ◆ Food in a can
- ◆ The emergence of our national cuisine
- ◆ Innovations that changed the way we cook
- ◆ Foods that comfort us in troubled times
- ◆ How restaurants have influenced what we cook

For hundreds of years, America didn't have a national cooking style. Food specialties were regional, dependent on geography, climate, and the religion and culture of early settlers in a particular locale. But our cuisine gradually evolved into what would be called mainstream American cookery. The influx of immigrants had a lot to do with this transformation, but there were other factors as well.

New innovations such as baking powder and gelatin, which were available to everyone, made home cooking easier and more convenient. Frozen, canned, and packaged foods introduced Americans to regional and ethnic fare they never had tasted. Manufacturers provided recipe booklets for new foods, which housewives throughout the country were eager to try. Modern kitchen equipment liberated home cooks everywhere from boring, labor-intensive, time-consuming kitchen drudgery. Travel became easier and faster, enabling people to discover what others were eating elsewhere. Cookbooks, magazines, TV shows, World's Fairs, and the Internet brought the country even closer with the exchange of culinary ideas.

If our cuisine was influenced by the innovations in good times, it also was affected during times of trouble. During Prohibition, the Depression, and two World Wars, we came together gastronomically with foods that stretched the budget and nourished the emotions.

The impact of restaurants was enormous, too, as many of their famed dishes were the ones we wanted to copy at home. To this day, restaurants help define the style of cooking in favor at any particular moment.

Foods That Changed Culinary History

The Pilgrims would have starved in America if they hadn't found piles of dried corn to eat their first winter. (Native Americans would later show them how to plant corn.) Salmon saved the pioneers on the Oregon Trail. But when hunger was no longer the issue, enterprising Americans created new foods and innovated new culinary ideas that would make cooking simpler, easier, tastier, and more dependable. At a time when America was beginning to define itself as a national, cultural whole, these developments had impact beyond specific regions to home cooks throughout the land.

Kitchen Clue

When preparing quickbreads, mix the dry and liquid ingredients together as quickly as possible and just enough to blend them. Overbeating the batter makes the breads tough.

Baking 101

Baking got a big boost when women were able to buy Hecker's packaged flour in 1852 and uniformly consistent yeast in 1868. Thanks to the availability of baking soda and baking powder, no one had to beat eggs, batter, or dough for interminable amounts of time in order to get cakes and biscuits to rise. A new category of breads called "quickbreads" was born, including cranberry-orange bread and blueberry muffins.

Fitting a New Mold

About 100 years ago, the only way to prepare foods in aspic was to use homemade gelatin made by poaching calves' or pigs' feet (or by using products such as agar-agar or Irish moss). Wealthy folks had cooks to do the job, but the rest didn't make many molded salads. Enter Knox unflavored gelatin. It saved hours of time and was afford-able. Molded salads that encased fruits and vegetables became widely popular. About the same time that Knox hit the shelves, a cough medicine manufacturer in New York was tinkering with a flavored-gelatin recipe; his wife called it Jell-O. They sold the recipe, which was mostly sugar, for $450. Since then, Jell-O, intended as dessert, has been used in all sorts of dishes. Molded salads, even while considered passé by some sophisticated cooks, are still popular at potlucks, church suppers, and casual parties.

Fat in the Can

Today's health-conscious home cooks shudder at the amounts of saturated fat in hydrogenated vegetable shortening, but before Crisco (1911), the only firm fats available for baked goods were lard and chicken fat. Vegetable shortening wasn't an instant success, but it gradually gained wide appeal, especially during war years, when butter was in short supply. Oatmeal cookies, which commonly use shortening, not butter, first became popular during World War II. Although you may not wish to indulge often, if you want tender pie crust and tasty fried chicken, shorten-ing will help you do the job deliciously.

Kitchen Clue

Different types of fat can make a big differ-ence in pie crust. Butter-only crusts taste best, but they aren't tender. Old-fashioned lard crusts and all-shortening crusts are tender, but can be greasy. The ideal is a mix of mostly butter and a small quan-tity of shortening and/or lard. (See the Basic Pie Crust recipe in Appendix C.)

Convenience: Five Foods That Changed Our Lives

Frozen and processed foods made a considerable difference in defining a more unified national cuisine. While hundreds of convenience items have come along—cake and pancake mixes, packaged pudding, crackers, American cheese, and boxed breakfast cereal, to name just a few—five stand out because of their special impact.

Dip of Ages

Anyone over a certain age could wax rhapsodic about Lipton's Onion Soup Mix. It was made into a dip by mixing the contents of the package with two cups of dairy sour cream. Lipton's Onion Soup Dip was the rage of the 1950s, and is the classic must-bring to every retro party. Home cooks, always looking for a way to cut down on kitchen time, also used the dehydrated soup to flavor pot roast, meatloaf, and any number of casseroles.

Gee Whiz!

Cheez Whiz (1953) was created as a replacement for Welsh Rabbit (or rarebit; both names are correct) and was more successful than anyone dreamed (does anyone cook Welsh Rabbit?). Homemakers found hundreds of uses for this product, including macaroni and cheese, chili cheese dogs, and nachos.

> **Fein on Food**
>
> Fondue was fashionable in the 1960s. This elegant Swiss dish was "Americanized" by many home-cooks-in-a-hurry, who substituted processed cheese, including Cheez Whiz, for imported Emmenthaler, and milk or canned soup for the wine. Supermarkets even sold fondue cheese in a jar.

The National Cookie

Thanks to packaged chocolate morsels, Americans have been able to stuff themselves with what has become the national cookie. In 1930, the Nestlé company, eager to know why its chocolate sales soared in Boston, learned that Ruth Wakefield's *Toll House Cook Book* had a really good recipe for cookies with chunks of chocolate in them. At first the company manufactured scored chocolate and sold it with a tiny chopper; Chocolate Chip cookies got even easier to bake after 1939 when the morsels first appeared.

A Real Smoothie

Where would we be without Hellmann's mayonnaise, introduced in 1915? Before it came along, mayo was made drop by drop, by hand—no blenders and food processors then. All of a sudden it was easy to prepare potato salad, macaroni salad, and any number of dressings including Russian (mayo with ketchup and pickle relish), Thousand Island (mayo with chili sauce, onion, olives, and green and red peppers) and Tartare (mayo with onion, olives, capers, parsley, and tarragon). During the Depression, Hellmann's created a recipe for a chocolate cake that used mayonnaise in place of expensive butter and milk. Chocolate Mayonnaise Cake became a trendy, cult favorite.

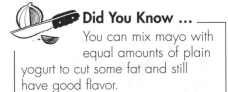

Did You Know ...

You can mix mayo with equal amounts of plain yogurt to cut some fat and still have good flavor.

A Good Piece of Bread

It was wonder enough when a new, soft, packaged white bread appeared in the stores in 1921, and even more of a wonder when it was sold pre-sliced a few years later! Americans couldn't get enough of the stuff, and lunch time in America was never the same. If it weren't for Wonder Bread, zillions of kids wouldn't have had their peanut butter-and-jelly sandwiches. Would we have known the joys of BLTs and Grilled Cheese? After Wonder Bread, all kinds of pre-sliced packaged loaves appeared, paving the way for some of America's classic sandwiches: Dagwoods, Reubens, and Tuna Melts, to name a few.

It Comes in a Can

Canned food, which has been around since the early part of the nineteenth century, can be invaluable. In the days before fast transport and refrigeration, some of America's first canned products were salmon and tuna, which let people who lived inland get a taste of foods that otherwise would have been unavailable to them. Canned vegetables, tomatoes, and fruit gave people greater variety and more choices when making meals. Beans, Spam, and other canned foods helped feed soldiers during wartime. Of course, canned food has its limitations, too, particularly when it is used regularly in place of fresh ingredients.

Mmm, Mmm, Good!

The canned product that has had the most influence on American cooking is condensed soup. John T. Dorrance couldn't have predicted what would happen when he invented this new item in 1897 for the Joseph Campbell Preserve Company. In 1916, Campbell's began to publish recipe booklets that became the most liberating literature in America: They showed homemakers how to use condensed soup in recipes. Housewives quickly caught on and began to open cans instead of preparing homemade sauces. Cream of Mushroom and Cream of Chicken soups (1933), in particular, had a huge impact in the kitchen. Two American culinary icons, Tuna Casserole and Green Bean Bake, are often prepared with condensed soup. By the 1950s, home cooks throughout the land used canned soup for all kinds of dishes, including shortcut versions of famous entrees such as Chicken Divan and Chicken Tetrazzini.

Aluminum foil, a neat and handy invention, was first available in 1947—just in time to wrap those all-in-one canned-soup-frozen-vegetable-meat dishes.

Mini-Recipe
1950s Party Cheeseball
(12 servings)   Mix an 8-ounce package of cream cheese with 2 tablespoons finely chopped green pepper, 2 tablespoons finely chopped onion, 4 ounces drained, canned crushed pineapple, and 1¹/₂ teaspoons seasoned salt. Shape into a large ball and roll in a cup of finely chopped nuts.

Gourmet with a Can Opener

As varieties of canned, packaged, and frozen foods burgeoned, so did recipes for down-home fare such as Three-Bean Salad, Cheeseballs, and Pineapple upside-down Cake. Cooks also used convenience foods to cut cooking time of otherwise long, intricate recipes. Beef Wellington, so *de rigeur* in the 1960s, was interpreted using canned mushrooms, liver paste, and refrigerator biscuits or frozen pie dough. Chicken à la King was prepared with canned soup, canned mushrooms, and jarred pimiento.

Foods That Brought Us Closer

After the Civil War ended in 1865, people still cooked regional dishes, but a national cuisine began to emerge. Several factors encouraged more standardized fare: faster travel, better means of communication, and a World's Fair or two.

Trains, Planes ...

The completion of the first transcontinental railroad in 1869 put an end to the pioneer era. Travelers could journey from coast to coast, sleep in comfortable Pullman cars, and dine on local meats, fish, and produce picked up en route. It was many people's first chance to taste foods of different regions. A century later, Americans traveled abroad and tasted their first authentic foreign foods. They came back with a longing for the local, ethnic, fresh flavors of the places they had visited. They took cooking lessons, read cookbooks, and sought out products that would help them prepare Pasta Pesto, Tiramisu, Roasted Red Peppers, Gazpacho, and other foods they had enjoyed abroad.

Kitchen Clue
Any red bell pepper is suitable for roasting, but the dark, claret-red Holland peppers are the sweetest and most flavorful. You can use your oven broiler, but for even better results, use an outdoor grill, which permeates the peppers with a rich, smoky taste.

... and Automobiles

The automobile, above all, tied the country together gastronomically, but in a different way than trains and planes. Rather than spur an interest in the local, fresh, and different, it encouraged the familiar—consider the ubiquitous foods available along our highways and byways. This predictable, safe sameness started as soon as cars first hit the road. Entrepreneurs believed that drivers would need a place to eat along the way and that what they wanted was something so well known they could choose easily, eat quickly, and be on their way. Hamburgers tasted pretty much the same no matter who made them. The automobile paved the way for the cult of all fast food: hamburger, fries, pizza, fried chicken, and sandwiches.

World's Fair Wonders

World's Fairs may introduce wonders of science and industry, but for folks who like to eat, the event is all about the food. People at the 1876 fair in Philadelphia got their first tastes of Heinz ketchup and breads made with Fleischmann's yeast. In 1893, fairgoers in Chicago tried Aunt Jemima Pancake Mix for the first time, and at Chicago's 1933 fair they drank canned pineapple and orange juices. At the 1964 fair in New York, visitors gobbled up Belgian waffles. But food connoisseurs will always speak of 1904 as a vintage World's Fair year, when our most iconic food, the hamburger on a bun, was popularized. An enterprising vendor sold the grilled meat on a soft roll so fairgoers could eat as they made their way through the grounds. Iced tea and ice cream cones also made their debuts at the 1904 fete in St. Louis, as did popcorn, puffed rice, and peanut butter.

> **Did You Know ...**
>
> If you want the best iced tea, make it fresh, with loose or bagged tea and just-boiled water. Use about twice the amount of tea as for hot tea and let the brew cool before pouring it over ice cubes. You needn't stick to standard tea types. Consider green teas, flavored varieties such as Earl Grey and herbals. Or innovate by steeping the tea with fresh herbs such as mint or rosemary, dried spices such as cardamom pods or cinnamon stick, or bold flavorings such as orange slices or chunks of crystallized ginger.

Reading for Recipes

Although food manufacturers publish recipes, most of us turn to professionally written cookbooks when we want to learn the basics or cook something new (see Appendix B for a good selection). Cookbooks can reflect a nation's culinary character, but the best ones are those that set a new style and are useful to all home cooks. Thousands of cookbooks have been written. While many are worthy, the following deserve special mention:

- Amelia Simmons's *American Cookery* (1796) was the first American cookbook. It called for American ingredients rather than English ones.

- *The Virginia Housewife* (1824) by Mary Randolph was the first regional cookbook.

- *The Boston Cooking School Cook Book* by Fannie Merritt Farmer (1896) was the first to give recipes with precise, level measurements, rather than specifying "a handful of flour" or "butter the size of a walnut."

- *The Joy of Cooking* by Irma Starkloff Rombauer offered enormous amounts of information and inspired confidence; originally self-published in 1931, several editions have made this the best-selling cookbook of all time.

- *Mastering the Art of French Cooking* (1961) forever changed the way Americans cooked. This two-volume tome by Julia Child, Simone Beck, and Louisette Bertholle gave home cooks the confidence to prepare even the most sophisticated French food.

- James Beard's many books, particularly *American Cookery* (1972), were resolutely pro-American and focused on fresh, regional ingredients.

Better Cooking Through TV

TV food shows invigorated an interest in cooking. Julia Child's popular TV program, *The French Chef*, aired for the first time in 1963. She was always fun to watch and her program provided years of quality home instruction. She was followed over the years by many who nurtured the American love affair with food. Today, thanks to cookbooks, TV, food magazines, and the Internet, cooking is revered as an art form, rather than as drudgery. People attend cooking schools for personal pleasure and for serious career study. Kitchen equipment has become big business. Premium cookware and good knives are considered essentials, and whisks, copper bowls, food processors, and electric mixers are staples for those who take an interest in the culinary arts.

Kitchen Clue

Cookware can be very expensive, but don't be tempted by large multi-piece sets that contain sizes you don't need. Buy a small set of all-purpose cookware. Fill in with other pans that are more suitable for specific types of cooking: an enamel pan for long-simmering sauces, for example. Premium stainless-steel cookware is the most versatile. Brands with an aluminum core are the best performers.

Time Savers

These days we take cooktops, ovens, refrigerators, and freezers for granted, but these appliances are relatively new. Most people cooked with wood and coal stoves until the 1920s. Before the first icebox was built (1803) people stored food in underground cellars; iceboxes were eventually replaced by refrigerators, which weren't available until 1916, and they cost a small fortune, so most people didn't buy them then. These appliances were groundbreaking tools, enabling us to preserve and prepare a larger variety of foods. Thousands of other appliances and gadgets have come to market. Some are silly, trendy toys, while others are useful implements that save time and work. Pressure cookers, microwave ovens, toasters, electric coffeemakers, and bread machines are among the more helpful ones.

Three cooking tools stand out because they changed food preparation significantly. They are also exceptional for their versatility, function, performance, and widespread use in the American kitchen:

♦ Blenders began as barware back in the 1930s but broke new ground in the 1950s when they were redesigned for kitchen use. Because they could chop and purée solid foods, blenders liberated housewives from tedious, time-consuming cooking tasks. They are still tops for puréeing and mixing liquids.

♦ Electric mixers got their start with a patent by Hobart for a commercial mixing machine in 1918. Today, home cooks who bake regularly couldn't do without this appliance. A good mixer is unsurpassed for creaming butter, for whipping cream and egg whites, and for blending pastry and kneading dough. Electric hand-held mixers are practical, too, and do many of the same kitchen tasks, but they don't have the power and sturdiness of a standing model. The best standing mixers work by means of planetary action, in which a beater moves around a stationary bowl. Models with stationary beaters and bowls that spin don't gather ingredients as quickly or as efficiently.

♦ Food processors were introduced at Chicago's Housewares Show in 1973. They were intended for gourmet cooks, but very quickly became one of the most dependable, depended-on appliances for all cooks. A true workhorse, a food processor chops, shreds, grates, slices, and purées food in a flash with the touch of a button. They save hours of time and work. Few home cooks like to be without one.

Two other major innovations changed the American table. The supermarket (first was King Kullen, on Long Island, in 1930) let customers make their own choices from among thousands of products. Before supermarkets, people shopped at grocery stores, where the grocer selected goods for customers. Shopping carts (1937) allowed people to buy loads of food in one trip instead of the usual few items at a time.

Comfort Foods

Foods bring us together when times are good. In the Gilded Age of the 1890s, fabulous restaurants catered to the rich and famous. In boom times like the 1960s, we set our sights on exotic, foreign fare. And during the Reagan years, people spent a fair amount of money trying every new food in every new restaurant that came along.

But certain foods have brought us together as a nation in times of trouble. During Prohibition the cocktail party came of age, and people throughout the country drank more soft drinks. Cocktail nibbles became popular to counteract the effects of "bathtub gin." During the Depression, when everyone was careful about pennies, through the World Wars, when certain foods were scarce, and in periods of inflation when prices for many foods were prohibitive, Americans used leftovers in hash, soup, or sandwiches. Home cooks devised dozens of ways to stretch ground meat into meatloaf, meatballs, Sloppy Joes, and so on. So-called lesser cuts such as tongue and lamb shoulder became the stuff of daily meals. Starchy foods and creamy ones, whether they were rich dishes made with meat, fish, or poultry (Creamed Chicken and Waffles, Creamed Chip Beef on Toast) or meatless fare such as Macaroni and Cheese, Welsh Rabbit, Spanish Rice, or Mashed Potatoes, were comforts to everyone. For dessert, people counted on pudding and cookies. Amazingly, while these are the foods of frugality, they are also the ones we cling to when we feel in need of emotional nourishment.

> **Did You Know ...**
>
> There are all sorts of ways to prepare meatloaf. For rich flavor, substitute some ground pork for beef; for less saturated fat, use some ground turkey. Mix in fresh basil, chopped pignoli nuts, and Parmesan cheese; hoisin sauce, soy sauce, and Chinese rice wine; or fresh cilantro, chili powder, cumin, and oregano. Cover the meatloaf with strips of bacon, bottled salsa, or chutney.

The Restaurant Influence

American home cooks have always taken cues from professional chefs. In recent times, two of America's best-known dishes were restaurant creations: Blackened Redfish (K-Paul's, New Orleans), and Pasta Primavera (Le Cirque, New York). We often serve salad before, not during, a main course, an innovation of Lawry's Prime Rib restaurant (Beverly Hills). Lawry's was also where Americans first learned about baked potatoes with sour cream and chives, and were introduced to Lawry's Seasoned Salt.

Chicken Divan, a home cook's favorite in the 1950s, was invented at New York's Divan Parisien restaurant. And Rumaki was a favorite nibble that homemakers copied from Trader Vic's and Don the Beachcomber. Restaurants gave us the flambé, too: Cherries Jubilee and Bananas Foster, all perfect for the chafing dishes people had at home.

In the Beginning

In America's earliest days, there were no restaurants. Travelers ate at inns, while the locals gathered at taverns. There was no such thing as a menu. Customers ate whatever the owner served. New York's Fraunces' Tavern was the only upscale eatery, serving elegant fare and fine wines. This is probably why George Washington chose to give his farewell address there in 1783, followed by dinner.

A New Concept

At the end of the eighteenth century, when restaurants were a new concept in France, several opened in America. One that created a totally new vision was Delmonico's in New York City. It set the standard for upscale dining for centuries to come, with fine tablecloths, china and silverware, well-prepared food, and impeccable service. It was the first restaurant where people went to be seen. Presidents, royals, dignitaries, and entertainers dined there. It was the favorite of singer Jenny Lind and businessman Diamond Jim Brady, whose gargantuan appetite made him the establishment's best patron. Another regular was Samuel F.B. Morse, who sent the first transatlantic telegram from his table. Charles Dickens, who wrote about the lack of refinement in American cookery, apologized for his glibness after he ate there.

It was Delmonico's wisdom, in a practice followed by some restaurateurs to this day, to name certain dishes after special customers and events. Many are among America's classics:

- Lobster Newberg, named for Bud Wenberg. This dish of lobster in cream-sherry sauce was such a winner that "Lobster à la Wenberg" became a daily menu item. Unfortunately, the tycoon had a falling out with the owners, who promptly renamed the dish.

- Chicken à la King, with chunks of chicken in a cream-sherry sauce, was probably invented for Foxhall P. Keene, son of a Wall Street speculator and among Delmonico's most valued patrons.

◆ Baked Alaska was invented to honor the purchase of Alaska, which would eventually become our forty-ninth state. Some people called the dish "Alaska-Florida," presumably because the inside ice cream layer is frozen-cold while the outside meringue layer is hot.

Fein on Food _____

History is full of Olympic-scale gastronomes. But America's trencherman, Diamond Jim Brady, probably wins the gold medal. He dined daily at Delmonico's or Rector's, another famous old New York restaurant. His gigantic breakfasts, lunches, and mid-day snacks were legendary. For dinner Brady would eat dozens of oysters and crabs, several lobsters, terrapin (turtle) soup, and steak, followed by coffee, pastries, and a couple of pounds of candy. Restaurateur George Rector called him "the best 25 customers we had."

Down New Orleans Way

In New Orleans, Antoine's fabulous fare attracted the rich and famous. It also named foods for celebrities:

◆ Oysters Rockefeller, a dish of oysters, greens, and cream, was so rich that the chef decided to name it after the then-richest man in the world, John D. Rockefeller.

◆ Pompano en Papillote, to honor Alberto Santos-Dumont, a famous balloonist who visited New Orleans at the turn of the twentieth century, is made with fish, shellfish, and sauce and enclosed in parchment paper. As the food cooks, steam trapped within causes the paper to inflate like a balloon. The paper is pierced at tableside, revealing moist, succulent fish and releasing an intense aroma.

South of the Border

One famous dish that we think of as American was actually invented outside the United States. Restaurateur Caesar Cardini created Caesar Salad when several celebrities dined at his place in Tijuana, Mexico, one night in 1924. The restaurant's big draw was that it was south of the border, where Prohibition wasn't the law and liquor was legal. The food was fine, the booze even better, and the new salad an instant success.

Classic Caesar Salad is made with a coddled egg; that is, an egg cooked for about one minute. But because undercooked eggs are risky to eat, you might wish to make Caesar Salad without it. A food processor can be a real help emulsifying the dressing.

Hotel Dining

Several of America's renowned dishes came from the kitchens of upscale hotels:

◆ Boston Cream Pie and Parker House rolls were made famous in the nineteenth century at Boston's Parker House Hotel.

◆ Vichyssoise was the creation (1917) of Louis Diat, the chef at New York's elegant Ritz-Carlton.

◆ Green Goddess salad dressing was created by the chef at San Francisco's Palace Hotel to honor a smash-hit play of the 1920s, *The Green Goddess*.

◆ Waldorf Salad, from the kitchens of New York's old Waldorf Hotel, is a concoction of apples, celery, and walnuts cloaked with mayonnaise. It was invented in 1893 by Oscar Tschirky, America's first celebrity chef, whose haughty bearing was probably as famous as his food.

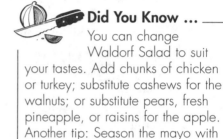

Did You Know ...

You can change Waldorf Salad to suit your tastes. Add chunks of chicken or turkey; substitute cashews for the walnuts; or substitute pears, fresh pineapple, or raisins for the apple. Another tip: Season the mayo with chopped fresh tarragon.

A Famous Sandwich

One of America's best-known sandwiches was invented at a hotel, or maybe at a deli. Some say that Reuben Kulakofsy, who played cards at Omaha's Blackstone Hotel in the 1920s, created the sandwich, and that the hotel owner, also a regular in the game, liked it so much he put it on the hotel's menu. But New Yorkers claim the sandwich was invented by Arnold Reuben, owner of Reuben's Deli. Everyone thanks the inventor, whoever it is, for this classic, made with corned beef, Swiss cheese, and sauerkraut and Russian dressing on rye bread.

The French Influence

The era of gastronomy that began with Delmonico's faded in the twentieth century, done in by Prohibition, World War I, and the Depression. American fare became settled, with little to inspire enthusiasm or creativity until the 1939 World's Fair. The French Pavilion there caused a sensation with its exquisite food and first-rate service. Henri Soule, *maître d'hôtel* at the pavilion, opened Le Pavilion restaurant in New York a few years later. It was even more opulent than Delmonico's had been. Le Pavilion spawned many other fine French restaurants, and new generations of Americans learned about gracious dining and fine food. After Julia Child surfaced on TV, some even cooked these dishes at home.

Chinatown, My Chinatown

By the late 1960s and 70s, people were getting bored with the same old food, even their favorite Chinese restaurant fare. Americans seemed especially happy with changes in the law that allowed immigration from mainland China. The newcomers brought recipes for regional Chinese dishes, and Americans particularly loved the hot and spicy foods of Sichuan and Hunan. Chinese food and cooking became a national mania. Chinese cooking schools opened and classes were filled to capacity. At the height of the Chinese cooking craze, a new piece of equipment emerged: the flat-bottomed stir-fry pan. With its greater stability, the stir-fry pan became more popular than the traditional rounded Chinese wok, and is now among the basic items in every cook's kitchen.

The stir-fry technique caught on like a Velcro zipper. It had great appeal because it seemed easy to do and featured foods that could be cooked quickly and with little fat. Today, even if most Americans no longer cook Chinese cuisine at home, many still prepare quick stir-fries for dinner.

Nouvelle Cuisine

Americans also tired of the same French food they had been eating. In the 1980s, a handful of French chefs rebelled against old-fashioned classics and created a new style of cooking that was lighter and easier. Nouvelle (literally, "New") Cuisine took off with rocket speed in America. At its best, it spurred an interest in new ingredients, a focus on fresh local products, and a reexamination of American food.

Kitchen Clue

While they may not have exactly the same flavor, you can substitute dried herbs for fresh ones. Use about one third the amount, and crush the dried herbs slightly between your fingers before adding them to food.

Nouvelle American

Chez Panisse, which opened in 1971, was as influential and as visionary as Delmonico's had been in its day. At this California restaurant, chef-owner Alice Waters focused on fresh vegetables and fruit, and she included fresh herbs in her recipes. This was a real novelty. For decades, Americans had relied on canned or frozen produce, and many used perhaps one or two well-known dried herbs to season their food—or relied only on salt and pepper. (For more on Alice Waters and Chez Panisse, see Chapter 7.)

Back to Regional

Chef Paul Prudhomme was among the first restaurant chefs to reinvigorate regional cuisine. His New Orleans restaurant, K-Paul's (opened in 1979), made Cajun food famous and word of his signature dish, Blackened Redfish, spread faster than Morse's cable from Delmonico's. Not since Chicken à la King has a dish been duplicated so often in so many American kitchens. Americans began to consider other localized cuisines. These days, chefs and home cooks are once again looking to dishes that exemplify the best of a region. Traditional specialties such as Succotash and Pecan Pie may be given new interpretations, and classic but less-familiar dishes such as Buttermilk Pie and Lady Baltimore Cake may be re-emerging on the culinary horizon. Here we are, back where we started, but it's not quite the same.

The Least You Need to Know

- Convenience foods have been instrumental in giving American cuisine its national character.

- In America's early days, canned foods allowed people in different parts of the country to taste regional foods; later they became convenience ingredients for use in casseroles and other dishes.

- Besides the refrigerator, freezer, stove, and oven, the three most exceptional and valuable kitchen appliances are the blender, electric mixer, and food processor.

- During the Depression, wars, and other troubled times, Americans like to eat economy-minded but emotionally satisfying dishes such as pudding and mashed potatoes.

- Some of America's favorite recipes were developed in restaurants.

Rumaki

These old-fashioned tidbits are still big winners at cocktail parties.

Prep time: less than 30 minutes • Makes 18 to 20 pieces

1 lb. chicken livers

$^1/_4$ cup soy sauce

$^1/_4$ cup molasses

3 TB. water

2 TB. crystallized ginger, crumbled

1 clove garlic, slightly bruised (gently crushed with the flat side of a knife)

$^1/_2$ star anise (or use $^1/_4$ tsp. anise extract)

$^1/_2$ lb. bacon

1 can whole water chestnuts

Remove any fat and gristle from chicken livers. Cut livers into large bite-size pieces and set aside.

Combine soy sauce, molasses, water, ginger, garlic, and anise in a saucepan. Bring to a simmer. Add livers and poach for 5 minutes.

Let livers cool, then remove them with a slotted spoon. Discard the poaching liquid and let cool. Cut bacon slices in half. Wrap 1 water chestnut and 1 piece liver with a $^1/_2$ slice bacon. Secure with a toothpick.

Preheat a grill or broiler. Broil or grill Rumaki for several minutes, turning occasionally, until bacon is browned and crispy.

Caesar Salad Without Eggs

This famous salad has endured over the decades because the romaine lettuce is so crunchy and the dressing so satisfyingly rich and tangy. You can add grilled chicken or shrimp to make it a main course, but even plain, this dish is a big winner.

Prep time: less than 30 minutes, plus 15 minutes to make the croutons   •   Makes 6 servings

Special equipment: food processor or blender

1 large head romaine lettuce, washed and dried

1 large clove garlic

2-oz. can anchovies, drained

1 tsp. Dijon mustard

$^1/_2$ cup extra-virgin olive oil

$^1/_4$ cup fresh lemon juice

$^1/_2$ cup Parmesan cheese, freshly grated

Salt and freshly ground black pepper, to taste

2 cups croutons, homemade (recipe follows) or packaged

Tear lettuce leaves into pieces and place in a salad bowl. Place garlic clove, anchovies, and mustard in a food processor or blender. With the machine on, slowly add olive oil through the feed tube or lid opening.

Add lemon juice and process for several seconds to blend ingredients. Pour dressing over greens. Sprinkle with cheese. Toss ingredients to coat lettuce. Add salt, pepper, and croutons (recipe follows) and give salad a final toss. Serve immediately.

For the croutons:

2 cups $^1/_2$" thick homestyle white bread or Italian bread cubes

$^1/_4$ cup olive oil

2 cloves garlic, peeled and sliced

2 TB. butter

Trim crust from bread and cut bread into cubes. Heat oil over moderate heat and add garlic. Cook for a few minutes to flavor oil. Discard garlic. Add butter. When melted, add bread cubes. Cook over moderate heat, turning frequently, until cubes are golden brown on all sides.

Hot Tip
Use the bread crusts to make fresh bread-crumbs; store in a plastic bag in the freezer.

Lime and Walnut Gelatin Mold

My mom (Lily Vail) loved this molded salad. She served it as a buffet dish at parties and for many family gatherings.

Prep time: less than 15 minutes • Makes 8 to 10 servings

2 (3-oz.) packages lime gelatin

1 cup boiling water

1 (15-oz.) can crushed pineapple, undrained

2 cups dairy sour cream

²/₃ cup walnuts, chopped

²/₃ cup maraschino cherries, chopped

Mix gelatin and boiling water together until gelatin dissolves. Stir in pineapple and mix thoroughly. Refrigerate for about 30 minutes or until mixture is thickened to a syrupy consistency.

Add sour cream and beat in with a whisk or electric beater until mixture is foamy and sour cream is evenly dispersed. Stir in walnuts and cherries. Pour mixture into a six-cup mold. Refrigerate for several hours or until mold is set. Unmold and serve.

Grilled Chicken Waldorf Salad

This salad updates the original and makes it more substantial by adding grilled chicken. It's a terrific buffet or lunch dish. To make traditional Waldorf Salad, eliminate the chicken and tarragon, and cut down on the mayonnaise by using about ¹/₃ cup, or mix the mayo with equal parts plain yogurt.

Prep time: less than 15 minutes • Makes 4 servings

2 large chicken breast halves

1 TB. olive oil

Salt and freshly ground black pepper, to taste

2 stalks celery, diced

2 tart apples, peeled, cored, and diced

¹/₂ cup walnuts, chopped

1 TB. fresh tarragon, chopped

¹/₂–³/₄ cup mayonnaise

Preheat an outdoor grill or oven broiler.

Trim fat and cartilage from chicken breasts, rinse, and dry. Rub breasts with olive oil, and sprinkle with salt and pepper. Grill chicken over moderate heat for 12–15 minutes, depending on thickness, or until cooked through. Turn chicken occasionally.

Remove chicken and cut into dice. Combine chicken, celery, apples, walnuts, and tarragon, and toss ingredients. Moisten with mayonnaise.

Vichyssoise

This is an opulent, velvety soup that makes an elegant first course for a special dinner.

Prep time: less than 30 minutes   •   Makes 8 servings

Special equipment: blender or food processor

4 TB. butter

4 large leeks, white part only, cleaned and chopped

1 medium onion, chopped

6 medium all-purpose potatoes, peeled and sliced

4 cups chicken stock

1 TB. salt, or to taste

2 cups whole milk

2 cups whipping cream

White pepper, to taste

2 TB. fresh chives, chopped

Melt butter in a soup pot over moderate heat. When butter has melted and looks foamy, add leeks and onion, and cook for 3–4 minutes or until vegetables have softened. Do not let vegetables brown. Add potatoes, stock, and salt. Partially cover the pan and simmer for 45 minutes, or until vegetables are tender.

Purée mixture in a blender or food processor. Strain mixture through a strainer. Return soup to the pot. Add 1 cup milk and 1 cup cream, and stir to blend ingredients. Bring to a simmer. Remove the pan from heat.

Chill thoroughly. Stir in remaining milk and cream. Taste for seasoning. Add salt and white pepper to taste. Serve garnished with chives.

Hot Tip

Try these variations:

♦ Lobster Vichyssoise: Steam a 1- to $1^1/_2$-lb. lobster over $2^1/_2$ cups water. Use the steaming liquid to replace an equal amount of the stock called for. Chop the lobster and add it to the cold soup. Garnish with fresh dill instead of chives.

♦ Avocado Vichyssoise: Add 3 large, seeded tomatoes with the potatoes; add 3 large ripe, peeled avocados when you purée the cooked soup; add $1/4$ cup lemon juice and cayenne pepper to taste just before serving.

Cheese Fondue

This is the classic lush version of Swiss fondue. Serve it for casual gatherings of good friends—dunking into one pot inspires conviviality.

Prep time: less than 15 minutes • Makes 4 to 6 servings

1 large clove garlic, sliced in half

1½ cups dry white wine

½ lb. Gruyere cheese, grated

½ lb. Emmenthaler cheese, grated

4 tsp. all-purpose flour

3 TB. kirschwasser

French bread, cut into chunks

Rub inside of the fondue pot with cut sides of garlic. Discard garlic. Pour wine into the fondue pot and set it over low heat.

Combine two cheeses and toss gratings in flour to coat. Add cheese to the fondue pot gradually, stirring constantly with a wooden spoon. When all cheese has been added and melted, stir in kirschwasser. Keep the flame at the lowest possible. Skewer chunks of bread and dunk.

Hot Tip

Try these variations:

- ◆ Use 1 lb. Monterey Jack cheese and stir in 2 chopped jalapeño peppers.
- ◆ Use brandy, lemon juice, vodka, or tequila instead of the kirschwasser.

Macaroni and Cheese

This tangy, creamy dish is an American classic. You can eat it immediately after mixing the macaroni and sauce, or make it into a baked, crispy-topped casserole.

Prep time: less than 15 minutes • Makes 4 servings

1½ cups elbow macaroni

2 TB. butter

2 TB. all-purpose flour

2 cups milk

½ tsp. salt

Black pepper and freshly ground nutmeg, to taste

8 oz. sharp cheddar or American cheese (about 2 cups grated)

Cook macaroni in lightly salted water until al dente. Drain and set aside.

While macaroni is cooking, heat butter in a saucepan over low heat. When butter has melted and looks foamy, add flour and cook, stirring constantly (preferably with a whisk), for 2–3 minutes. Gradually add milk, stirring almost constantly for 3–4 minutes, or until sauce has thickened.

Stir in salt, pepper, and nutmeg. Add cheese and continue to cook, stirring occasionally, for 2 minutes or until cheese has melted and sauce is thick and smooth. Pour sauce over cooked macaroni and mix thoroughly. Serve immediately.

For baked macaroni and cheese: Preheat the oven to 350°. Place macaroni and cheese in a baking dish. Combine 1½ cups of fresh breadcrumbs and 3 tablespoons melted butter. Mix with your fingers and sprinkle over macaroni. Bake for 25–30 minutes or until crust is golden brown.

Grilled Cheese

Here are two recipes for the famous sandwich. The first one, my mom's version, is the one I grew up eating. It is open-faced and broiled. My mom frequently topped the cheese with bacon and tomato. Following that is the more well-known, two-sided, pan-fried classic.

Grilled Cheese with Tomato and Bacon

Prep time: less than 15 minutes   •   Makes one sandwich

1 slice white bread

1 tsp. softened butter

3 or 4 slices American cheese

1 or 2 slices tomato

2 pieces of cooked bacon

Preheat the broiler.

Place white bread on a piece of aluminum foil. Smear bread on one side with butter. Cover with cheese. Place tomato on top.

Place sandwich on a broiler pan set 4" away from the heat source. Broil for a few minutes until cheese is melted and bubbly. For the last minute, place bacon on top. (The sandwich can also be cooked in a toaster oven, using the top-brown feature.)

Classic Grilled Cheese

Prep time: less than 15 minutes   •   Makes one sandwich

2 slices white bread

1½ TB. softened butter

3 or 4 slices American cheese

Butter both slices of bread on the outside with butter. Place cheese between two dry sides of bread.

Place sandwich in a small frying pan, cover the pan, and cook over low-moderate heat for 3–4 minutes, or until bread has browned. Turn sandwich over and cook until browned.

Hot Tip
The traditional grilled cheese sandwich is made with American cheese on white bread, but you can substitute any type of meltable cheese, such as Swiss, Monterey Jack, Havarti, or mozzarella, and use any kind of sliced bread you like.

Sloppy Joes

Great for a quick, casual dinner. Kids love these, too.

Prep time: less than 15 minutes • Makes 4 to 6 servings

2 TB. vegetable oil

1 medium onion, chopped

1 small celery stalk, chopped

1½ lbs. ground beef

⅔ cup bottled chili sauce or bottled barbecue sauce

1 TB. Worcestershire sauce

¾ cup water

Salt and pepper, to taste

4–6 hamburger or sandwich buns, lightly toasted

Heat vegetable oil in a skillet. Add onion and celery and cook over moderate heat for 2–3 minutes. Add meat and cook, breaking the pieces apart, until meat has browned. Drain excess fat from the pan.

Add chili sauce, Worcestershire sauce, and water. Simmer over low heat for about 30 minutes, stirring occasionally, or until mixture has thickened. Taste for seasoning and add salt and pepper as desired. Spoon meat over toasted bun bottoms and top with other half of bun to serve.

Tuna Casserole

Rather than using canned soup, this casserole is made with a fresh, creamy white sauce. It's a nice Sunday supper dish. If you prefer, use grilled fresh tuna. If you love the old-fashioned canned-soup kind of Tuna Casserole, though, see the Hot Tip that follows.

Prep time: less than 15 minutes • Makes 4 servings

$^1/_2$ lb. egg noodles

3 TB. butter

1 medium onion, chopped

1 stalk celery, chopped

1 large clove garlic, chopped

$^1/_4$ cup all-purpose flour

$2^1/_4$ cups milk

Salt and pepper, to taste

2 (6-oz.) cans tuna, drained and cut into chunks

1 cup frozen peas, thawed

3 TB. breadcrumbs

$^1/_4$ cup Swiss cheese, grated

3 TB. Parmesan cheese, grated

Preheat the oven to 350°.

Cook egg noodles in lightly salted water until tender but firm. Drain and set aside.

Heat butter in a skillet over moderate heat. When butter has melted and looks foamy, add onion and celery, and cook for 3–4 minutes or until vegetables have softened slightly. Add garlic and cook briefly.

Stir in flour and cook, stirring constantly, for 2 minutes. Gradually add milk and cook, stirring constantly, for 5 minutes or until sauce has thickened. Remove the pan from heat and stir in salt and pepper to taste.

Combine mixture with noodles. Fold in tuna and peas. Place mixture into a $1^1/_2$ quart casserole. Sprinkle top with breadcrumbs and cheeses. Bake for 15 minutes or until lightly crispy on top.

Hot Tip

To make an old-fashioned canned-soup Tuna Casserole, preheat the oven to 350°; cook 2 cups elbow macaroni and mix it with two 6-ounce cans (drained) tuna, 1 can condensed cream of mushroom or cream of celery soup, and 1 cup milk. Spoon into a casserole and top with $^1/_2$ cup crushed potato chips. Bake for 25–30 minutes.

Chicken à la King

You might think of this dish as college dormitory food, but this recipe is rich and lavish, prepared in its original way.

Prep time: less than 30 minutes   •   Makes 4 servings

2 TB. vegetable oil	1 cup chicken stock
1 small onion, chopped	1 cup cream
2 cups mushrooms, sliced	2 TB. sherry
$^1/_2$ small red bell pepper, chopped	1 TB. lemon juice
$^1/_2$ small green bell pepper, chopped	3 cups chicken, cooked, sliced
2 TB. butter	Salt and freshly ground black pepper, to taste
3 TB. all-purpose flour	Steamed white rice or cooked egg noodles

Heat vegetable oil in a skillet over moderate heat. Add onion, mushrooms, and red and green peppers, and cook for 4–5 minutes, stirring occasionally, or until vegetables have softened and mushroom juices have evaporated. Set the pan aside.

Heat butter in a saucepan over moderate heat. When butter has melted and looks foamy, add flour, lower the heat, and cook, whisking ingredients for 1–2 minutes. Gradually stir in stock and whisk ingredients for about 2 minutes or until a smooth, thickened sauce has formed. Stir in cream and cook for about 5 minutes, or until sauce is smooth and thick.

Add sherry and lemon juice and cook another minute. Add chicken and reserved vegetables. Cook until hot.

Add salt and pepper to taste. Serve over steamed white rice or cooked egg noodles.

Pasta Primavera with Shrimp

For this dish, use any vegetables that look fresh and wonderful. This recipe uses purple onion, green asparagus, and bright red tomatoes, which give it visual appeal, so bear that in mind when shopping. If you prefer to make a vegetarian meal, leave out the shrimp.

Prep time: less than 30 minutes • Makes 4 servings

12–16 oz. fresh shrimp, shelled and deveined

6-7 TB. olive oil

1 lb. pasta

2 TB. salt

1 small purple onion, peeled and chopped

1 lb. asparagus, cut into bite-size pieces

1 pint grape or cherry tomatoes

2 TB. chopped fresh basil, optional

Salt and freshly ground black pepper, to taste

Preheat and outdoor grill or oven broiler. Wipe shrimp dry and toss with 2 tablespoons of the olive oil. Grill for 5–6 minutes, turning once. Bring a large pot of water to a boil. Add the 2 tablespoons salt. Add pasta and cook until al dente. While pasta is cooking, heat 2 tablespoons olive oil in a skillet. Add onion and cook over moderate heat for 2 minutes, until onion has softened slightly. Add asparagus pieces and continue to cook, stirring occasionally, for 2–3 minutes. Add tomatoes and basil, if used, and cook another minute. Add shrimp to the pan.

Remove the pan from heat. Drain pasta. Put pasta into the skillet and return the pan to the stovetop over moderate heat. Add 2 tablespoons more of olive oil, toss ingredients, and cook for about a minute until hot. Add another tablespoon olive oil (or cooking water) if you like pasta a bit moister. Taste pasta and add salt and pepper as desired.

Stir-Fried Chicken with Vegetables

The Chinese stir-fry technique is perfect for all kinds of tender foods that cook quickly, like the chicken and vegetables in this recipe. Serve over steamed white rice.

Prep time: less than 30 minutes   •   Makes 4 servings

4 TB. vegetable oil

2 whole skinless, boneless chicken breasts, cut into thin strips

2 carrots, thinly sliced

1 small yellow squash or zucchini, thinly sliced

$1/2$ medium red bell pepper, cut into thin strips

$1/2$ medium purple onion, sliced

2 cloves garlic, finely chopped

2 TB. fresh basil, chopped or 1 tsp. dried

1 TB. fresh oregano, chopped or $1/4$ tsp. dried

$1/4$ cup white wine or chicken stock

Salt and freshly ground black pepper

Heat 2 tablespoons vegetable oil in a wok or skillet. Add chicken and stir-fry over moderate heat for 3–4 minutes or until white and almost cooked through. Remove chicken and set aside.

Heat remaining 2 tablespoons oil in the pan. Add carrots and stir-fry for 2 minutes. Add squash, red pepper, and onion, and stir-fry for 2 minutes. Add garlic, basil and oregano and stir-fry for another minute or until vegetables are tender but still crispy. Return chicken to the pan. Pour in white wine, sprinkle with salt and pepper, and stir-fry for another minute.

Hot Tip _____

If you use dried herbs, add them when you begin to stir-fry the chicken.

Rich Mashed Potatoes

Better make lots of this because every morsel will be gone! These mashed potatoes are lush and fluffy. If there is any left over, shape it into small cakes, dredge them in some flour, and fry them until crispy.

Prep time: less than 15 minutes • Makes 4 to 6 servings

2 lbs. all-purpose potatoes	6–8 TB. sour cream
3 TB. butter	Salt and pepper, to taste
3 TB. cream cheese	

Wash, peel, and cut the potatoes into chunks. Cook in lightly salted water until fork-tender. Drain potatoes and add butter and cream cheese. Mash with a potato masher or ricer until no lumps remain. Add enough sour cream to make mixture smooth and fluffy. Taste for seasoning; add salt and pepper to taste.

Hot Tip

Don't use a food processor or blender to mash potatoes, because it will turn potatoes into a gummy mess!

Cranberry Bread

This traditional loaf is sweet and moist. It's perfect when served plain, or as an accompaniment to coffee or tea, and it also makes a fine breakfast. Or use it at your next turkey dinner.

Prep time: less than 15 minutes   •   Makes 1 loaf

Special equipment: cake rack

2 cups all-purpose flour	4 TB. butter
1 cup sugar	1 egg
1 tsp. salt	³/₄ cup orange juice
1¹/₂ tsp. baking powder	1 TB. freshly grated orange rind
¹/₂ tsp. baking soda	1 cup fresh cranberries, chopped

Preheat the oven to 350°.

Sift together flour, sugar, salt, baking powder, and baking soda. Add butter in chunks, and cut into dry ingredients until mixture resembles coarse meal.

In a separate bowl, beat egg, orange juice, and orange rind together until mixture is uniform. Add liquid ingredients to dry ones. Stir only until ingredients are blended. Stir in cranberries. Pour into a greased 9"×5"-inch loaf pan. Bake for about 1 hour or until a cake tester inserted into middle comes out clean.

Cool in the pan for 10 minutes, then remove to a cake rack to cool completely.

Iced Tea

Refreshing and flavorful, nothing beats this beverage on a hot summer day. It takes minutes to make; prepare a batch in advance and store it in the fridge.

Prep time: less than 15 minutes • Makes 8 servings

6 cups fresh cold water

2 TB. sugar or honey, optional

4 TB. (mounded) tea leaves (or use 12 tea bags)

Bring water to a boil. Place tea leaves or bags in a teapot and pour boiling water over them. Let steep for 6–7 minutes.

Strain tea or remove tea bags. Stir in sugar or honey. Let mixture cool. Pour over ice cubes into tall glasses.

Hot Tip _____

Try these variations:

- ◆ Herbal Iced Tea: Steep tea with ¼ cup fresh mint or rosemary leaves.
- ◆ Orange and Ginger Flavored Iced Tea: Steep tea with 1 sliced navel orange and 2 tablespoons crushed crystallized ginger.

Tiramisu

A fabulously creamy, rich, lush dessert—no wonder it's so popular! Try it with some fine, hot espresso coffee. Use bakery ladyfingers for this dish. They soften, but packaged supermarket varieties become overly soggy and pasty.

Prep time: less than 30 minutes   •   Makes 6 to 8 servings

3 eggs, separated	32–36 ladyfingers, approximately
¹/₂ cup sugar	³/₄ cup cold brewed espresso
12 oz. Mascarpone cheese	2 TB. unsweetened cocoa powder
2 TB. rum or brandy	

Place egg yolks and ¹/₄ cup sugar in the top part of a double boiler set over simmering water. Beat with a hand mixer set at medium speed for 4 minutes, or until mixture is hot, thick, and pale. Remove the pan from heat and let cool slightly.

Add cheese and rum or brandy and beat for 1–2 minutes, until smooth. Line a 9"×5" loaf pan with as many ladyfingers as necessary to form a single layer on the bottom. Brush ladyfingers with coffee. Place another layer of ladyfingers on top and brush with more coffee (half the coffee should be used for this layer).

Beat egg whites until frothy. Gradually add remaining sugar and beat whites until they stand in stiff, glossy peaks. Fold into cheese mixture. Spoon half the cheese mixture over ladyfingers. Sprinkle 1 tablespoon cocoa powder over cheese. Repeat with another double-layer of ladyfingers, coffee, and cheese. Refrigerate for at least 4 hours. Just before serving, dust with remaining cocoa powder.

Hot Tip

This recipe contains egg whites that are uncooked. Uncooked eggs can be a slight health risk for some people, particularly very young children, the elderly, and anyone with a weak immune system. If you wish to avoid eating raw eggs for health and safety reasons, substitute ³/₄ cup heavy cream, whipped until thick. Don't forget to add the remaining sugar.

Chocolate Chip Cookies

These are crunchy, warmly seasoned, and fragrant, a little different from the recipe on the back of the morsels bag. Great for dunking into cold milk!

Prep time: less than 30 minutes • Makes about 30 cookies

¹/₂ cup butter	1 tsp. baking soda
³/₄ cup brown sugar	1 tsp. cinnamon
¹/₄ cup white sugar	¹/₂ tsp. salt
1 egg	1 cup regular or quick-cooking oats
1 tsp. vanilla extract	1 cup chocolate chips
³/₄ cup all-purpose flour	

Heat the oven to 350°.

Place butter, brown sugar, and white sugar in an electric mixer bowl. Beat at medium speed for 3–4 minutes, or until thoroughly blended, scraping the sides of the bowl occasionally. Add egg and vanilla extract, and blend in.

Combine flour, baking soda, cinnamon, and salt and add to butter mixture. Blend thoroughly. Stir in oats and chocolate chips, and stir to distribute evenly through dough. Drop by heaping teaspoonfuls onto a greased cookie sheet, leaving 1¹/₂" between each cookie. Bake for about 12–15 minutes or until lightly browned.

Homemade Vanilla Pudding

This tastes like the kind my grandma made from the box, before the days of additives and preservatives. It is smooth, creamy, and wonderful, best when served slightly warm with real, chilled heavy cream.

Prep time: less than 15 minutes • Makes 4 to 6 servings

3 cups whole milk

$^1/_2$ cup sugar

$^1/_3$ cup cornstarch

$^1/_4$ tsp. salt

1 TB. butter

2 tsp. vanilla extract

Heat milk in a saucepan over moderate heat for a few minutes until bubbles appear around edges of the pan. Sift sugar, cornstarch, and salt together in a small bowl. Add $^1/_2$ cup heated milk and stir ingredients to form a smooth paste. Transfer paste to the saucepan of heated milk. Cook ingredients, stirring constantly, for a minute or so or until mixture is thick and smooth. Remove the pan from the heat.

Let pudding cool for a few minutes. Stir in butter and vanilla extract. Pour into 4–6 dessert dishes and chill thoroughly. (If you like a "skin" on top of pudding, do not cover the dish; otherwise, cover the dish with plastic wrap.)

Hot Tip

Try these variations:

- Chocolate pudding: Increase sugar to $^2/_3$ cup, add $^1/_3$ cup unsweetened cocoa powder, and sift with the other ingredients; reduce vanilla extract to $1^1/_2$ teaspoons.

- Butterscotch pudding: Substitute brown sugar and increase to $^2/_3$ cup, use $1^1/_2$ tablespoons butter, and reduce vanilla extract to $1^1/_2$ teaspoons.

Baked Alaska

This famous dessert is very impressive. Serve it for special company. It looks difficult to make, but isn't.

Prep time: less than 45 minutes • Makes 8 to 10 servings

Special equipment: cake rack

For the cake:

3 TB. butter

3 large eggs

$^{1}/_{2}$ cup sugar

$^{3}/_{4}$ tsp. vanilla extract

$^{1}/_{2}$ cup all-purpose flour

$^{1}/_{4}$ tsp. salt

Preheat the oven to 350°.

Grease an 8" or 9" cake pan. Melt butter and set aside to cool. Beat eggs, sugar, and vanilla extract together in an electric mixer bowl set at medium speed for about 5 minutes or until mixture is thick and pale. Sift flour and salt together and fold gradually into egg mixture. Fold in melted butter.

Pour batter into the prepared pan. Bake for 25 minutes or until a cake tester inserted into center comes out clean. Let cake cool in the pan for 10 minutes, and then invert onto a cake rack to cool completely. Brush cooled cake with syrup and spread preserve mixture on top (recipes follow).

For the syrup:

$^{1}/_{4}$ cup sugar

$2^{1}/_{2}$ TB. water

2 TB. brandy

Place sugar and water in a small saucepan, bring to a boil, and remove from heat. Stir in brandy. Let cool.

For the preserve mixture:

$^{1}/_{2}$ cup jam or preserves such as apricot, strawberry, blackberry, or raspberry

2 TB. brandy

Using a small pan, heat jam until melted. Remove pan and stir in brandy. Let cool.

For the ice cream, meringue, and final assembly:

1 quart vanilla or peach ice cream, slightly softened

6 egg whites at room temperature

Pinch of salt

$^{1}/_{2}$ tsp. cream of tartar

$^{3}/_{4}$ cup sugar

Shape ice cream into dome about 1" smaller in diameter than cake layer. Place ice cream dome on top of cake. Wrap cake and ice cream in plastic wrap and place in the freezer for at least 1 hour.

Preheat the oven to 450°.

Beat egg whites and salt together in an electric mixer bowl set at medium speed until mixture is foamy. Add cream of tartar and beat until soft peaks form. Gradually add sugar and continue to beat until mixture stands in stiff, glossy peaks.

Place cake and ice cream mound on an oven-proof platter or cookie sheet. Spread meringue all over ice cream and cake, including sides of cake, making sure to seal in ice cream completely. Bake for 45–60 seconds or until meringue end swirls have become golden brown. Serve immediately.

Hot Tip

The meringue in this recipe contains egg whites that are cooked only briefly. Undercooked eggs can be a slight health risk for some people, particularly very young children, the elderly, and anyone with a weak immune system. Unfortunately, there is no substitute for the meringue when making authentic Baked Alaska. You can skip it altogether and pile sweetened whipped cream on top of the ice cream and cake for a completely different but equally delicious dessert.

Glossary

Al dente Slightly chewy and resilient; used to describe the proper point at which pasta should be cooked.

American cheese A processed product, not true cheese. It begins as pasteurized cow's milk cheddar, which is milled, shredded, cooked, and colored, and then molded into brick shapes.

Americanitis A nineteenth-century term coined to describe a growing population of sedentary city-dwellers and an epidemic of national obesity and indigestion.

Andouille A hot and peppery Cajun pork and garlic sausage that has been smoked over sugar cane and pecan wood.

Applejack An apple brandy, similar to French Calvados.

Baba ghanoush A spread based on pureed eggplant and seasonings; a Middle Eastern specialty.

Baking blind Baking or partially baking a pie crust before it's filled.

Bison The correct culinary term for buffalo. The meat has a rich, luxurious texture and tastes similar to beef, but contains less fat and cholesterol.

Black-eyed peas Small beige dried beans that have a distinctive black mark or "eye."

Bodega A small grocery store that offers Latino specialties.

Boudin A spicy sausage made with pork, rice, chicken, and vegetables.

Bourbon   Corn whiskey that must be at least 51 percent corn, and must be aged at least two years in charred white oak barrels that can never be reused. Bourbon is never more than 160 proof.

Broiler-fryer chicken   A chicken that weighs 2¹/₂ to 4 pounds, developed to cook quickly under the intense heat of a broiler or grill or in deep, hot fat.

Brown bread   A tender, grainy loaf that contains some rye and wheat flours and molasses; a New England specialty.

Cajun cooking   Cooking of the descendants of the French Canadians who settled in Louisiana. It is rustic cooking that relies heavily on fish, shellfish, and rice and is usually hot and spicy, with lots of chili peppers.

California cuisine   A fusion of foods and methods that focuses on light dishes and fresh local produce and herbs.

Cane syrup   A byproduct of sugar cane production, made by boiling the juices extracted from the sugarcane plant. It is very sweet, thick, and dark brown and tastes somewhat like molasses.

Cappuccino   Espresso coffee sometimes mixed with steamed milk and always capped with a thick layer of frothed milk.

Chaurice   A hard, spicy pork sausage similar to Spanish chorizo; used in Louisiana cookery.

Chicken fried steak   Thin steaks, breaded and fried like chicken, and served with a creamy gravy.

Chili powder   A blend of spices including dried, powdered chili peppers, garlic, oregano, and cumin. It is different than powdered chili, which is the pure, ground form of a particular dried chili pepper.

Chitterlings   Pig intestines that are cleaned, poached, and fried or used in soup.

Chorizo   A firm, spicy, paprika-laden sausage usually made of pork.

Chowder   A thick, chunky soup.

Cobbler, pandowdy   Fruit pies covered with classic shortcrust pastry; the dough is crushed before serving. Sometimes cobblers are made with streusel toppings.

Country hams   Dry-cured hams, not necessarily smoked, which are lean, firm, and well seasoned, similar in style to Italian prosciutto.

Crawfish   Shellfish that look like tiny lobsters. The meat is white, sweet, and lobster-like. Crawfish are often used in Cajun and Creole cooking.

Creole cooking   Cooking of the descendants of the original aristocratic and wealthy French and Spanish who came to New Orleans. It is based in the French classics but uses local ingredients and the tastes of other cultures—Spanish peppers, Italian tomatoes, African okra, West Indian fruits and vegetables, and Native American file powder.

Dutch oven   A deep, large, dome-topped skillet used for stew and braised foods.

Etouffee   A Louisiana specialty; it means "smothered," and it refers to dishes cloaked with a thick sauce and served over rice.

Falafel   Deep-fried chickpea fritters, a Middle Eastern specialty.

File powder   Ground, dried sassafras leaves. It is aromatic and spicy and is used as a thickening agent in Cajun and Creole cooking.

Fricassee   A stew-like dish in which an ingredient is sautéed in butter or vegetable oil to brown the surface, and then cooked with liquid in a covered pan until the dish is done.

Funnel cake   A squiggly doughnut, made by squeezing sweet batter through the bottom of a funnel into hot fat. It is a Pennsylvania Dutch snack.

Fusion cuisine   The blending of ingredients, seasonings, and cooking styles of two or more cultures, first used in the United States to mean French-Asian.

Grits   Ground hominy, similar to cornmeal, used in southern cuisine.

Hominy   Dried corn, whose hull has been removed with a solution of lye or slaked lime and water.

Hoppin' John   A dish that combines black-eye peas, rice, and salt pork or ham hock.

Hummus   A Middle Eastern spread made with puréed chickpeas, tahini (sesame paste), and seasonings.

Hushpuppies   Fried balls of cornmeal dough, a southern specialty.

Indian pudding   Cornmeal mush mixed with eggs, milk, molasses, and spices.

Jonnycakes (ashcakes, hoecakes)   Flat, fried breads made with cornmeal; among the earliest foods of the first settlers in America.

Kosher   Jewish dietary laws governing which foods are fit to eat (kosher) and which are prohibited (treyf).

Lagniappe   A Cajun tradition of giving something "extra," such as an extra cookie at the bakery or the mention of a special technique or other tip when sharing a recipe.

Latke   A Jewish word for pancake or fritter.

Latte   Espresso mixed with steamed milk.

Luau   A Hawaiian barbecue whose main dishes are pit-roasted pig, salted salmon, and poi.

Macchiato   Espresso with a dollop of steamed milk on top.

Maine lobster   A lobster with two large claws; rock or spiny lobsters have no claws.

Maryland fried chicken   Deep-fried chicken, similar to southern-fried chicken but served with a cream-based gravy made from the pan drippings.

Moonshine   Corn liquor made without regard to proof or age.

Nouvelle Cuisine   A cuisine that endeavored to simplify the French classics and to focus on light, fresh, uncomplicated foods.

Oenophile   Someone who loves and appreciates wine.

Pareve   A neutral ingredient that Jews may eat with either meat or dairy. Pareve ingredients include eggs, vegetables, grains, and fish.

Pennsylvania Dutch   A Protestant Christian sect, mainly Amish and Mennonites.

Philadelphia ice cream   A version of ice cream that traditionally is made without eggs.

Pilaf   A dish made by sautéing rice in butter or vegetable oil, and then adding stock, wine, or another flavorful liquid to moisten and soften the grains.

Piñons   The tiny nuts of the piñon tree, similar to pignoli nuts.

Plantain   Used mostly in Latino cooking, this fruit is a cousin to the banana. It is used in all states of ripeness from dark green to black-ripe, and may appear at any point of a meal, from appetizer to dessert. Plantains are almost always cooked before being eaten.

Potlatch   A Native American custom during which a host would give away possessions and serve a feast that always included salmon. Guests brought other seasonal foods to be shared. The custom of potlatch, which means "gift," became the American potluck dinner.

Pu-Pu platter A selection of Hawaiian hors d'oeuvres usually presented with a hibachi grill that keeps the tidbits warm.

Quickbreads Breads and muffins that are leavened with baking powder and/or baking soda.

Red flannel hash A New England specialty made with chopped corned beef, potatoes, and beets.

Roux A blend of fat and butter, used for enrichment and thickening. French roux uses butter and is always pale in color. Louisiana roux is usually made with vegetable oil, and the mixture is slow-cooked to tan or even dark brown, depending on how it will be used.

Salsas Vegetable and/or fruit mixtures used in southwest cookery. They are frequently uncooked (salsa fresca or salsa cruda) and are usually served as a condiment to accompany food.

Scoville scale A heat index for food such as chili peppers, which can range from zero or negligible units to over 800,000 units.

Scrapple A highly seasoned mixture of pork scraps and cornmeal packed as a compact loaf; a Pennsylvania Dutch specialty.

Shoofly pie An ultra-sweet confection with a sticky molasses center and streusel top; a Pennsylvania Dutch specialty.

Shortcrust pastry Standard pie dough.

Slumps, grunts Fruit pies topped with biscuit dough.

Smithfield ham A type of country ham, with a distinctive flavor; traditionally made from peanut-fed pigs.

Succotash A vegetable casserole made with corn and lima beans and sometimes other ingredients.

Wild rice A brownish-black aquatic grass whose narrow, tapered shape looks similar to rice.

Yam A plant similar to sweet potatoes, but is not grown commercially in the United States; American markets sell different varieties of sweet potatoes, which differ botanically from true yams.

Bibliography

Anderson, Jean. *The American Century Cookbook*. New York: Clarkson Potter, 1997.

Beard, James. *James Beard's American Cookery*. Boston, New York, London: Little, Brown and Company, 1972.

Better Homes and Gardens Books. *Heritage Cookbook*. Des Moines, Iowa: Meredith, 1975.

———. *Heritage of America Cookbook*. Des Moines, Iowa: Meredith, 1993.

Bittman, Mark. *How to Cook Everything*. New York: Macmillan, 1998.

Brown, Dale, and the Editors of Time-Life Books. Foods of the World, *American Cooking: The Northwest*. New York: Time-Life Books, 1970.

———. Foods of the World, *American Cooking: The Melting Pot*. New York: Time-Life Books, 1971.

Butel, Jane. *The Best of Mexican Cooking*. New York: Barron's, 1984.

Casey, Kathy. *Pacific Northwest the Beautiful Cookbook*. San Francisco: Collins Publishers, 1993.

Corriher, Shirley O. *CookWise*. New York: Willaim Morrow and Company, Inc., 1997.

Diner, Hasia R. *Hungering for America*. Cambridge, Massachusetts: Harvard University Press, 2001.

Feibleman, Peter S., and the Editors of Time-Life Books. Foods of the World, *American Cooking: Creole and Acadian*. New York: Time-Life Books, 1971.

Fein, Ronnie. *The Complete Idiot's Guide to Cooking Basics, Third Edition*. Indianapolis: Alpha Books, 2000.

Harbutt, Juliet, and Roz Denny. *The World Encyclopedia of Cheese*. New York: Lorenz Books, 1998.

Jamison, Cheryl Alters and Bill Jamison. *American Home Cooking*. New York: Broadway Books, 1999.

Jenkins, Steven. *Cheese Primer*. New York: Workman Publishing, 1996.

Jones, Evan. *American Food*. Woodstock, New York: The Overlook Press, 1974, 1975, 1981, 1990.

Jones, Judith and Evan Jones. *The L.L. Bean Book of New England Cookery*. New York: Random House, 1987.

Kolpas, Norman. *Southwest the Beautiful Cookbook*. New York: HarperCollins, 1994.

Lee, Hilde Gabriel. *Taste of the States*. Hong Kong: Howell Press, 1992.

Leonard, Jonathan Norton, and the Editors of Time-Life Books. Foods of the World, *American Cooking: The Great West*. New York: Time-Life Books, 1971.

———. Foods of the World, *American Cooking: New England*. New York: Time-Life Books, 1970.

Lovegren, Sylvia. *Fashionable Food*. New York: MacMillan, 1995.

Mariani, John. *America Eats Out*. New York: William Morrow and Company, 1991.

Nathan, Joan. *Jewish Cooking in America*. New York: Alfred A. Knopf, 2001.

Nix, Jan. *The Book of Regional American Cooking Southwest*. New York: HPBooks, 1993.

Prudhomme, Paul. *Chef Paul Prudhomme's Louisiana Kitchen*. New York: William Morrow and Company, 1984.

Rosengarten, David. *The Dean & Deluca Cookbook*. New York: Random House, 1996.

Stern, Jane and Michael Stern. *American Gourmet*. New York: HarperCollins, 1991.

———. *Square Meals*. New York: Alfred A. Knopf, 1984.

Stevens, Patricia Bunning. *Rare Bits*. Athens, Ohio: Ohio University Press, 1998.

The Art Institutes. *American Regional Cuisine*. New York: John Wiley & Sons, 2002.

Trager, James. *The Food Chronology*. New York: Henry Holt and Company, 1995.

Wilson, José, and the Editors of Time-Life Books. Foods of the World, *American Cooking: The Eastern Heartland*. New York: Time-Life Books, 1971.

Basic Recipes

The following are some recipes that will always come in handy. They are the basic, standard foods that we use often enough to be part of our general repertoire, no matter what kind of food we like to cook.

Crumb Crust for Pie

Crumb crusts were invented in an effort to cut down on the fat needed for basic pie dough. They are often used for no-bake pies (you could fill the crust with Homemade Vanilla Pudding, for example; see Chapter 10).

Prep time: less than 15 minutes • Makes enough for one 9" open-face pie crust

1½ cups packaged cookie crumbs   6 TB. melted butter

1–5 TB. sugar, optional

Combine cookie crumbs, sugar if used, and melted butter. Press buttered crumbs onto the bottom and sides of a 9" pie pan. Chill crust for one hour or bake in a preheated 350° oven for 10 minutes before filling.

Hot Tip _____

You can use any kind of cookie, including graham crackers, chocolate or vanilla wafers, or gingersnaps.

Basic Pie Dough

Use this basic dough to make any kind of baked pie, such as Strawberry Rhubarb (see Chapter 8), or to make open-face tarts such as Macadamia-Date Tart (see Chapter 7).

Prep time: less than 30 minutes • Makes enough for 1 two-crust 9" pie

2½ cups all-purpose flour	½ cup butter, chilled
¾ tsp. salt	⅓ cup shortening, chilled
½ tsp. sugar	4–5 TB. cold milk

Combine flour, salt, and sugar in a large bowl. Cut butter and shortening into chunks and add to flour mixture. Using your fingers, a pastry blender, or two knives, work fat into flour mixture until ingredients resemble crumbs. (You can also use a food processor; add ingredients to the workbowl and mix with 24 to 36 quick, short pulses—enough for mixture to resemble coarse meal.)

Add milk, using just enough to form pastry into a soft ball of dough. (If you use a food processor, add 4 tablespoons milk. Process ingredients for several seconds until mixture forms itself into a ball of dough.) Add remaining milk, if necessary, to help shape dough. Cut dough in half and flatten each half to make a disk shape. Wrap dough in plastic wrap and let stand at least 30 minutes before using.

French Fries

Everyone's favorite! For a real treat, sprinkle the hot potatoes with seasoned salt. This recipe will work with any number of potatoes that you need, about one per person. The number you can cook at any one time will depend on how big your wire basket is. Be sure the potatoes are completely immersed in the hot fat. The best potatoes to use are Russets (see Chapter 7). Be careful when cooking these; the fat may spatter. And be sure to use a large, thick potholder to protect your hands.

Prep time: about 15 minutes for 4–6 potatoes • Makes 1 potato per person

Baking or Idaho potatoes
Vegetable oil for frying

Peel potatoes and cut into strips, $^3/_8$-inch thick for regular fries, or $^1/_8$-inch for matchstick. Place some of potatoes in a wire basket. Heat enough vegetable oil or shortening in a deep fryer to come halfway up the sides of the pan. When the temperature reaches 350°, immerse the basket and cook potatoes for a few minutes until they begin to brown. Drain potatoes, set aside, and repeat with remaining potatoes.

To finish cooking, heat the oil to 375°, put all potatoes in the basket, and cook for several minutes until golden brown and crispy. Drain the potatoes on paper towels. Serve hot.

Poached Fruit

Poached fruit is a simple, lovely dessert. Serve it plain, with ice cream, or topped with whipped cream or a dessert sauce. The poaching liquid in this recipe can be used for any kind of fruit, and you can vary the recipe by adding a cinnamon stick or 3 or 4 whole cloves or a tablespoon of crystallized ginger. Refrigerate the poaching fluid to use again (within one week), or boil it down until it is syrupy to serve over the fruit (let it cool first). If you use vanilla extract, do *not* add it until you remove the pan from the heat. Heat dissipates the intensity of extract.

Prep time: less than 15 minutes • Makes enough for $1^1/_2$ to 2 pounds of fruit

$1^1/_2$ cups sugar

6 cups water

3 strips of lemon peel

1 (4") piece of vanilla bean, or 1 TB. vanilla extract

Fruit, such as pears, peaches, apricots, plums, nectarines, or blueberries

Combine sugar, water, lemon peel, and vanilla bean or extract in a saucepan. Bring mixture to a boil over high heat. Reduce the heat to low and simmer for 10 minutes.

Add fruit. Fruit must be completely immersed in poaching liquid. You can cut large fruit such as pears or peaches in half. (Remove seeds or pit first.) Cook fruit until barely fork-tender. The time depends on fruit. Remove the pan from the heat, and let fruit cool in poaching liquid.

Hot Tip

You can peel the fruit before you poach it, but you don't have to. The skin of peaches and pears comes off easily after the fruit is poached. To serve, peel the fruit, remove the seeds, and core.

Tomato Salsa

Sometimes called Salsa Fresca, this spicy salsa goes well with tortilla chips or as a garnish for grilled steak or chicken.

Prep time: less than 30 minutes   •   Makes 3 cups

4 large ripe tomatoes, chopped

1 small onion, chopped

2 scallions, chopped

1 large jalapeño or serrano pepper, seeded and chopped

3 or 4 TB. fresh cilantro, chopped

2 TB. lime juice

Salt and pepper

Combine all ingredients and let chill for 3–4 hours in the refrigerator to blend flavors.

Basic Tomato Sauce

Serve this basic sauce over any kind of pasta for a simple but delicious meal, or use it in dishes like Veal Parmigiana (see Chapter 9).

Prep time: less than 30 minutes • Makes about 2 to 2½ cups

1 (2-lb. 3-oz.) can Italian plum tomatoes, drained (or use tomatoes in thick puree, undrained, and cook the sauce a little longer)

3 TB. olive oil

1 small onion, chopped

4 large cloves garlic, finely chopped

2–3 TB. fresh basil, chopped or 1½ tsp. dried

Salt, to taste

Freshly ground black pepper, to taste

Chop tomatoes and set aside. Heat olive oil in a saucepan over low-moderate heat and add onion. Cook for 3 minutes or until onion has softened. Add garlic and cook for another minute.

Add tomatoes, basil, salt, and pepper. Simmer 45 minutes, or until it reaches the desired consistency, taste for seasoning, and add salt and pepper to taste. Serve sauce chunky, or puree in a food processor or blender.

Hot Tip

Try these variations:

- ◆ Mushroom: Add 1 cup sliced mushrooms with the onion and garlic.
- ◆ All'Arrabbiata: Add 4 slices crispy cooked bacon (crumbled) and ½ teaspoon red pepper flakes with the tomatoes.
- ◆ Sausage: Add 2 or 3 fried Italian-style sausages cut into small pieces with the tomatoes.

Vinaigrette Dressing

This is the mother of so many recipes! Use it as a salad dressing or a marinade. Keep some in your fridge; it lasts up to a week. Once you have homemade vinaigrette dressing in your house, you won't want to be without it.

Prep time: less than 15 minutes • Makes about ¾ cup

¹⁄₂ cup olive oil

3 TB. red-wine vinegar

1¹⁄₂ tsp. Dijon mustard, or ¹⁄₄ tsp. powdered mustard

1 medium garlic clove, minced (optional)

Salt and pepper, to taste

Combine all ingredients in a bowl and whisk together until well blended, or place in a covered container and shake for several seconds until well blended. Taste for seasoning, and add salt and pepper as desired.

Hot Tip

Try these variations:

- Balsamic vinaigrette: Use 2 tablespoons Balsamic vinegar instead of 3 tablespoons red-wine vinegar.
- Shallot vinaigrette: Add 1 finely chopped shallot, which is about 1 tablespoon of chopped shallot.
- Herb vinaigrette: Add 1 tablespoon minced fresh herbs such as marjoram, oregano, basil, thyme, savory, chervil, or dill, or 1 teaspoon dried herbs.
- Mustard vinaigrette: Add 1¹⁄₂ teaspoon additional Dijon mustard.
- "French" dressing: Add 1 tablespoon mayonnaise and ¹⁄₂ teaspoon paprika.
- Lemon vinaigrette: Use lemon juice instead of vinegar.

Index

G

H

I